Proceedings of the Sixth International Workshop on
Digital Forensics & Incident Analysis (WDFIA 2011)

London, UK
7-8 July 2011

Editors

Nathan Clarke
Theodore Tryfonas

Centre for Security, Communications & Network Research
University of Plymouth

ISBN: 978-1-84102-285-7

© 2011 University of Plymouth
All rights reserved
Printed in the United Kingdom

No part of this book may be reproduced, stored in a retrieval system, or transmitted in any form or by any means – electronic, mechanical, photocopy, recording or otherwise, without the prior written permission of the publisher or distributor.

Preface

The field of digital forensics is rapidly evolving and continues to gain significance in both the law enforcement and the scientific community. Being intrinsically interdisciplinary, it draws upon a wide range of subject areas such as information & communication technologies, law, social sciences and business administration.

With this in mind, the workshop on Digital Forensics and Incident Analysis (WDFIA) specifically addresses this multi-facetted aspect, with papers invited from the full spectrum of issues relating to the theory and practice of digital forensics and incident analysis.

This book represents the proceedings from the 2011 event, which was held in London, UK. A total of 14 papers are included, spanning a range of topics including systems and network investigation, services and applications and supporting the forensic process. All of the papers were subject to double-blind peer review, with each being reviewed by at least two members of the international programme committee.

We would like to thank the authors for submitting their work and sharing their findings, and the international programme committee for their efforts in reviewing the submissions and ensuring the quality of the resulting event and proceedings. We would also like to thank Christopher Wills for acting as the local Chair. His support was invaluable in making this workshop a success.

Nathan Clarke & Theodore Tryfonas
Editors, WDFIA 2011

London, July 2011

International Programme Committee

P. Bednar	University of Portsmouth	United Kingdom
C. Bolan	Edith Cowan University	Australia
S. Bradford	LSBsoft Ltd	United Kingdom
S. Brenner	University of Dayton	USA
A. Cerezo	University of Malaga	Spain
T. Chen	Swansea University	United Kingdom
B. Crispo	University of Trento	Italy
J. Evans	QinetiQ	United Kingdom
C. Fuhrman	Ecole de technologie superieure	Canada
S. Furnell	University of Plymouth	United Kingdom
J. Haggerty	Liverpool John Moores University	United Kingdom
C. Hargreaves	Cranfield University	United Kingdom
C. Hennell	British Telecom Openreach	United Kingdom
B. Hutchinson	Edith Cowan University	Australia
C. Illioudis	ATEI of Thessalonki	Greece
A. Irons	University of Sunderland	United Kingdom
A. Jones	Khalifa University	UAE
	Edith Cowan University	Australia
S. Karatzouni	University of Portsmouth	United Kingdom
M. Karyda	University of the Aegean	Greece
T. Karygiannis	National Institute of Standards and Technology (NIST)	USA
V. Katos	Democritus University of Thrace	Greece
G. Kessler	Champlain College	USA
S. Kokolakis	University of the Aegean	Greece
I. Kotenko	SPIIRAS	Russia
C.T. Li	University of Warwick	United Kingdom
J. Lopez	University of Malaga	Spain
T. Martin	Khalifa University	UAE
M. Merabti	Liverpool John Moores University	United Kingdom
I. Mitchell	Middlesex University	United Kingdom
L. Mitrou	University of the Aegean	Greece
J. Niccolis	Avon & Somerset Police	United Kingdom
G. Pangalos	Kingston University	United Kingdom
A. Patel	University of Kebangsaan	Malaysia
G. Pernul	University of Regensburg	Germany
G. Quirchmayr	University of Vienna	Austria
G. Richard III	University of New Orleans	USA
V. Roussev	University of New Orleans	USA
P. Sommer	London School of Economics	United Kingdom
I. Sutherland	University of Glamorgan	United Kingdom
H. Tamman	Staffordshire University	United Kingdom
P. Thomas	University of Glamorgan	United Kingdom
D. Tsaptsinos	Kingston University	United Kingdom
C. Valli	Edith Cowan University	Australia
S. Venkatesan	The University of Texas at Dallas	USA

Contents

Exploring Solutions Put Forth to Solve Computer Forensic Investigations of Large Storage Media
A.Z. Tabona and W.B. Glisson
 — 1

Proposing a Digital Operational Forensic Investigation Process
M.A. Bihina Bella, M.S. Olivier and J.H.P. Eloff
 — 17

Digital Forensics: the Need for Integration
P. Sant and M. Hewling
 — 33

A Formal Logic for Digital Investigations: A Case Study Using BPB Modifications.
I. Mitchell
 — 44

Reconstructive Steganalysis by Source Bytes Lead Digit Distribution Examination
A. Zaharis, A. Martini, T. Tryfonas, C. Illioudis and G Pangalos
 — 55

Combating Information Hiding Using Forensic Methodology
C. Balan, D.S. Vidyadharan, S. Dija and K.L. Thomas
 — 69

Forensic Analysis of Navman GPS Devices
D. Jones
 — 76

Active Detection and Prevention of Sophisticated ARP-Poisoning Man-in-the-Middle Attacks on Switched Ethernet LANs
K. Kalajdzic and A. Patel
 — 81

Towards a Forensically Ready Cloud Storage Service
T. Spyridopoulos and V. Katos
 — 93

Requirements for Wireless Sensor Networks in Order to Achieve Digital Forensic Readiness
F. Mouton and H.S. Venter
 — 108

A Signature Detection Scheme for Distributed Storage
R. Hegarty, M. Merabti, Q. Shi and R. Askwith
 — 122

LUARM – An Audit Engine for Insider Misuse Detection
G. Magklaras, S.M. Furnell and M. Papadaki
 — 133

Issues on Selecting Image Features for Robust Source Camera Identification
Y. Hu, C-T. Li, C. Zhou and X. Lin
 — 149

A Social Network Discovery Model for Digital Forensics Investigations   160
A. Karran, J. Haggerty, D. Lamb, M. Taylor and D. Llewellyn-Jones

Exploring Solutions Put Forth to Solve Computer Forensic Investigations of Large Storage Media

A.Z. Tabona and W.B. Glisson

School of Humanities
University of Glasgow
e-mail: 1005599z@student.gla.ac.uk, brad.glisson@glasgow.ac.uk

Abstract

The capacity of digital storage media is growing at a phenomenal rate, leading to an increase in the overall time it takes to process a typical digital forensics investigation. Conventional tools and techniques simply do not cater for the size of potential evidence that investigators have to analyse. With digital evidence being available on an increasing number of digital media types, ranging from portable media players, to Global Positioning System (GPS) devices, to rack-mountable servers, in addition to the fact that there is a rising trend for digitizing information in the business world, the problem is only getting worse. This paper endeavours to initiate an investigation into the current solutions put forth to solve computer forensic investigations of large storage media for the purpose of stimulating ideas and encouraging expansion of current solutions within the research community.

Keywords

Forensics, Analytics, Datasets, Triage, Search, Distributed Processing, Hashing, Large-Scale, Data Mining

1. Introduction

Storage media vendors are answering calls from the market to have more compact devices that give customers increased storage for their dollar value. At the time of writing, a 3TB (Terabytes) hard disk drive costs £140 ($220) (dabs.com, 2011). The past few years have seen a decrease in the physical size of storage media but an increase in the storage capacity at the same time. Nowadays, it is not uncommon to find pervasive media devices that hold between 16GB to 160GB (Gigabytes) worth of data (Apple, 2011), or entry-level desktop computers that come pre-built with at least 250GB hard disk drives (Dell, 2011). This increase in storage media has a direct impact on the proliferation of digital evidence in a typical computer forensic investigation. Statistics from the FBI (FBI, 2010a) show that the number of Terabytes they processed for the 2009 Financial Year doubled from two years prior to reach a staggering 2334 Terabytes worth of data. By way of comparison, think of the entire contents of an academic research library (each and every book, journal, transcript, etc.) being the equivalent of 2 Terabytes. The notion of data doubling every two years is further corroborated by Roussev (2009).

The traditional approach to a computer forensics investigation (seize, image, search) is no longer viable for large-scale examinations (Rogers, 2006; Rowlingson, 2004). Storage media capacity has increased at such a rate that computer forensic investigators are unable to keep up. Their productivity throughput and ability to maintain a reasonable backlog have also suffered as a result of storage media being too large for manual analysis (FBI, 2010a). In addition, a typical forensic investigation is likely to encompass multiple devices or machines, ranging from smartphones to laptops to large-scale financial database servers. Gone are the days when a digital forensics team had the resource to analyze each and every piece of storage media looking for potential evidence.

Investigators might agree that current implementations of industry tools (such as AccessData's FTK and Guidance Software's EnCase) have failed to implement any substantial time saving techniques. Their inability to sufficiently handle terabyte datasets leaves investigators in a situation where even preliminary forensic tasks take an inordinate amount of time. Researchers have proposed a number of solutions to the problem, including hash lists of known files (Roussev, 2009), triage tools and models (AccessData, 2011; FBI, 2000; IDEAL Technology Corp., 2011, Rogers, 2006; Microsoft, 2011; SPEKTOR Forensic, 2011), de-centralized parallel processing (van den Hengel, 2008; Richard and Roussev, 2006; Liebrock, 2007; Roussev et al., 2009), data mining (Beebe and Clark, 2005; Rao, 2010; Abraham, 2006), data sampling (Mora and Kloet, 2010), data analytics and traditional search, filter and categorization techniques (Tanner and Dampier, 2010; Beebe and Clark, 2005; Beebe and Dietrich, 2007; Beebe, 2009; Pollitt, 2010), implementing layers of abstraction within the system (Carrier, 2003) and a methodology that promotes the sharing and re-use of knowledge gained from past forensic examinations (Tanner and Dampier, 2010). As well as the technical challenges faced by investigators when dealing with the increasing capacity of storage media, there are also the legal challenges to contend with (Spafford, 2006; Sommer, 2004). Investigators are under increasing pressure from the justice system to provide evidence quickly, when they do not understand the scale of the data that investigators need to analyse. In addition, the economics of handling evidence are also a challenge; the costs associated with printing terabytes worth of data as well as managing and maintaining the evidence itself (Sommer, 2004). There is a dire need for solutions that assist digital forensic investigators in reducing the dataset that they analyse by removing 'noisy' data and helping them to quickly visualize only data of relevance. This notion is further corroborated by Riley et al. (2008) who demonstrate how traditional preliminary forensic analysis tasks such as imaging eat into investigation time. Experiments by these authors show that imaging a 250GB hard drive takes in excess of 1.5 hours.

This paper is organized as follows. Section 2 looks at hashing techniques and Section 3 discusses triage. Section 4 discusses the different methods that involve the retrieval and analysis of data, while Section 5 contains a discussion about distributed forensics and the importance of parallel processing. Section 6 highlights the way things stand now and future work, whilst exploring a holistic design that allows various solutions to work as a cohesive unit. Finally, the author's conclusions are documented in Section 7.

2. Hashing

Hashing is a technique used for data integrity and verification matching of known data. The way hashing works it to take a random string of binary data as input and generate a unique alphanumeric value (known as the message digest) as output, typically in a SHA1 or MD5 format (Carrier, 2005). Hashing is uniformly applied in the computer forensics world to hard drive volumes or individual files for data integrity purposes or to compare files to determine if a dataset contains "known" objects (Carrier, 2003; Roussev, 2009). The concept is to compare the hashes of every file found on a hard disk with a database of hashes to see which ones match with a hash that is known to be "good" or "bad". Such hash databases would be pre-compiled and verified manually.

The National Software Reference Library (NSRL) (National Software Ref. Library, 2011), maintained by the US National Institute of Standard and Technology (NIST), is a comprehensive list of hashes belonging to common operating systems and applications as well as software that may be considered malicious. Unlike the US National Drug Intelligence Center's HashKeeper database (USDOJ, 2011), the NSRL does not contain a list of illicit data, such as known child pornography images. Both these databases are used extensively by investigators around the world to filter out 'noisy' data that does not need to be examined because it can quickly be determined if that data is considered to be good or bad. In addition to NSRL and HashKeeper, vendors of commercial forensics tools also maintain their own versions of hash databases that contain a list of known hashes for other software.

Hashing forms the basis of many commercial and open source forensic software packages. AccessData's FTK software, for example, has what they call the KFF (Known File Filter) which uses the NSRL and HashKeeper databases, allows you to import your own set of file hashes and customize the alerting options for different types of hashes (AccessData Forensic Toolkit. 2010). There are typically two approaches to this data reduction technique; 'known objects' which performs a comparison to determine if there is a direct match and, 'similar objects' which compares whether file 'A' is similar to any other file within the given dataset. These approaches are usually called 'simple hashing' and 'fuzzy hashing'.

2.1. Simple Hashing

Simple hashing involves comparing the hashes of known files, such as those found in the NSRL (National Software Ref. Library, 2011) and HashKeeper (USDOJ, 2011), with those found within the dataset. If a set of file hashes match then that data is 'removed' from the dataset that is displayed to the investigator. Simple hashing also allows file fragments to be found by splitting the file into multiple blocks and keeping a list of the hashes of each individual block to compare with data fragments found in unallocated space, for example (Roussev, 2009). The disadvantage of hashing is that, since the hash list is processed in memory in a sequential manner, the larger the dataset grows the worse the query performance throughput will be. While hash databases such as NSRL and HashKeeper aim to facilitate the fast processing of the hash list by already coming as a sorted set, this does little to help in the long term as the hash database grows.

Roussev (2009) suggests using Bloom Filters to counteract this problem which operate by using a set of independent hash functions to generate a value for elements in a vector of size m based on a given input string. By using each hash function to generate a hash on a specific element, a comparison can then be made to see whether the element has its bits set to 1 or 0 when a lookup is made. Bloom Filters allow for fast processing of hash lists, but may generate a minimal rate of false positives. Roussev (2009) gives an example of increasing the number of hashes in a set from 50 million to 500 million and only having a false positive rate of 0.2 per cent. While simple hashing techniques allow known files to be filtered out at a faster rate than a manual analysis, they do not assist an investigator in finding files of a similar type.

2.2. Fuzzy Hashing

Fuzzy hashing allows two datasets to be compared for similarity. Characteristics are drawn from each object in the dataset and then compared for likeliness. The way it operates is to split each file into multiple chunks and generate a corresponding 6-bit hash for each chunk which are then concatenated into one larger base64 encoded hash. Roussev (2009) points out that fuzzy hashing techniques are successful in finding small objects and similar versions of files, but they suffer when it comes to finding similarities in larger files.

Related to fuzzy hashing is the concept of data fingerprinting, which generates a signature of file data that is more tolerant to changes in the original file (Roussev, 2009). This is different to the design of hashing which generates a different output if even one bit of the input is changed. Fingerprinting operates on the same lines as fuzzy hashing whereby characteristic features are selected for each object and then collated and compared for similarity at a binary level. This is highly beneficial in determining if a file has changed format. For example, consider a static XML file that is viewed in a web browser and then saved as a TXT file. Even though the tags will be removed as part of the conversion, the text should remain the same and produce the same set of characteristics as the original static XML file, allowing the versions to be correlated.

Lejsek et al. (2010) argue that hash lists are unsuitable for the purposes of video identification due to the lack of resources available to build and maintain a hash database of video content and that since there are so many different variations of such content, hashing video files would simply not be scalable in the long term. The authors propose a video identification solution whereby the video file is split into different points, each of which are encoded to have a unique fingerprint which can then be compared with a database of known video fingerprints. This automated process would save the investigator having to watch each and every video file to determine its category; it would essentially allow them to pinpoint video files that were of a pornographic nature for example. Lejsek et al.'s experiments show that in a sample dataset containing over 25,000 hours of video content, they were able to classify the files 70% faster than a manual analysis. This is advantageous in allowing the investigator to get the job done in less time while saving on productivity costs. The disadvantage of such a technique is that as the size of the collection increases, the quality of the results decreases, therefore requiring constant fine tuning by the investigator.

3. Triage

Adapting the Oxford English dictionary's (2011) definition of 'triage' to the field of computer forensics, it could be interpreted as: 'A method whereby items are ranked in order of priority or importance in order to determine which should be processed first'. In investigations that involve kidnap or murder, time is of the essence as it could mean the difference between life and death. Rogers et al. (2006) propose The Cyber Forensics Field Triage Process Model (CFFTPM), a formalized methodology that was built upon years of real-world experience where various approaches have been tried and tested in the field. The authors demonstrate how their model can be used to collect various evidentiary materials and be used in several specific cases including child pornography, drug, and fraud based investigations. A benefit of this methodology is that it allows for a feedback loop between first and second line investigators. Information can be fed back to each other, allowing keyword and file type searches to be fine-tuned based on new information that is gathered from the initial triage process.

Industry tools such as AccessData's AD Triage (AccessData, 2011), the FBI's ACES (Automated Computer Examination System) (FBI, 2000) and Microsoft's COFEE framework (Microsoft, 2011), as well as triage devices like SPEKTOR (SPEKTOR Forensic, 2011) and STRIKE (IDEAL Technology Corp., 2011), allow first responders to collect relevant data quickly and in a forensically sound manner. Such tools can however be considered immature and will require time to evolve, based on user experience and technology advancements.

3.1. Image Recognition

Choudhury et al. (2008) propose a novel skin tone detection algorithm that analyses images to determine if they could be of a pornographic nature. The results of their experiments are encouraging and show accuracy rates of over 78%. Such a technique would be useful for first responders in a child pornography case where they could quickly run a 'triage' scan using a tool that implements this algorithm to determine which storage media is likely to contain illicit images. The investigator would then only have to seize, image and analyse those drives.

Chen et al. (2005) offer a Content Based Image Recognition (CBIR) technique that extracts properties from previously identified illicit images and uses these properties when searching target drives for contraband. The process will identify those images that share the same properties as other contraband and that may have had their orientation, quality, or size properties altered. This is useful in a triage scenario when the investigator needs to quickly determine if a storage media contains illegal images.

3.2. Selective Data Acquisition

Lee et al. (2009) propose a methodology that promotes selective data acquisition, alleviating the need to duplicate or image the entire storage media and allowing for the investigation of relevant data only. Indeed, the process of selective data acquisition is considered to be one of the solutions to the challenges investigators face of dealing with significant amounts of data (Beebe, 2009). The Phased Investigation Methodology (PIM) is broken down into four steps; target selection and pre-investigation, tracing recent computer usage, computer usage pattern analysis, investigation of user-based file contents. At each step, the investigator can analyse only the data that is required and decide whether to move onto the next step or if all or parts of the system should be excluded from analysis altogether.

The drawback of using triage is the potential of missing some exculpatory evidence during the preliminary stages of deciding which machines or devices should be examined first. Additionally, forensic triage tools often come pre-configured with 'default' options or require pre-investigation customization. Opening up tools to investigator customization is beneficial in terms of allowing them to define what data is to be collected, but at the same time generates a risk of investigator bias.

4. Data Analytics

4.1. Scoped Search Methods

The feature set of the current generation of forensic tools already offer some time saving techniques for dealing with large data sets that are built around search mechanisms. File carving, for example, is a process whereby the tool automatically carves out files of interest based on their starting and ending file signature (Richard and Roussev, 2006). This alleviates the investigator from needing to manually sift through large amounts of hexadecimal values looking for obfuscated data. The disadvantage of such a process is that it may end up carving out duplicate files; thumbnails from larger JPEG files, images within PDF documents, etc. Consequently, with carving there is a tradeoff between looking at certain files twice versus missing a possibly crucial piece of evidence that is hidden amongst unallocated space.

File categorization techniques allow the investigator to focus on particular pieces of evidence. Sorting, filtering and file categories are often used in current forensic toolsets to search for particular information and reduce the dataset being displayed to the investigator. Sorting allows the investigator to group files by various fields, including file type, size, hash value, path, etc. Filtering allows only data that meets certain criteria to be displayed and file categorization displays files in a hierarchical format based on their category (e.g. Documents, Images, Deleted Items, etc.).

Searching allows the investigator to look for evidence containing a specified keyword or set of keywords using the 'AND' or 'OR' logical operators.

There are typically two types of search; what is known as 'live' search where the entire dataset is searched in real-time and 'indexed' search where the dataset, having previously been indexed, is searched for items that correspond to a given keyword. Garfinkel (2010) refers to these techniques as the "Visibility, Filter and Report" model and argues that while the investigator is able to search for specific items, they are not able to quickly prioritize the data that they find. Parallelizing such an approach is also not possible with current tools (Garfinkel, 2010), meaning that the problem is going to get worst as the capacity of storage media continues to increase. Furthermore, encrypted data, compressed files and embedded text formats cannot be evaluated using search utilities because they operate based on a string of plain text. Regular expressions can help with this by offering a method of finding text that matches a given data pattern. For example, the following regular expression will find all IP addresses in a search: \b\d{1,3}\.\d{1,3}\.\d{1,3}\.\d{1,3}\b.

A problem associated with the use of a search utility is that it is assumed that the computer forensic investigator knows explicitly what keywords and phrases to use in the search. In addition, the time it takes for them to manually review these results is also a problem (Beebe, 2009). Relying on the human factor alone for each individual case would be unwise. This is where having pre-defined keyword lists based on the type of case being investigated would be beneficial, in addition of course to the investigator's intuition and an automated collection of keywords derived from the evidence itself.

Being dependent on conventional search methods will only make the problem worse in the long term, as datasets continue to grow at astounding rates. One approach to the problem of analysing large datasets is to improve the efficiency of the analytical approaches used today (Beebe, 2009; Pollitt, 2010). Beebe (2009) discusses how the current analytical approaches result in "underutilization of available computational power and high information retrieval overhead". The present-day implementations of search, retrieval and analytic algorithms are underutilized and do not scale to the full potential of today's computing platforms. It would be wise to borrow a leaf out of the information retrieval group's expertise and utilize an advanced algorithm for intelligent search mechanisms in digital forensics applications. This would allow relevant data to be presented to investigators more quickly whilst reducing the "noisy" results.

Text string searches occur at the physical level of the storage media, meaning the specified search string can be found in locations that are independent of the logical data structures, partitioned volumes, and data allocation flags (Beebe and Dietrich, 2007). This poses as another problem for conventional text based search tools in that they return an extremely high number of 'hits' (Beebe and Clark, 2007; Beebe and Dietrich, 2007), a lot of which bear no relevance whatsoever to the case in question. To solve this problem, there is a need for the search tool to either reduce the number of irrelevant search hits returned or present the results in a way that allows the investigator to locate relevant hits quickly (Beebe and Clark, 2007).

Beebe and Clark (2007) propose an approach that builds on the latter and allows the investigator to locate more relevant hits more quickly by thematically clustering digital forensic text string search results. The algorithm would be responsible for automatically grouping false positives that are generated as part of a generalized keyword search, allowing the investigator to skip these false positives as they analyse the results. Beebe and Dietrich (2007) propose an approach which introduces additional system state transitions and operators. Additional levels of computer information processing (CIP) operators gather, classify, index and rank the hits before they are presented to a human for information processing. This is beneficial since less relevant evidence will be missed and can scale to large datasets. The disadvantage of such a technique is that there is a risk that the investigator will become over reliant on the computer interpreted information and bias towards certain hits.

Tanner and Dampier (2010) suggest a socio-technical approach to the problem of investigating evidence on large storage media. This approach involves the use of concept maps to generate and represent the relationships between information and expert knowledge. They argue that this knowledge can then be shared with other investigators and re-used in future examinations for selecting better search terms. The pros to such a solution are that it will help to narrow down the results that need to be analysed and offer a visual representation of them. The cons to this approach are that it is initially time consuming, requires a comprehensive learning curve and may result in duplicating work processes.

4.2. Random Data Sampling

To help reduce backlog produced as a result of investigators having to analyse large storage media, random data sampling can be used to calculate the number of items that the investigator needs to review from a given dataset. This will allow the investigator to have x% confidence that between n% and n% of the items on the storage media are contraband. The formula used to calculate the sample size that the investigator is required to analyse is shown below (Mora and Kloet, 2010):

$$n = \frac{N}{1 + N(e)^2}$$

n is the sample size, N is the population size, and e is the level of precision required. The formula above assumes a degree of variability of 0.5 and a confidence level of 95%. As an example, consider a dataset containing 2000 items (this is the population size) where the investigator wanted to know how many items he or she would need to review to be 95% confident that the remainder of the dataset contained contraband. Using the formula above, the sample size would be 333, meaning the investigator would only need to review this amount of items from the population as opposed to the entire population itself (Mora and Kloet, 2010).

The lack of random data sampling techniques in commercial forensic applications like Guidance Software's EnCase and AccessData's FTK, are putting the investigator at a disadvantage by requiring them to analyse a large set of data when, based on statistical theorems, they should really be able to only analyse a sample of that data to give them confidence that there is a specific type of material present on the evidence drive. Mora and Kloet (2010) propose using random data sampling as a triage technique whereby the first responder would review a given sample size from a data collection to determine whether that storage device or computer needed to be seized and taken back to the lab for further analysis.

4.3. Data Mining

Data mining is the process of finding and retrieving data from large datasets and presenting that data to the user in a useful and comprehendible format. Data mining can be sub-divided into three classes; (1) descriptive data modelling, (2) predictive data modelling, and (3) content retrieval (Beebe and Clark, 2005).

Descriptive data modelling involves the summarization and comparison of data with the aim of aggregating it into a smaller subset of data. Summarization is unsuitable for digital forensic purposes due to the risk of data loss during the aggregation stage. Comparison is more suited however, since it only involves determining the differences between two datasets. Predictive data modelling involves identifying specific data characteristics with the aim of anticipating future observations, and content retrieval data mining involves the retrieval of unstructured or semi-structured data sets (Beebe and Clark, 2005).

Data mining techniques for multimedia are of the utmost importance for digital forensics. Child pornography cases can involve thousands upon thousands of illicit images (FBI, 2010b), which is often too much of a burden for the investigator(s) to analyse manually. By using data mining, images of interest can be classified by type (human, building, car, etc.) and retrieved and displayed to the investigator accordingly.

One of the key benefits of data mining is the possibility to rank documents based on relevance to the investigation and prioritize the search 'hits' that the investigator will analyse. In addition, by using data mining techniques, costs and system and human processing time can be reduced and data analysis quality improved. Enhanced utilization of computing power and the ability to discover trends within a dataset that are normally hidden to humans, are also benefits (Beebe and Clark, 2005). The drawbacks of data mining potentially include advanced training to know how to mine properly and proper interpretation of the data. Since data mining converts data at a higher abstraction level error calculations are possible (Beebe and Clark, 2005).

Abraham (2006) builds on the data mining framework by proposing a methodology for analysing sequence events from data in order to determine if there were any unusual occurrences happening on the system and build an investigate profile to help the investigator determine if a particular machine should be considered suspicious.

Meanwhile, Rao et al. (2010) suggests a framework for data analysis (using data mining) that employs a statistical approach to validating the data at the pre-processing stage to ensure the reliability of the data being displayed within the application. The authors state that the proposed model can be adapted to identification of illegally stored data, identification of hidden and encrypted data and identification of renamed file extensions in the future. While digital forensics research into incorporating data mining techniques for large data sets has been limited (Beebe and Clark, 2005), initial studies indicate positive results and highlighting its relevance.

5. Distributed Forensics

The processing power of a single machine does not scale to meet the time-sensitive requirements that are needed to handle most large scale digital forensic operations. Hence, the concept of utilizing the processing power of multiple systems to aid in the handling of a forensics investigation is an attractive proposition for the digital forensics community. Having multiple machines running in parallel and processing the same task (searching or indexing of a large scale dataset, for example) will reduce the overall case investigation time and allow the investigator to focus on what is really important. Indeed, it is easy to see how running tasks such as evidence identification and imaging in parallel would be beneficial in allowing the investigator to focus on acquiring the most relevant data at an early stage of the investigation (Nance et al., 2009).

Van den Hengel et al. (2008) propose a system that uses distributed computing and image processing techniques to quickly extract relevant pieces of data, bringing the important events within the video content to the forefront of the investigator's analysis. The system uses a series of agents to execute tasks on the processing servers, and then return the results to the user in a low-bandwidth format which can be accessed via a pervasive mobile device such as a smartphone.

Roussev et al. (2009) provide a proof of concept that demonstrates how the MPI MapReduce model can be adapted for use in a digital forensic environment for tasks such as indexing, image processing and analytics. The system is based on shared memory that is spread over multiple nodes. The authors argue that by using this model to process forensic related tasks in parallel, terabyte sized datasets can be handled in real-time.

Liebrock et al. (2007) discuss the design of a system that uses parallelism and visual analytics to help reduce the dataset and better handle the imaging of large datasets. Richard and Roussev (2006) discuss a similar distributed processing environment which supports the processing of data in RAM (Random Access Memory) and utilizes more CPU (Central Processing Unit) cycles by spreading the load over multiple nodes. This de-centralized approach helps make investigations more efficient, but does come at a price. Given the need for more hardware, power, associated maintenance and operational aspects, distributed forensics processing incurs higher cost.

AccessData offers a form of parallel data processing in the shape of its PRTK based Distributed Network Attack (DNA) product (AccessData Forensic Toolkit, 2010) by using multiple machines to run the password recovery process in parallel, but more work needs to be done to allow other digital forensics tasks such as imaging, indexing and searching to utilize parallelism over multiple machines and speed up the overall investigation process. Currently AccessData only has multi-core support as part of their Forensic Toolkit (FTK) product (AccessData Forensic Toolkit, 2010) and, while this is a step in the right direction, it is still a way away from a fully-fledged distributed forensic computing environment.

It is worth mentioning that the rapid adoption of cloud computing services as a storage medium is changing the way investigators perceive and deal with digital evidence (Pollitt, 2010). The method and complexity of evidence collection and analysis in a cloud computing environment is a cause for concern. Currently, the digital forensics community lacks the tools required to acquire and analyse data that resides on cloud storage (Pollitt, 2010), which highlights it as an area for future research that is expected to grow in the years ahead.

6. Discussion and Future Work

The following table gives a high-level review of each solution category based on conclusions derived from an extensive literature survey. Future research should involve interviewing practitioners to validate the indications perceived in the literature. An in-depth examination of each implementation is also warranted. Table 1 uses a 3 level rating scale where H = High, M = Medium, and L = Low.

Criterion	Hashing	Triage	Analytics	Distributed Forensics
Accuracy	H	M	M	H
Speed	M	H	M	H
Risk of evidence omission	M	H	M	L
Ease of use	H	M	L	M
Ease of implementation	M	M	M	L

Table 1: Solution Categories Review

Table 1 supports the idea that investigators should not rely on a single technique alone and that the overall solution will probably use a blend of techniques that are dependent on the type of investigation. One area of future research would be to focus on automating forensic analysis tasks over distributed environments. This research should investigate incorporating advanced data analytic techniques and different levels of abstraction to make the investigation of large scale datasets more manageable and less time consuming. A logical order for the implementation of these techniques would be as follows:

1. Identify and assess evidence relevance (triage)
2. Reduce the dataset by removing 'noisy' data (hashing and analytics)
3. Process the dataset

Another idea for future research would be to look into the implementation of standard data analytic techniques into triage tools. Is it possible to increase the accuracy of the triage tools with these techniques? These techniques could also be considered for use in data set processing. It would also be interesting to test the Information Retrieval (IR) techniques in a distributed computing environment to see if they are effective. These research areas could be coupled with fuzzy hashing, data fingerprinting or categorization methods to identify and remove similar items from the data set being investigated.

All the proposals put forth thus far are centred on data reduction techniques that attempt to eliminate the 'noisy' data from the dataset so that investigators do not waste valuable time analysing evidence that is of no significance. A system that incorporates multiple such solutions and applies a funnel approach to narrowing the scope of the data would be beneficial. The key to this investigative strategy would be to implement an automated data reduction technique at each level of the funnel in a parallelized fashion, until only the relevant data is revealed. This would allow the investigator to have more thinking time when dealing with the case.

7. Conclusions

As Fred Brooks indicated, there is "no silver bullet" (Brooks, 1987). The same is true for solving the large scale data analysis issue in computer forensics. The increase in time taken and data storage capacities are driving the need for additional research in this area. Industry collaboration with the research community to investigate new and innovative approaches to working with large scale digital storage media for digital forensic investigations would benefit both communities.

This paper discusses the challenges faced by investigators when dealing with large storage media and the different solutions put forth thus far to help combat the problem. These solutions include hashing, fingerprinting, triage, data analytics (searching, categorization, filtering, random data sampling, data mining), and distributed forensics (parallel processing). When using such techniques, there is always going to be a trade-off between missing a possibly crucial piece of evidence versus saving time which, by way of human nature can also be the case even if the investigator manually sifted through each and every bit on the evidence drive.

8. References

Abraham, T. (2006), "Event sequence mining to develop profiles for computer forensic investigation purposes", *In Proceedings of the 2006 Australasian workshops on Grid computing and e-research*, Buyya, R., Ma, T., Rei, S.N., Steketee, C., and Susilo, W. (Eds.), Vol. 54. Australian Computer Society, Inc., Darlinghurst, Australia, 2006, pp. 145-153.

AccessData Website (2011) *AD Triage* (Online). Available from: http://accessdata.com/products/forensic-investigation/ad-triage (Accessed: 29 March 2011)

AccessData Forensic Toolkit (2010) *Sales and Promotional Summary* (Online). Available from: http://accessdata.com/media/en_us/print/techdocs/Forensic%20Toolkit.pdf (Accessed: 29 March 2011)

Apple Website (2011) iPod Products (Online). Available from: http://www.apple.com/uk/ipod (Accessed: 29 March 2011)

Beebe, N. and Clark, J. (2007), "Digital forensic text string searching: Improving information retrieval effectiveness by thematically clustering search results", *Digital Investigation*, Vol. 4, Supplement 1, 2007. pp. 49-54.

Beebe, N., Dietrich, G. (2007), "A New Process Model for Text String Searching", *Advances in Digital Forensics III, IFIP International Federation for Information Processing.* Craiger, P. and Shenoi, S. (Eds.), Vol. 242. National Centre for Forensic Science, Orlando, Florida, 2007. pp. 179-191.

Beebe, N. and Clark, J. (2005), "Dealing with Terabyte Data Sets in Digital Investigations", *Advances in Digital Forensics, IFIP International Federation for Information Processing*, Pollitt, M. and Shenoi, S. (Eds.), Vol. 194. National Centre for Forensic Science, Orlando, Florida, 2005. pp. 3-16.

Beebe, N. (2009), "Digital Forensic Research: The Good, the Bad and the Unaddressed", *Advances in Digital Forensics V,* Boston, USA, 2009. pp. 17-36.

Brooks, F. P. Jr. (1987), "No silver bullet: essence and accidents of software engineering". Computer, Vol. 20, No. 4, 1987. pp. 0-19.

Carrier, B. (2003), "Defining Digital Forensic Examination and Analysis Tools Using Abstraction Layers", *International Journal of Digital Evidence,* IJDE Vol. 1, No. 4, 2003. pp. 1-12.

Carrier, B. (2005), *File System Forensic Analysis*. Addison-Wesley. Indiana, USA. 2005. Chapter 1, p. 6.

Chen, Y., Roussev, V., Richard, G., Gao, Y. (2005), "Content-Based Image Retrieval for Digital Forensics", *Advances in Digital Forensics, IFIP International Federation for Information Processing*, Pollitt, M. and Shenoi, S. (Eds.), Vol. 194. National Centre for Forensic Science, Orlando, Florida, pp. 271-282.

Choudhury, A., Rogers, M., Gillam, B., and Watson, K. (2008), "A Novel Skin Tone Detection Algorithm for Contraband Image Analysis". *In Proceedings of the 2008 Third International Workshop on Systematic Approaches to Digital Forensic Engineering (SADFE '08)*. IEEE Computer Society, Washington, DC, USA, 2008, pp. 3-9.

Dabs.com Website (2011) Seagate 3TB FreeAgent GoFlex USB 2.0 3.5" Black Desktop Hard Drive (STAC3000200). Available from: http://www.dabs.com/products/seagate-3tb-freeagent-goflex-usb-2-0-3-5--black-desktop-hard-drive-73QP.html (Accessed April 04 2011)

Dell Website (2011) Optiplex 380 Desktop (Online). Available from: http://www.dell.com/uk/business/p/optiplex-380/pd?oc=x0238004&model_id=optiplex-380&~ck (Accessed: 29 March 2011)

Federal Bureau of Investigation Website (2010) Regional Computer Forensics Laboratory Program Annual Report FY2009 (Online). Available from:

http://www.rcfl.gov/downloads/documents/RCFL_Nat_Annual09.pdf (Accessed 28 March 2011)

Federal Bureau of Investigation Website (2000) Laboratory: Computer Analysis and Response Team (Online). Available from: http://www2.fbi.gov/hq/lab/org/cart.htm (Accessed: 27 March 2011)

Federal Bureau of Investigation Website (2010) Press Release: Muncie Man Sentenced to Seven Years for Distributing Child Porn (Online). Available from: http://indianapolis.fbi.gov/dojpressrel/pressrel10/ip031010.htm (Accessed: 29 March 2011)

Garfinkel, S.L. (2010), "Digital forensics research: The next 10 years", *Digital Investigation*, Volume 7, Supplement 1, In Proceedings of the Tenth Annual DFRWS Conference, August 2010, pp. 64-73.

Guidance Software EnCase Website (2011) (Online). Available from: http://www.guidancesoftware.com/computer-forensics-fraud-investigation-software.htm (Accessed: 29 March 2011)

IDEAL Technology Corp. Website (2011) STRIKE Overview (Online). Available from: http://www.idealcorp.com/products/index.php?product=STRIKE (Accessed: 29 March 2011)

Lee, S., Bang, J., Lim, K., Kim, J., Lee, S. (2009), "A Stepwise Methodology for Tracing Computer Usage", *NCM '09. Fifth International Joint Conference on Networked Computing, Advanced Information Management and Digital Content and Multimedia Technologies*, 2009. pp. 1852-1857.

Lejsek, H., Þormóðsdóttir, H., Ásmundsson, F., Daðason, K., Jóhannsson, Á., Jónsson, B. and Amsaleg, L. (2010), "Videntifier Forensic: large-scale video identification in practice", *In Proceedings of the 2nd ACM workshop on Multimedia in Forensics, Security and Intelligence (MiFor '10)*, ACM, New York, NY, USA, pp. 1-6.

Liebrock, L.M., Marrero, N., Burton, D.P., Prine, R., Cornelius, E., Shakamuri, M., and Urias, V. (2007). "A preliminary design for digital forensics analysis of terabyte size data sets", *In Proceedings of the 2007 ACM symposium on Applied computing (SAC '07)*, ACM, New York, NY, USA, pp. 190-191.

Microsoft Website (2011) Computer Online Forensic Evidence Extractor (COFEE) (Online). Available from: http://www.microsoft.com/industry/government/solutions/cofee/default.aspx (Accessed: 29 March 2011)

Mora, R.J. and Kloet, B. (2010), *Digital forensic sampling* (Online). Available from: http://blogs.sans.org/computer-forensics/files/2010/03/statisticalforensictriage.pdf (Accessed: 27 March 2011)

Nance, K., Hay, B., and Bishop, M. (2009), "Digital Forensics: Defining a Research Agenda", *Proceedings of the 42nd Hawaii International Conference on System Sciences*. 2009. pp. 1-6.

National Software Ref. Library Website (2011) (Online). Available from: http://www.nsrl.nist.gov (Accessed: 30 March 2011)

Oxford Dictionaries Website (2011) 'triage' definition (Online). Available from: http://www.oxforddictionaries.com/definition/triage?view=uk (Accessed: 29 March 2011)

Pollitt, M. (2010), "A History of Digital Forensics", *Sixth Annual IFIP WG 11.9 International Conference on Digital Forensics*. University of Hong Kong, Hong Kong. 2010. pp. 3-15.

Rao, P.G., Bhat, V.H., and Shenoy, D. (2010), "A Data Mining Approach for Data Generation and Analysis for Digital Forensic Application", *IACSIT Int. Journal of Engineering and Technology*, Vol. 2, No. 3 June 2010. pp. 313-319.

Richard, G.G. III and Roussev, V. (2006), "Next-generation digital forensics", *Commun. ACM 49*, 2 (February 2006), pp. 76-80.

Riley, J., Dampier, D., Vaughn, R. (2008). "Time Analysis of Hard Drive Imaging Tools", *Advances in Digital Forensics IV, IFIP International Federation for Information Processing*, Indrajit, R. and Shenoi, S. (Eds.), Vol. 285. National Centre for Forensic Science, Orlando, Florida, 2008, pp. 335-344.

Rogers, M.K., Goldman, J., Mislan, R., Wedge, T., Debrota, S. (2006), "Computer Forensics Field Triage Process Model", *Journal of Digital Forensics, Security and Law*, Vol. 1, No. 2, 2006, pp. 19-38.

Roussev, V. (2009), "Hashing and Data Fingerprinting in Digital Forensics", *Security & Privacy*, IEEE, vol.7, no.2, March-April 2009. pp. 49-55.

Rowlingson, R. (2004), "A Ten Step Process for Forensic Readiness", *International Journal of Digital Evidence*. IJDE Vol. 2, No. 3, 2004. pp. 1-28.

Roussev, V., Wang, L., Richard, G. and Marziale, L. (2009). "A cloud computing platform for large-scale forensic computing", *Advances in Digital Forensics V. Fifth IFIP International Conference on Digital Forensics*, Orlando, Florida, USA, 2009. pp. 201-214.

Spafford, E. (2006), "Some Challenges in Digital Forensics", *Advances in Digital Forensics II, IFIP Advances in Information and Communication Technology*, Olivier, M. and Shenoi, S. (Eds.), Vol. 222. National Centre for Forensic Science, Orlando, Florida, 2006, pp. 3-9.

SPEKTOR Forensic Website (2011) Intelligence Forensic Triage (Online). Available from: http://www.evidencetalks.com/spektor.html (Accessed: 29 March 2011)

Sommer, P. (2004), "The challenges of large computer evidence cases", *Digital Investigation*, 1 (1), 2004, pp. 16-17.

Tanner, A.L. and Dampier, D.A. (2010), "An Approach for Managing Knowledge in Digital Forensic Examinations", *International Journal of Computer Science and Security*, (IJCSS), Vol. 4, No. 5, 2010. pp. 451-465.

The Sleuth Kit (2011) (Online). Available from: http://www.sleuthkit.org/sleuthkit (Accessed: 29 March 2011)

US Department of Justice Website (2011) National Drug Intelligence Center: HashKeeper (Online). Available from: http://www.justice.gov/ndic/domex/hashkeeper.htm (Accessed: 29 March 2011)

van den Hengel, A., Hill, R., Detmold, H., and Dick, A. (2008), "Searching in space and time: a system for forensic analysis of large video repositories". *In Proceedings of the 1st International Conference on Forensic Applications and Techniques in Telecommunications, Information, and Multimedia and Workshop (e-Forensics '08)*. ICST (Institute for Computer

Sciences, Social-Informatics and Telecommunications Engineering), ICST, Brussels, Belgium. pp. 1-6.

Proposing a Digital Operational Forensic Investigation Process

M.A. Bihina Bella[1], M.S. Olivier[1] and J.H.P. Eloff[1,2]

[1]ICSA Research Lab, Department of Computer Science, University of Pretoria, Pretoria, South Africa
[2]SAP Research Pretoria, Pretoria, South Africa
e-mail: mbihina@yahoo.fr

Abstract

The increasing complexity of IT systems can lead to operational failures with disastrous consequences. In order to correct and prevent the recurrence of such failures, a thorough post-mortem investigation is required to localise their root causes. However, the currently used troubleshooting approach fails to provide sound analysis of these causes. A promising alternative approach is the emerging field of operational forensics, which applies digital forensic techniques to failure analysis with a view to improve the faulty system. This paper proposes a process for an operational forensic investigation, and shows how the process could be applied to a real-life IT failure to provide the correct diagnosis of the problem quicker and with more accuracy than troubleshooting. It also revisits the current definition of operational forensics in order to make it more specific.

Keywords

Troubleshooting, operational forensics, digital forensics, forensic science, root cause analysis, failure analysis

1. Introduction

IT systems are getting more and more complex due to the advancement of technology and customer demands for innovative products to simplify or enhance their daily activities. This is evident with the increasing demand for convergent IP-based Next-Generation Network (NGN) services and mobile applications (Bihina Bella *et al.* 2009). The NGN services are developed from the integration of various applications from a range of vendors, adding complexity to the resulting products. This creates more security loopholes and potential malfunctions once the system is in operation, even though thorough testing has been performed during its development (Bihina Bella *et al.* 2009).

As incidents often originate from a sequence or combination of events and not a single action (Noon, 1992), identifying the root causes of a failure can be challenging and even more so in such composite systems. This may lead to longer system downtime and lost revenue (Trigg & Doulis, 2008), as well as various litigation issues over the liability of the different parties involved. Without an understanding of the underlying cause of the problem, preventing its reoccurrence will be hampered.

Currently, general system failures are usually handled through troubleshooting. A failure can also be addressed by an incident response program although this typically deals with security related incidents (Jordan, 2008), which is not the focus of this paper. Troubleshooting relies heavily on the investigator's experience with the target system and focuses primarily on restoring it to its operational state as quickly as possible (Turner, 2007). In so doing, valuable information that could pinpoint the root cause of the problem is often lost during rebooting and little time is given to a proper investigation (Trigg & Doulis, 2008).

However, various regulations, standards and best practices advocate for a root cause analysis of IT incidents (Stephenson, 2004). The following are examples of such recommendations.

- In Principle 14 of its section on Risk Management for Electronic Banking, the Basel Committee on Banking Supervision clearly specifies that banks should establish "a process for collecting and preserving forensic evidence to facilitate appropriate post-mortem reviews of any e-banking incidents as well as to assist in the prosecution of attackers" (Basel Committee on Banking Supervision, 2003).

- The ISO/IEC 27002 information security standard also recommends the post-incident collection and analysis of forensic evidence for future improvements in Part 13, control 13.2: "Responsibilities and procedures are required to manage incidents consistently and effectively, to implement continuous improvement (learning the lessons), and to collect forensic evidence" (ISO/IEC, 2007).

- The American National Institute of Standards and Technology (NIST) also stipulates that an incident post-mortem be conducted for improvement purposes. They mandate organisations to "emphasize the importance of incident detection and analysis throughout the organization" and to "use the lessons learned process to gain value from incidents" in their Incident Handling Guide (Scarfone et al. 2008).

Despite these strong regulatory requirements, root cause analysis is poorly addressed in the IT industry (Trigg & Doulis, 2008; Shedden et al. 2010). The absence of an in-depth investigation of the root cause of a significant system's failure can have disastrous consequences. This was the case with the Therac-25, a computer-controlled cancer radiation therapy machine. The poor initial investigation of the machine's malfunction through informal troubleshooting carries at least part of the blame for the series of massive overdoses of radiation which killed several patients (Leveson and Turner, 2002).

Operational forensics has the potential to prevent such disasters by providing a sound methodical approach to failure analysis. Corby (2000a), who coined the term *Operational Forensics*, defines it as "the application of digital forensic techniques to the identification of occurrences and underlying causes of observed computer based events." Note that operational forensics applies to events that occur once a system is in production, thus after the design, development and testing phases. Unlike troubleshooting, operational forensics is based on objective scientific analysis methods, which increases the reliability of its results and makes the process repeatable.

After considering the issues above-mentioned in more detail, we provide our own definition of Operational Forensics in Section 4 as the following: *the application of scientific methods and legal principles to failure analysis of IT systems.*

Since the term Operational Forensics was coined in 2000 (Corby, 2000a), little research has been done in the field and it has remained at a conceptual level with no clearly defined end-to-end process.

The purpose of this paper is two-fold. It proposes a more specific definition of operational forensics and presents a process for an operational forensic investigation as this does not yet exist.

The remainder of the paper is organised as follows: Section 2 provides background on previous research on operational forensics. Section 3 presents how the forensic approach is applied for failure analysis in other fields. Section 4 defines operational forensics based on its two main component fields: digital forensics and troubleshooting. It explains its commonalities and differences to these fields. Section 5 describes the proposed process to be followed during an operational forensic investigation. We apply this process to a case study of a real-life system failure in Section 6, the Therac-25 accidents mentioned earlier. The paper ends with a conclusion in Section 7.

2. Review of previous work on operational forensics

Operational forensics is an emerging field with little available literature. To the best of our knowledge, only the following two authors have addressed it in formal publications: Michael Corby (Corby, 2000b) and Barry Hodd (Hodd, 2010).

The first publication on operational forensics from Corby (2000a) defines the field and scope of this new discipline. His second publication (Corby, 2000b) presents a pre-incident operational forensic program to ensure that potential evidence is preserved and admissible in court. However, it does not indicate how to identify the root cause of the incident nor does it present a process for the investigation.

Hodd (2010), which references Corby's seminal work (Corby, 2000a), investigates the use of modeling tools such as Petri Nets for operational forensic analysis. His research is solely on crime investigation, mainly cases of insider threats and social engineering, while the present research focuses on general system failures. While his paper focuses on the formal modeling of a failure it does not indicate the investigation process.

In addition to the above research, the concept of applying digital forensic techniques to the investigation of computer failures has been explored before but mainly in the area of incident response (i.e. only for cases of security incidents). The possibility to extend it to more general cases of system failures is usually an afterthought (Kent *et al*. 2006; Turner, 2007).

Stephenson (2003) proposes a digital investigation process for security incidents based on the Digital Forensic Research Workshop (DFRWS) investigation framework (Palmer, 2001). The process, called EEDI (End-to-End Digital Investigation), is used to create narratives of the planned investigation steps. The narratives are then translated into the Digital Investigation Process Language (DIPL), which creates a structured model of the investigation process. The DIPL model can be used to simulate the possible outcome of the investigation. Although the EDDI could be applied to non-security related events, its scope is limited to the collection and analysis of evidence, rather than to the entire investigation which must include preservation of the evidence, presentation of the findings, and recommendations for improvements.

The NIST published a guide on how to use digital forensic techniques to assist in incident handling and troubleshooting (Kent *et al*. 2006). The guide explains how to establish a forensic capability but does not provide a process for the investigation nor does it mention the concept of operational forensics.

Turner (2007) unites the forensic approach with the incident response procedure through a Digital Evidence Bag to preserve digital evidence used in the investigation. It highlights the benefits of such an approach but, like Kent *et al* (2006), maintains the distinction between forensics and incident response.

Although it remains essentially conceptual and is not yet operational in the IT industry, the usage of forensics is wide spread in the domain of failure analysis and improvement in other industries from which valuable lessons can be learnt. This is the topic of the next section.

3. Lessons learned from other forensic disciplines

Although the field of operational forensics in the IT industry is still new with limited research available, the application of forensic science to investigations for improvement purposes in other industries is not a new concept. It is, for example, a professional field of practice in the engineering industry under the name of *forensic engineering* (Noon, 2001). Some specialised areas of forensic engineering even exist as disciplines of their own such as *forensic structural engineering* for failed structures (e.g. buildings, bridges) (Ratay, 2010), or *tire forensics* for tire failures (Gioppani, 2008). In each case, the goal is to improve product quality and limit litigation which is also the intention for operational forensics.

The emergence of formal failure investigations as currently conducted in forensic engineering can be traced to the Industrial Revolution during which many complex machines were introduced. The added complexity led to many accidents that required expert analysis to understand their causes and prevent their reoccurrence. The types of accidents evolved as engineering products developed: from steamboats, railway trains and steel bridges in the 1800's to automobiles, home appliances and airplanes in the 1900's (Brown *et al.* 2003). Forensic engineering is now applied to significant failures of any engineering product; just as operational forensics could be used for any type of major IT system malfunction. As stated, the increasing complexity of IT systems also requires more formal investigations than are currently available with troubleshooting.

Forensic engineering has successfully demonstrated its effectiveness by applying various scientific examination tools and techniques, simulations and event reconstruction methods to identify the source of failure in numerous engineering disasters such as the Challenger Space Shuttle accident in 1986 (Rogers, 1986) and the Columbia Space Shuttle tragedy in 2003 (McDanels, 2006). Technical as well as organisational failures were found to be responsible for each accident which could not have been identified without a thorough forensic investigation.

Forensic engineering has evolved from its initial focus on legal investigations in product liability cases to its current focus on failure analysis for product and system quality improvement purposes. Presently, most forensic engineering investigations do not reach the courtroom and are done mainly with a view to prevent similar future accidents (Carper, 2000). One example is the forensic investigation of the September 11, 2001 World Trade Center collapse which was undertaken to understand the impact of the fire on the collapse of the twin towers although the responsible parties were already known (Usmani *et al.* 2003). Various elements such as the construction design, fire properties of materials used, and their thermal expansion were examined through simulations and computer-based structural analysis. Based on this analysis it was determined that using reinforced concrete instead of lightweight steel as well as providing an energy absorbing structure could prevent the collapse of such tall buildings in the future (Zhou, 2004).

In this regard, forensic engineering is comparable to forensic pathology, another application of forensic science to the improvement of a field's procedures and products. Forensic pathology is a branch of medicine that investigates the cause of death upon a legal request. However, when applied to public health and safety, it is used for the prevention and control of diseases. For instance, a forensic autopsy may uncover a previously undetected contagious disease to prevent an outbreak or pandemic. It may also help identify an hereditary condition that will enable family members proactively to seek treatment (Dolinak *et al.* 2005).

In summary, as demonstrated for many years in the engineering and medical fields, through the integration of scientific methods and legal principles, the forensic approach has ensured objective, comprehensive investigations producing reliable results and has created opportunities for improving product quality.

In light of the above benefits in other fields of practice, we can expect similar benefits for the IT industry based on the application of operational forensics. The next section defines the scope of operational forensics based on its relation to its two components: digital forensics and troubleshooting.

4. Link between digital forensics, operational forensics and troubleshooting

In order to define operational forensics as a new field, it helps to relate it to existing fields with which it shares certain elements. As its definition suggests, operational forensics uses digital forensic techniques to analyse the cause of an event. It thus contains elements of both digital forensics and troubleshooting. Section 4.1 presents the link between operational forensics and digital forensics and Section 4.2 explains the link between operational forensics and troubleshooting.

4.1. Link between digital forensics and operational forensics

The Digital Forensics Research Workshop defines digital forensics as "the use of scientifically derived and proven methods toward the preservation, validation, identification, analysis, interpretation, documentation and presentation of digital evidence derived from digital sources for the purpose of facilitating or furthering the reconstruction of events found to be criminal, or helping to anticipate unauthorized actions shown to be disruptive to planned operations" (Palmer, 2001).

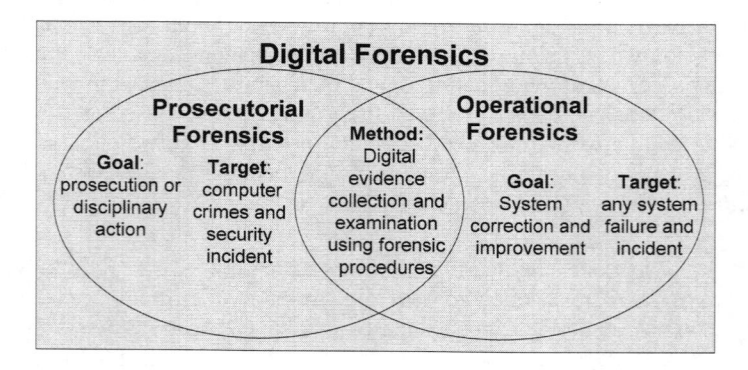

Figure 1: Relationship between prosecutorial forensics and operational forensics

According to Corby (2000b), digital forensics can be categorised into two branches based on the goal of the investigation: operational forensics and prosecutorial forensics. Traditionally, digital forensics has been prosecutorial by nature with the objective of collecting evidence for prosecution or disciplinary action. By contrast, the main goal of operational forensics is to gather evidence for system correction and improvement (Hodd, 2010). Unlike prosecutorial forensics, which only deals with computer crimes and security incidents, operational forensics handles any kind of computer event. It can be argued that in prosecutorial forensics, the stress is placed on the legal aspect of the investigation, while in operational forensics the emphasis is on the scientific approach of the analysis. We have summarised the distinctions between the two branches of digital forensics in Figure 1.

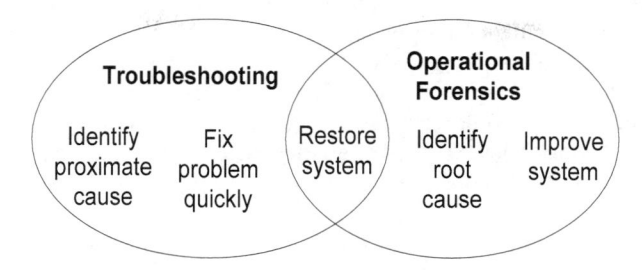

```
        Troubleshooting                    Operational Forensics

     Identify    Fix      Restore    Identify    Improve
     proximate   problem  system     root        system
     cause       quickly             cause
```

Figure 2: Relationship between operational forensics and troubleshooting

Figure 1 shows the differences between the two branches and highlights their commonality, which is the collection and examination of digital evidence using forensic procedures. A more detailed comparison of operational forensics and prosecutorial forensics is provided in Table 1. The table shows our analysis of the two fields and presents the differences that have a direct impact on the outcome of the investigation.

Operational forensics	Prosecutorial forensics
Similarities	
Digital evidence collection and examination	
Use sound forensic process and techniques	
Evidence admissible in court	
Differences	
Applicable in any computer-based event	Applicable only in computer crimes and security incidents
Used for system improvement and correction	Used for prosecution and disciplinary action
Proactive collection of evidence (mostly "live" forensics)	Reactive collection of evidence (mostly "dead" forensics)
System usually remains operational during the investigation	System is frozen during the investigation
Investigation sequence affected by internal factors (the system or company)	Investigation sequence affected by external factors (e.g. trial)
Investigation can be extended to other domains relevant for improvement (e.g. organisation culture and management)	Investigation focused only on the crime scene
Finding (root cause identification) and decision (recommendation for improvement) are an integral part of the investigation.	Identifying and sanctioning the perpetrator are not part of the process, but are determined in trial outside the digital investigation
Conclusion drawn by investigator	Conclusion drawn by judge

Table1: Operational forensics versus prosecutorial forensics

4.2. Link between operational forensics and troubleshooting

Troubleshooting is a logical search for the source of a problem in order to fix it so the system can immediately resume working. Isolating the cause of the problem typically involves a process of elimination which starts with the most visible or easiest problem to fix depending on the investigator's experience (TechTerm.com, 2011). Operational forensics, meanwhile, focuses on improving the system so the failure does not reoccur, and uses scientific forensic techniques to identify the origin of the problem. In order to prevent the reoccurrence of the issue, its root cause must be identified. Troubleshooting can be satisfied with a proximate cause as long as it helps solve the problem at hand.

These distinctions are summarised in Figure 2. The diagram shows from left to right the main stages of an investigation in both fields. Troubleshooting starts by identifying a proximate cause of the problem based on the investigator's suspicion and ends with a system restoration, while operational forensics first restores the system, identifies its root cause based on an analysis of the acquired digital evidence, and ends with recommendations to improve the system.

As shown in Figure 2, the common denominator between the two fields is to restore the system to its working state. A more detailed comparison of operational forensics and troubleshooting is provided in Table 2. The table shows our analysis of the two fields and presents the differences that have a direct impact on the outcome of the investigation.

Operational forensics	Troubleshooting
Similarities	
Used to solve the problem at hand	
Includes system restoration	
Differences	
Find root cause (s)	Find proximate cause (s)
Relies on scientific forensic analysis	Relies on investigator's experience with the target system
Focus on improving the system	Focus on restoring the system
Includes a formal post-event investigation	No formal post-event investigation
Process is repeatable	Process is not repeatable, case by case
Evidence collected and documented before, during and after the event in a planned manner	No evidence collected

Table 2: Operational forensics versus troubleshooting

Based on the above analysis, we can establish that operational forensics is an interdisciplinary discipline which lies between the fields of troubleshooting and prosecutorial forensics. It is a new area of digital forensics aimed at addressing the limitations of conventional troubleshooting with regard to complex IT systems. This is illustrated in Figure 3, which only shows the main connections between operational forensics and the other two disciplines.

As we recall from Section 1, our own definition of operational forensics, which stems from the above mentioned interrelation, is as follows: *the application of scientific methods and legal principles to failure analysis of IT systems.*

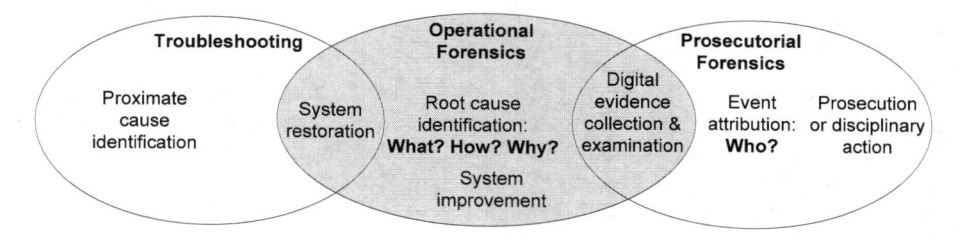

Figure 3: Link between operational forensics, troubleshooting and prosecutorial forensics

Like in other fields, an operational forensic investigation follows a specific process, which is described in the next section.

5. The operational forensic investigation process

As demonstrated in previous sections, operational forensics is composed of digital forensics and troubleshooting and can be compared to forensic engineering. It is therefore expected that an operational forensic investigation combines elements of those three fields. Operational forensics has two facets: the forensic preparation and the investigation. Section 5.1 presents the forensic preparation and Section 5.2 describes our suggested high-level investigative process.

5.1. The operational forensic preparation

In order to maximise the effectiveness and speed of the investigation, a forensic capability needs to be established in the organisation prior to the investigation. The organisation must be "forensic ready" by taking the following actions: (a) equip personnel with necessary forensic skills; (b) identify, acquire and maintain potential evidence such as log files and (c) develop supportive policies and procedures (Corby, 2000a; Kent *et al.* 2006). The organisation must also ensure that all system documentation is available and up-to-date. This includes system specifications, user manuals, licensing information, test plans, and a history of changes and reported incidents (Trigg & Doulis, 2008). This operational forensic program ensures that when a problem occurs, information that can be used as evidence during the investigation is readily available and the responsible parties know how to collect it in a forensically sound manner.

5.2. The operational forensic investigation process

The proposed investigative process consists of three basic stages. The first two occur during the event or immediately after it has been detected: firstly, collect evidence and secondly, restore the system. The third phase is the root cause analysis which is conducted once the system has been restored.

Phase 1: **Information collection**

This phase corresponds to the first step of a digital forensic investigation. Shortly after a failure has been detected, all information that can assist in the investigation needs to be collected in a forensically sound manner by maintaining the chain of custody and preserving its integrity. For the purpose of this paper, we classify the information to be collected as either primary or secondary. The primary information is the electronic data that can serve as potential evidence (e.g. audit logs, network and system configuration settings) while the secondary information is background information regarding the system and the issue at hand. This includes the documentation indicated previously in the forensic readiness program as well as a recording of the state of the scene (e.g. screenshot of the error message) and interviews with the system administrator and the users who reported the failure (Kent et al. 2006).

Phase 2: **System restoration**

Once all relevant information has been acquired, the problem is fixed and the system is restored to its operational state as quickly as possible. This reduces its downtime, which limits any associated negative consequence such as financial loss. A restoration might be as simple as rebooting the system or it might necessitate some preliminary diagnostic of the failure to fix it. This will follow a typical troubleshooting process, which requires a recreation of the problem to isolate its cause (Juniper Networks, 2011).

Phase 3: **Root cause analysis**

An operational forensic investigation is a failure analysis of an IT system. It follows closely the process of a forensic engineering investigation, which includes laboratory examination, simulations and reconstruction of the incident to determine its root cause (Brown, 1995). These steps are also applicable to the analysis of an IT event and are thus part of our process. The electronic data collected in the 1st phase of the investigation is examined in a computer lab in conjunction with the secondary information to understand the failure. The examination follows the scientific method, which consists of formulating hypotheses for all the probable causes of the failure and predicting and testing evidence for each hypothesis. The root cause is the hypothesis that accounts for most of the evidence (Noon, 2001).

In case the responsibility for a system failure is attributed to a criminal or malicious intent, the investigation becomes a prosecutorial forensic case to identify and prosecute the perpetrator. A representation of the complete investigation process is provided in the flowchart in Figure 4.

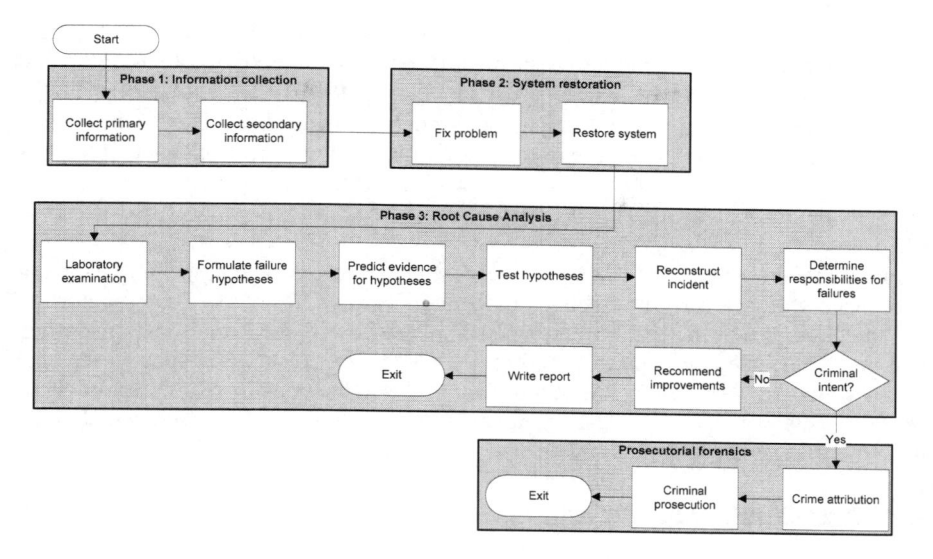

Figure 4: The operational forensic investigation process

The process does not indicate a technique to examine the collected evidence but rather steps that can lead to a thorough investigation of all possible sources of the problem and how to choose the best one. As it is a lengthy process it is best suited to significant failures with high impact.

6. Case study: Therac-25 accidents

This section illustrates the application of the proposed investigative process in a real-life scenario. The example used is the infamous disaster of the Therac-25, a computer-controlled radiation therapy machine used to treat cancer patients. The machine, designed by AECL (Atomic Energy of Canada Limited), was installed in 11 hospitals throughout the USA and Canada in the mid 1980's. Due to several software bugs in the machine, a series of six (6) severe overdoses of radiation occurred between 1985 and 1987 in different hospitals killing several patients (Leveson & Turner, 2002). The author chose this event as a case study as it is well documented with publicly available reports on the various accidents and resulting investigations. This is not the case for more recent incidents as companies keep this type of information confidential for legal reasons and to uphold their public image.

An in-depth investigation of the Therac-25 disaster is beyond the scope of this paper. Reports of such investigations are publicly available (Leveson, 1995; Leveson & Turner, 2002) and the root causes of the accidents have been identified. In this section, we demonstrate how our process could have been used for the investigation. The information presented is from Leveson (1995) and Leveson and Turner (2002).

The Therac-25 was used to administer a radiation beam to the patient in either one of two modes depending on the depth of the tumour:

- Low energy or electron therapy: electron beam of 200 rads aimed at patient directly. The computer controls the beam energy (5 to 25 MeV1) and current.
- High energy or X-ray: 25 MeV through a metal plate between beam and patient. Metal plate transforms beam into an x-ray. Electron beam 100 times greater than for low energy mode. The positioning of the metal plate is determined by a turntable.

Prior to the accidents, the Therac-25 had already been in use for two (2) years and had successfully treated hundreds of patients in various hospitals. The operators of the machine, however, had become accustomed to its frequent malfunctions which had never affected any patient before the deadly accidents. In such cases, the operator would call a hospital technician to reset the machine and restore it to service. This was the troubleshooting approach commonly used and which they initially followed after each accident.

First event: Kennestone Oncology Center, Marietta, Georgia, USA, 3 June 1985

The machine did not show any sign of unusual activity and did not generate an error message. However, the patient felt a high heat sensation after receiving treatment and accused the machine's operator of having burnt her. Shortly after returning home, the patient's skin reddened and swelled and she was in great pain. This was initially attributed to her disease. Weeks later, the patient's breast was removed, and her shoulder and arm were paralysed due to obvious radiation burn but the doctors could not explain its cause. It was later estimated that 15 000 to 20 000 rads had been administered instead of the set 200 rads.

No investigation was conducted for this accident as there was no information to indicate the machine was responsible for the patient's condition. The operational forensic process would not have yielded any result either as there was no primary or secondary information available. Indeed, the system was not forensic ready as the logs were not activated due to memory constraints. There was no system documentation available and no previous case had been reported. What could have been done (but was not done), however, was to interview the patient and the machine operator and file a report of the incident for future reference.

Second event: Ontario Cancer Foundation, Hamilton, Ontario, Canada, 26 July 1985

The machine paused after 5s of activation and displayed HTILT error message, NO DOSE and TREATMENT PAUSE. As the machine indicated that no radiation had been administered, the operator retried four (4) times until the machine stopped. The patient complained of burning electric sensation after the treatment. On 30 July, she was hospitalised as her skin was swollen and burnt and the machine was put out of service. She died on 3 November 1985 from cancer but the autopsy revealed that the radiation burn would have necessitated a complete hip replacement had she survived. It was later estimated that she had received 13 000 to 17 000 rads. Table 3 shows how this accident could have been investigated with our proposed operational forensic process.

Investigation	
What was done with troubleshooting	What could have been done with the operational forensic process
Phase 1: Information collection	
No information was collected.	- **Collect primary information**: No log files, but record error messages. - **Collect secondary information**: No system specification and test plans, but obtain user manual and case history. Also interview the machine's operator and the patient.
Phase 2: System restoration	
The machine was reset by the hospital's technician who did not find anything wrong. Operation of the machine was discontinued five (5) days later.	- First reset the machine so that it can resume working. - Discontinue usage of the machine once patient started developing skin reddening and swelling after the treatment. - Only put the machine back into service once the investigation has been completed and the implemented improvements have been tested.
Phase 3: Root cause analysis	
- AECL first tried to recreate the problem with no success. - AECL suspected a mechanical failure and hardwired its error conditions. They found some hardware design flaws and fixed them. - They also modified the software to better control the positioning of the turntable. - Based on these changes, AECL claimed a significant improvement of the machine, although they concluded that they could not ascertain the exact cause of the accident. The machine was put back into operation despite this uncertainty.	**Laboratory examination of collected data**: - *User manual*: the user manual's description of many error messages was cryptic. The meaning of HTLILT was unclear. NO DOSE indicates that no dose of radiation has been delivered. - *Report of 1st accident*: based on the patients' testimony and symptoms, a correlation could have been established between the two events. **Formulation of hypotheses**: 3 possible scenarios - *Electrical problem* since patients experienced electrical shock. - *Hardware failure*. E.g. Incorrect positioning of the metal plate - *Software error* since the software controlled the machine. **Prediction of evidence to support hypotheses** - The electrical shock theory was ruled out by a thorough inspection by an independent engineering company which did not find any electrical problem in the machine. - AECL's test identified some hardware design flaws, which supported the hardware failure theory. - AECL identified some weaknesses in the software, supportive of the software error theory. **Test the hypotheses** - Thorough testing of the improved machine with the corrected mechanical flaws would result in another overdose as other accidents followed the 2nd one despite this improvement. This would have ruled out the mechanical failure theory. - The only theory remaining was the software error. Further examination of the software would be necessary to identify the bugs responsible for the failure. The last four (4) steps of the investigation (**incident reconstruction, responsibilities for failures, recommendations for improvement and report writing**) depend on the results of the thorough examination of the software to identify the bugs. As this was done following the 6th and last accident, they are not covered in this paper.

Table 3: Operational forensic investigation of the 2nd Therac-25 accident

As this example demonstrates, the operational forensic process offers many advantages over the troubleshooting method used in the case of the Therac-25. It could have located the source of the problem as a software error and not a hardware failure as suspected by AECL. In addition, further software examination would have identified the software bugs responsible for the overdoses before other accidents occurred. Unfortunately, due to overconfidence in their software, AECL refused to consider this option until several other accidents occurred after they had fixed the hardware.

In essence, a comprehensive forensic investigation would have provided the following benefits. Firstly, ensure that the results of the investigation were reliable as they were based on objective scientific analysis. Secondly, ensure that the root cause and not a proximate cause for the failure was identified before restoring the machine to operation. This would have prevented further accidents. Thirdly, improve the quality of the machine and AECL's procedures for failure analysis. AECL had no forensic capability and no mechanism to follow-up on reported incidents. Besides, there was no audit log activated on the machine and documentation of the software design and test plan were lacking. The user manual was also poorly designed. In addition, late during the actual investigation, it was established that AECL did not perform a thorough testing of the software before installing the machine.

7. Conclusion

Operational forensics has the potential to solve some of the main limitations of troubleshooting for cases of complex IT system failures. The proposed process shows how the forensic method can lead to a proper diagnosis of the problem. It is not a silver bullet which guarantees the identification of the root cause but it ensures that all aspects of the problem are taken into account before reaching a conclusion. This is illustrated by the case study. The lack of an objective and sound failure analysis process supported by appropriate evidence was among the main errors AECL made that led to the multiple accidents. Based on their experience with the system, AECL engineers "diagnosed" the accidents without supporting evidence, which is typical of troubleshooting. Future research involves specifying appropriate methods to examine the evidence, reconstruct the failure and localise its root cause.

Acknowledgement

The support of SAP Research Pretoria/Meraka Unit of Technology Development towards this research is hereby acknowledged. Opinions expressed and conclusions arrived at are solely those of the authors and should not necessarily be attributed to SAP Research Pretoria/Meraka UTD.

8. References

Basel Committee on Banking Supervision (2003), "Risk Management Principles for Electronic Banking", Bank for International Settlements website, July 2003, http://www.bis.org/publ/bcbs98.pdf, (Accessed 21 February 2011).

Bihina Bella, M.A., Olivier, M.S. and Eloff, J.H.P. (2009). "A Fraud Management System Architecture for Next-Generation Networks", *Forensic Science International*, Vol. 185, pp.51-58.

Brown, J.F., Obenski, K.S. and Osborn, T.R (2003), *Forensic Engineering Reconstruction of Accidents*, 2nd edition, p4, Charles C. Thomas Publisher, Springfield, Illinois, USA.

Brown, S. (1995), *Forensic Engineering Part 1 – An Introduction to the investigation, analysis, reconstruction, causality, prevention, risk, consequence and legal aspects of the failure of engineered products*, ISI Publications, Texas.

Carper, K.L. (2000), *Forensic Engineering*, Second Edition, pp.2-4, CRC Press, Boca Raton.

Corby, M. J. (2000a), "Operational Forensics – The New Frontier", *Proceedings of the 23rd National Information Systems Security Conference*, Baltimore, USA, 16-19 October 2000, http://csrc.nist.gov/nissc/2000/proceedings/papers/317slide.pdf, (Accessed: 10 May 2010)

Corby, M. J. (2000b), "Operational Forensics", *Information Security Management Handbook*, 4th Edition, vol. 2, chapter 28, Auerbach Publications, Boca Raton.

Dolinak, D., Matshes, E.W and Lew, E.O. (2005), *Forensic pathology: principles and practice*, p68, Elsevier, Oxford.

Giapponi, T.R. (2008), *Tire forensic investigation: analyzing tire failure*, pp.xv-xvii, SAE International, Warrendale, USA.

Hodd, B. (2010), "Modelling for operational forensics", *Digital Forensics Magazine,* Issue 3, 1st February 2010.

ISO/IEC (2007), "Information technology - Security techniques - Code of practice for information security management", International Standard ISO/IEC 27002, ISO Copyright office, Geneva.

Jordan, S. (2008), "Mining gold... A primer on incident handling and response". *SANS Institute InfoSec Reading Room*, http://www.sans.org/reading_room/whitepapers/incident/mining-gold-primer-incident-handling-response_32818, (Accessed: 09 February 2011).

Juniper Networks (2011), "Basic Approaches to Troubleshooting", Juniper website http://www.juniper.net/techpubs/software/junos/junos42/swcmdref42/html/strategies2.html, (Accessed 26/02/2011)

Kent, K., Grance, T., Chevalier, S. and Dang, H. (2006), "Guide to Integrating Forensic Techniques into Incident Response", *NIST Special Publication 800-86*, National Institute of Standards and Technology, Gaithersburg, USA, http://csrc.nist.gov/publications/nistpubs/800-86/SP800-86.pdf, (Accessed 09 February 2011)

Leveson, N. (1995), "Medical Devices: The Therac-25", *Safeware: System Safety and Computers*, Appendix A, pp515-548, Addison-Wesley.

Leveson, N. and Turner, C. (2002), "An Investigation of the Therac-25 Accidents", *IEEE Computer*, Vol. 26, Issue 7, August 2002, pp.18-41.

McDanels, S. J. (2006), "Space Shuttle Columbia Post-Accident Analysis and Investigation", *Journal of Performance of Constructed Facilities*, Vol. 42, Issue 3, pp.159-163.

Noon, R.K. (1992), *Introduction to Forensic Engineering*, 1st edition, p1, CRC Press, Boca Raton.

Noon, R.K. (20001), *Forensic Engineering Investigation*, 1st edition, p1, CRC Press, Boca Raton.

Palmer, G. (2001), "A Road Map for Digital Forensics Research", *Report from the First Digital Forensics Research Workshop*, 7-8 August 2001, New York, http://www.dfrws.org/2001/dfrws-rm-final.pdf, (Accessed 25/02/2011).

Ratay, R.T. (2010), *Forensic structural engineering handbook*, 2nd edition, McGraw-Hill, New York. p.xi.

Roger, W.P. (1986), "Report of the Presidential Commission on the Space Shuttle Challenger Accident", US Government Accounting Office, http://history.nasa.gov/rogersrep/genindex.htm, (Accessed 27/02/2011).

Scarfone, K., Grance, T. and Masone, K. (2008), "Computer Security Incident Handling Guide", *NIST Special Publication 800-61*, Revision 1, March 2008, National Institute of Standards and Technology, Gaithersburg, USA, http://csrc.nist.gov/publications/nistpubs/800-61-rev1/SP800-61rev1.pdf, (Accessed 22 February 2011).

Shedden, P., Ahmad, A. and Ruighaver, A.B. (2010). "Organisational Learning and Incident Response: Promoting Effective Learning Through The Incident Response Process", *Proceedings of the 8th Australian Information Security Management Conference*, Edith Cowan University, Perth Western Australia, 30th November 2010.

Stephenson, P. (2003), "Modeling of Post-Incident Root Cause Analysis", *International Journal of Digital Evidence*, Vol. 2, Issue 2.

Stephenson, P. (2004), "The Application of Formal Methods to Root Cause Analysis 0f Digital Incidents", *International Journal of Digital Evidence*, Vol. 3, Issue 1.

TechTerm.com (2011), "Troubleshooting", computer and technology terms online dictionary, http://www.techterms.com/definition/troubleshooting, (Accessed 10 February 2011).

Trigg, J. and Doulis, J. (2008), "Troubleshooting: What Can Go Wrong and How to Fix It", *Practical Guide to Clinical Computing- Systems: Design, Operations, and Infrastructure*, chapter 7, pp 105-128, Elsevier Inc, London.

Turner, P. (2007), "Applying a forensic approach to incident response, network investigation and system administration using Digital Evidence Bags", *Digital Investigation*, Vol. 4, Issue 1, March 2007, pp.30-35.

Usmani, A. S., Chung, Y. C. and Torero, J. L. (2003), "How did the WTC towers collapse: A new theory", *Fire Safety Journal*, Vol. 38, Issue 6, pp.501-533.

Zhou, Q. And Yu, T.X. (2004), "Use of high –efficiency energy absorbing device to arrest progressive collapse of tall building", *Journal of Engineering Mechanics*, Vol.130, issue 10, pp.1177-1187.

Digital Forensics: the Need for Integration

P. Sant and M. Hewling

Institute for Research in Applicable Computing
University of Bedfordshire, Park Square, Luton, Bedfordshire
LU1 3JU, United Kingdom
e-mail: paul.sant@beds.ac.uk, moniphia.hewling@beds.ac.uk

Abstract

Digital forensics fast is becoming quite predominant within the legal court system which has had to deal with an increase of cases that involve the use of digital devices over the past decade. The procedures presently used in the digital forensic process were developed with a focus on the practitioner's expertise or interest. This resulted in very little regard for all fields that may be impacted by any one investigation. Such omissions have resulted in digital forensics seeming to be an ad hoc process resulting in a number of cases in which digital evidence has been deemed invalid, producing negative results. Alleviation of such issues is possible with the development of a standard framework flexible enough to accommodate the intricacies of all areas directly impacted by digital forensics. A complete framework incorporating views from computer scientists, lawyers, law enforcement officers and all other practitioners in related the field, needs to be developed. Such a framework should provide the basis from which a set of standards will be generated, defined and used to govern the acquisition of evidence from digital devices/sources, irrespective of their use in or to inform they will be used in a legal case. This paper proposes the development of such a framework integrating technical and legal dimensions.

Keywords

Digital Forensics, Computer Forensics, Digital Evidence, Digital Crime

1. Introduction

The apparent proliferation of digitally related crimes has been immense and is unavoidable in today's' technologically driven society. Increased connectivity has significantly increased the number of security related issues occurring and will continue to so do because of the dynamic nature of digital technology. In recent years there has been an increase in the use of digital devices as tools of convenience to access the World Wide Web to carry out activities such as banking, gaming, shopping and even studying. These activities have given rise to a number of security issues due to the fact that criminals have found a way to infiltrate their use. Additionally technology and digital devices facilitate these criminals by enabling more sophisticated methods of committing traditional crimes with a certain level of perceived invisibility. These developments have thus prompted the rise of fields such as Digital, computer, mobile, network and cyber forensics as well as cyber/internet, computer laws.

Digital forensics refers to the acquisition, preservation, analysis and presentation of digital evidence produced from the investigation of digital related crimes. Digital evidence recovered from the scenes of digital crimes are defined by Casey (2004) as "any data stored or transmitted using a computer that support or refute a theory of how an offence occurred or that address critical elements of evidence such as alibi". The basis of the investigation of any technological/digital related criminal act is reliant on digital evidence, which as alluded to before, is acquired through the digital forensics process. The definition or description of this process may vary depending on the expertise of the investigator or their background. This highlights one of the main issues in the field - the lack of a standard set of methodologies to carry out the digital forensics process.

The term 'forensics' refers to the application of science expertise in the form of knowledgebase and methodology within the court. This means that where evidence is gathered, the objective is for it to be used in legal proceedings. To ensure evidence is considered reliable when presented in courts, proper standards and procedures must be followed. This requirement is no different in the case of evidence acquired through all forensics fields and so it is for digital forensics The weaknesses identified above demonstrate the need for a comprehensive methodology that covers the multidimensional landscape of digital evidence. The remainder of this paper will address the limitations of existing approaches and propose a new framework that addresses the problems associated with existing models. The research commences by discussing the related work by researchers in the field and then goes on to explain the proposed approach. Section 2 will look at the aforementioned related work of other researchers, section 3 summarises the strengths and limitations of some of the existing models. The suggested framework will be highlighted in section 4 and the conclusion, in section five, present proposals for future work.

2. Related work

There are a myriad of existing digital forensic models some of which have been developed by organisations for their own use, or by law enforcement personnel for their own countries and even by other individuals based on their background, objective and even their employers' needs (Salemat et al 2008) and (Perumal 2009). These methodologies are in some part driven by the tools available to the investigator and focus on either the technical or legal aspects of the investigation. However, there are other models that focus solely on the acquisition of the evidence ignoring all other phases that may be required by a "forensic" investigation. These models all have positive and negative attributes most of which will be highlighted in this section.

2.1. Pollit et al. methodology

One of the earlier models to be developed was the Computer Forensics Process by Pollitt (1995). This model is comprised of four stages and stresses the point that the digital forensics process should conform to the law while remaining committed to the scientific principles. This model was however designed with the object of acquiring evidence from crimes committed in cyberspace and thus would need to be amended by the practitioner for use in other settings requiring such an acquisition.

2.2. Kruse & Heiser's methodology

Kruse and Heiser (2001) was also one of the earlier models to be developed, though coming approximately six year after Pollitt's. This model has three basic steps depicting the entire digital forensics process. The focus of this particular model is on the core aspects of digital evidence acquisition, acquiring, authenticating and analyzing the evidence. There is no mention of preparation, seeking authorization to acquire the evidence or identifying the evidence. Whereas these may have been assumed, as it seems with other models, to be discussed this is not enough especially where the legal issues are concerned.

2.3. H.C. Lee's methodology

Also in 2001 H. C. Lee in his book 'Henry Lee's Crime Scene handbook' suggested a model that included an additional stage when compared to that of Kruse and Heiser. This model is more systematic and follows four very pertinent stages, which are recognition, identification, individualization and reconstruction. This model is similar to the previous methodology proposed by Kruse and Heiser in that it assumes/ignores particular phases of the forensics process and does not include stages suggesting preservation or that of seeking authorization to access the evidence. This model focuses mainly on the analysis of the evidence.

2.4. The DFRWS methodology

The Digital Forensic research workshop (DFRWS) has also developed a model for the Digital Forensic process. This model is more extensive than the previous models highlighted. It has seven stages and makes far fewer assumptions than the previous models covering integral stages not previously covered. However like a number of the other models, it ignores or assumes some of the legal aspects of the investigation and focuses more on the technical aspects. It includes the stage "decision" which is somewhat out of the remit of the forensics process, which is concerned mainly with investigation and presentation of the findings.

2.5. Reith et al.

In 2002, Reith, Carr and Gunsch proposed a model that had a number of phases in which at least two phases overlap. This model is based on the one developed by DFRWS previously (DRFWS, 2002). The phases proposed include identify, prepare, approach strategy, preserve, collect, examine, analyse, present and return evidence. This model, despite addressing some of the core areas of forensics, such as it does not include any suggestion of getting authorisation to preserve and /or collect the evidence, which is very important with regards to the legal aspects of any forensics process.

2.6. Eoghan Casey's Methodology

Eoghan Casey (2004) proposes one of the more popular models as depicted in his book 'Digital Evidence and Computer Crime'. In this model Casey focuses on the investigation itself and presents only four stages that are recognition, preservation, classification and reconstruction. This model focuses main on the investigation of the device itself and like many of the other models ignores other elements such as the legal ones.

2.7. Ciarhuain's methodology

The Ciarhuain Model is one of the more comprehensive models developed and has approximately twelve (12) stages and sub stages. This model, unlike the others, does specify phases pertinent to a digital forensics investigation but has been developed to address cyber related crimes (cyber forensics) and developed specifically for the Malaysian context. A number of the stages are also redundant and the need for preservation of the acquired evidence is not mentioned which is integral in ensuring the admissibility of the evidence should it be required for use in court.

2.8. Bogen and Dampier's methodology

The model by Bogen and Dampier was developed in 2005 and has three distinct phases and is referred to as a multi-view computer forensics model. The views are investigative process view, domain View and evidence view. Each view has related products Including models and dependencies. This approach is quite different from the others identified and does not directly build or expand on a preceding model. It was designed from a software engineering standpoint and is thus focussed on the technical aspects of the digital forensics process.

2.9. Yong's methodology

Another model to be mentioned is Yong's, in 2008, has network forensics at its core and is not openly general, though it could possibly be adapted. Yong's model focuses on the investigation of cyber crimes and includes phases such as preparation, classification of the cybercrime, deciding investigation priority among others. It takes the investigator through summoning the suspect (which is not a core responsibility of a forensic expert) to writing the report. A comprehensive set of steps presented for investigation cyber crime however very little explanation is provided.

2.10. The Salemat and Perumal methodologies

Two of the more recent models Salemat et al (2008) and Perumal (2009) are the more comprehensive of the existing models. In an article entitled "The Mapping process of Digital forensics Investigations" (Salemat (2008), Salemat et al noted, "No formal theory exists for the digital examinations process". This is a point supported by Perumal (2009), Ricci (2006), among others. Salemat et al then proceed to produce what they term the "mapping process of the digital forensics investigations framework". The output of this process is a combination of the previous frameworks eliminating redundancies and detailed explanations of particular steps that were deemed vague. This has resulted in a five-phase step of activities with the headings, preparation, collection and preservation, examination and analysis, presentation and reporting. This structure of activities is written specifically for the Malaysian Criminal Justice system. It is very comprehensive and addresses key areas such authorization (but not continuous legal adherence or ethics), live and static data acquisition for use as evidence (not filtering of pertinent/relevant evidence) and storage of data. Overall Salemat's model is a very comprehensive methodology; however the focus seems to be on data acquisition as there is no mention of presentation which is critical part of any forensics process as one of the objectives of forensics is to present the findings of the investigation.

3. Strengths and weaknesses of Digital Forensics Models

Model/Designer	Year	Strengths (Includes)	Weaknesses (Excludes)
M. Pollitt	1995	Identification	Authorisation Live acquisition
W Kruse II., G Hieser	2001	Authentication	Authorisation Live acquisition
H. Lee	2001	Identification Reconstruction	Preservation Authorisation Presentation Moving of evidence to controlled area.
M. Reith, C. Carr, G. Gunsh	2002	Identification	Authorisation Live acquisition Moving of evidence to controlled area.
E. Casey	2004	Identification Reconstruction	Focus is on the investigation Authorisation Moving of evidence to controlled area.
S. O. Cuardhuian	2004	Awareness	Preservation Cybercrime Focus Overlapping of steps Live acquisition
C. Bogen & D. Dampier	2005	Includes various digital devices	Technical Oriented
FORZA – R. Ieong	2006	Legal inclusion	Focuses on legal aspects
Y.D. Shin	2008	Criminal profiling Classification of crime	Legal aspects
S. Perumal	2009	Archiving	Classification of crime

Table 1: Strengths and weaknesses of digital forensic models

3.1. Concerns

Some of the major concerns arising from examination of the models identified include:

a) Lack of legal authorisation to acquire and examine the evidence.
b) The need for preservation of all evidence immediately
c) The identification of the fact that a controlled environment is needed to carry out the investigation.
d) A step-by-step directive that can be followed by practitioners (usually provided with the tools but not good enough as the instructions are dependent on the developer of the tool).
e) Not having any particular tools identified to be used at the different stages. The methodology was written in isolation, separate from the tools. (NB Carrier has addressed this concern somewhat with sleuth kit)
f) Reconstruction of the crime scene to enable accurate criminal profiling is not addressed by most of these methodologies
g) Computer Scientists for some reason are intent on ignoring the legal aspects of "forensics".
h) Both live and static data needs to be captured in digital forensics.
i) Creation of logs to ensure proper presentation of the findings.
j) Lacks the identification of human resources training requirements

4. The Proposed Framework

4.1. Introduction

It is clear that for digital forensics to be recognised as a true division of the forensic science arena the evidence gathered through the process must be able to satisfy the Daubert testing criteria (among others). This becomes difficult with different personnel and organisations developing their own methodologies. Thus there needs to be standardised framework complete with a set of standards and a dedicated but flexible methodology which digital forensics practitioners, internationally, will use as a bench mark when carrying out their duties. This framework must not only satisfy technical and legal criteria but also adhere to ethical expectations, education and be flexible enough to meet the needs of a dynamic field. The proposed framework is flexible enough to be adapted for the various divisions in digital forensics for example, Mobile forensics, network forensics, cloud forensics and computer forensics

The proposed framework has three major phases that will be further broken down in to more specific categories. This proposed framework is designed to be prescriptive and rigorous while ensuring speed and accuracy. It is prescriptive because it includes recommendations of tools at particular stages in the process and is guided by standards. It is rigorous because it is expected that no phase will be excluded throughout the investigation. This measure ensures the model is accurate and reliable from a legal and scientific perspective and adaptable for any region.

4.2. Layout of the Framework

Educational training and qualification along with legal and ethical principles encompass the framework. These are addressed by the associated standards. From this framework the proposed methodology will be derived. The initial phase of the proposed methodology, the initiation phase comprises of those tasks involved in ensuring that all necessary actions are carried out and appropriate documentation produced before commencement of the actual investigation. Information ascertained at this phase includes, type of service required by the requester, type of intrusion, personnel involved in the intrusion and data type involved. From this stage is apparent what type of authorisation is needed to commence the investigation. The deliverable form this phase of the process is a formal document containing the results of the aforementioned information as well as documentation of any legal documents requested and/or received.

The investigation phase is very complex and critical to the overall process. During this phase the practitioner must be constantly aware of the fact that they are collecting evidence that may be used in a legal setting and thus "rules of evidence" will determine the admissibility of the evidence acquired. This stage needs to be carefully planned and coordinated to ensure that there is no spoliation of the evidence. Specific guidelines will be included to ensure this is alleviated. The investigation phase involves activities ranging from the locating of the devices involved in the incident through to the analysis of data pertinent to the investigation. On locating these devices the immediate environment should be physically preserved and protected. The scene should be diagrammatically captured with the use of drawings and/or photographs showing location of the devices. The investigation should then identify suspect devices and peripherals and proceed to preserve any live data. Another critical stage in this phase is the removal of devices to a controlled environment for analysis. Careful care and planning must be in place to ensure that the various laws are strictly adhered to. Once in the controlled area preservation and analysis of the data will proceed. Throughout this stage a standard code of ethics should be adhered to and there should be constant communication with all stakeholders.

The forensics process suggests application law and thus the practitioner must not only be aware but appropriately trained to produce a written and formal report. The final phase of this framework will focus on the production of report on the overall process specifying outputs from the previous phases. This phase will encompass much more than writing a formal report on the findings and should be relevant to apprehending a suspect. This phase will include the inventory of all items seized and/or analysed during the previous phases. All equipment and forensic tools used throughout the investigation will also be formally recorded. The methodology employed throughout the investigation as derived from the framework will have met the Daubert Standard. Other integral parts of the reporting phase include the virtual reconstruction of the crime scene and the creation of an attacker profile. These done in conjunction with the legal requirements will enable the production of a more detailed and relevant report that will positively support an expert witness in court.

4.3. Overview of the proposed framework

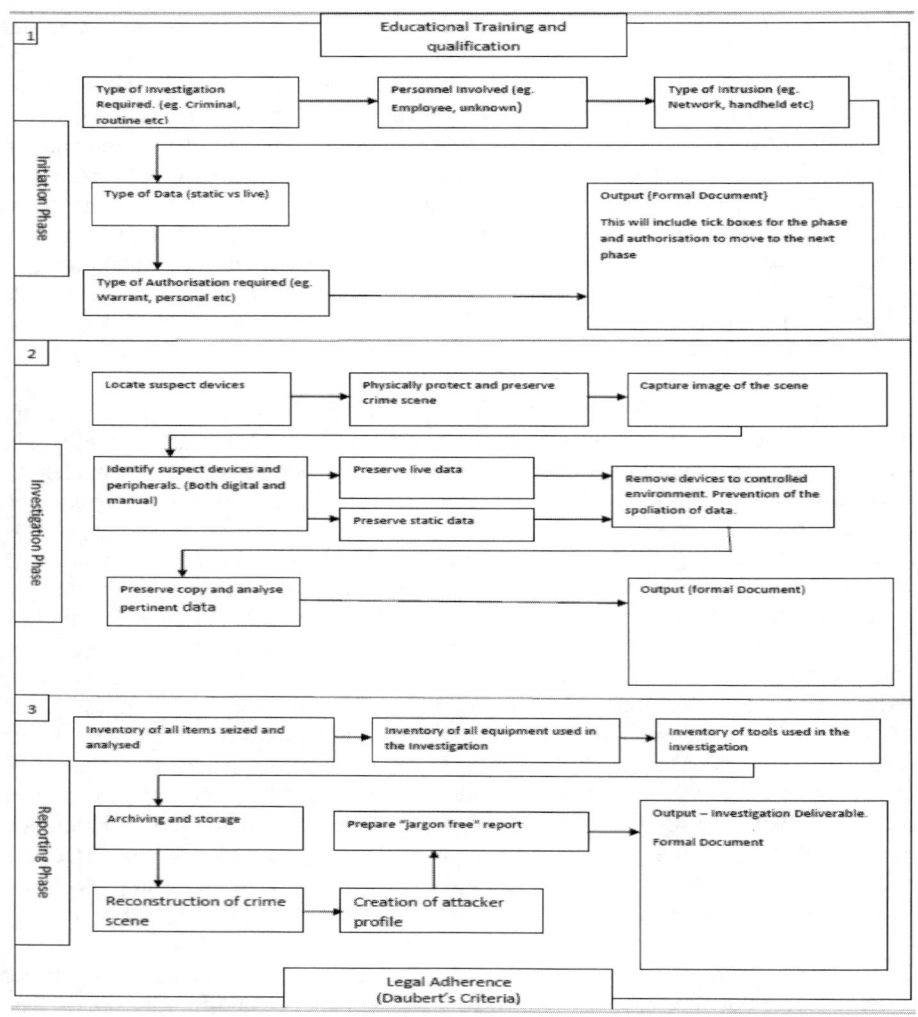

Figure 1: Proposed framework

4.4. Daubert's test

The mere number of models/methodologies identified in this paper suggest that there is very little or no formalization in the Digital Forensics Field. This present a huge problem for the development of Digital Forensics as a forensic science and digital evidence presented in courts are quite likely to fail the Daubert's test. Daubert's test is used to check whether or not forensic evidence presented in courts is sound. The Daubert's test is a legal standard used in courts to authenticate the statements of testifying experts. It refers directly to the methods used to acquire evidence in the various forensics fields. It seeks to ascertain whether the evidence/testimony being given is relevant, seeking to answer questions such as- was the data gathered using scientific methods and procedures, is the evidence based on mere assumptions or from a comprehensive knowledge base. It also seeks to ascertain whether the evidence being given is reliable, finding out if the practitioners is authorised, qualified and /or experienced in the particular field. The major questions comprising the Daubert's test include:

I. Has was the theory used been tested?
II. Has the theory been peer reviewed (less chance of error)?
III. What is the reliability/error rate of this particular theory?
IV. What is the extent of general acceptance by the scientific community?
V. Are there standards and controls in place governing its operation?

5. Conclusion

A standardized methodology (way of working) will be of benefit to all involved in the world of digital forensics. The definition of a framework that includes all aspects and core fields that are involved in the digital forensics process will help to alleviate some of the issues that exist within the discipline at present. It has been identified that although several subject areas are impacting on the field there is no collaborative and integrated approach. Digital forensics is a wide area and thus all professionals that are impacted must be able to communicate eliminating "area specific" jargon and assumptions that one field is more important than the other. Computer Scientists must accept that to be digital forensics practitioners they must become knowledgeable of the different laws that are related to the field. Legal experts must accept that digital forensics is more than just using a particular tool and become knowledgeable of the digital forensics field. Law enforcement officers must be cognisant of both of the above. Organisations must be made to realise though they may "forensics ready" (if there is such a term) and have various security personnel in place within the organisation it is not enough to use the Information technology department/technician to investigate a digital crime. The work proposed addresses these issues and lays the foundations of a framework that will accurately and rigorously address the multidimensional nature of digital forensics.

Digital forensics is a dynamic field that is currently faced with a number of issues. This study aims to highlight some of these issues and develop amicable solutions. The field of digital forensics encompasses various fields and criteria that must be satisfied before any evidence acquired can be accepted in a court. Facets include investigative, technical, ethical and legal. The digital forensic investigator must to ensure that at all times all aspects of the job are considered because ignoring any one area can impact significantly the outcome of an investigation. For example the main objective of a digital forensic investigation is to collect, analyze and preserve digital evidence that may be used in a legal case thus ignorance of any of the laws regarding the information technology/computer field can significantly impact on the case.

Whereas there has been some increase in research with regards to the digital forensics field there is still much more to be done. In his article Digital forensics research: The next 10 years Simon Garfinkel states simply, 'There is no standard set of tools or procedure" just 2 things that still need researching (Garfinkel, 2010). Two main areas are identified that need further research: i) the legal issues as they relate to digital forensic and ii) the evidence acquired and the issue of a methodology governed by a set of standards that may be used internationally by digital forensic investigators. Having a methodology governed by a set of standards will also help in satisfactory responses to the questions posed by the Daubert's test. The proposed framework addresses these key issues as well as the incorporation of the reconstruction of the crime scene and creation of an attacker profile. While this presents more assurance in digital evidence acquired through the digital forensics process being acceptable in courts internationally it also promotes the apprehension of the unknown attacker/s in digital related crimes.

6. References

Brill, A. Pollitt, M. (2006) *The evolution of Computer Forensics Best practices, An Update on Programs and Publications.* Journal of Digital Forensic Practice 2006; 1:3-11. Available from http://www.informatik.uni-trier.de/~ley/db/journals/jdfp/jdfp1.html#BrillPW06

Carrier B. D., (2003) Open Source Computer Forensic Manual. Available from: http://www.digital-evidence.org/

Casey, E. (2004). *Digital Evidence and Computer Crime, Forensic science, Computers and the Internet.* Academic Press, London, UK

Cuardhuain S. O., (2004) An Extended Model of Cyber Crime Investigation. Journal of Digital Evidence. Vol. 3. Issue 1

Garfinkel S., (2010) *Digital forensics research: The next 10 years. Digital Investigations 7.* 2010 S64-S73. Available from www.sciencedirect.com Accessed on August 20, 2010

Ricci I. S. C. (2006) *Digital Forensics Framework that incorporate legal issues.* Available from www.sciencedirect.com Accessed on October 20, 2010

Kruse W. Heiser J. G. (2001). Computer Forensics: Incident Response Essentials (1st ed.), Addison Wesley Professional. USA

Lee H, C., Palmbeach T. M., Miller M. T. (2001*) Henry Lee's crime scene handbook.* Elsevier Academic Press Available from: http://academic.evergreen.edu/curricular/social_dilemmas/fall/Readings/Week_06/Crime%20Scene%20Handbook.pdf

Meyers M., Rogers M. (2004) 'Computer Forensics: The need for standardization and Certification'*, International Journal of Digital Evidence*, Vol. 3, issue 2. Available from www.ijde.org

Pollitt M., (1995) *Principles, Practices, and Procedures: An approach to standards in computer forensics.* Available from; www.digitalevidencepro.com/resources/principles.pdf

Perumal S., (2009) Digital Forensics Model Based on Malaysian Investigation Process, IJCSNS Vol. 9 No. 8 Available from www.sciencedirect.com

Ricci I. S. C. (2006) *Digital Forensics Framework that incorporate legal issues.* Available from www.sciencedirect.com Accessed on October 20, 2010

Salemat S. R. Yusof R. Sahib S. (2008) *Mapping Process of Digital Forensic Investigation Framework.* International Journal of Computer Science and Network Security Vol. 8 NO 10 Available from www.sciencedirect.com

A Formal Logic for Digital Investigations: A Case Study Using BPB Modifications.

I. Mitchell

Middlesex University, UK

Abstract

A Formal Logic is developed and the following presented: i) Notation for Formal Logic; ii) developing the Formal Logic for Digital Investigations Experiments (FDIE); iii) Case study modifying BPB and demonstrating the Formal Logic in ii); and iv) extending the Formal logic to Digital Investigations (FDI). A case study using BIOS Partition Block (BPB) modifications to render the partitions unreadable is used to successfully demonstrate the FDIE. From this experiment the Formal logic (FDIE) is extended to Formal Logic for Digital Investigations (FDI).

Keywords

Formal Logic, Recovery, Anti-contamination, Evidential Integrity, BPB, FAT, NTFS.

1. Introduction

Recovery of data often leads to changes being made to digital evidence. During judicial proceedings such changes bring into question the integrity of the evidence, the reliability of the process or processes used to recover data, and the credibility, expertise and skills of the investigator (McKemmish, 1999). When a third party does not reproduce identical results it costs time to re-examine the original investigation. These events can become acrimonious with each party accusing the other of malpractice or incompetence. The formal logic implemented here indicates simple steps taken to certify digital evidence and is an attempt to satisfy cases where modifying evidence is necessary.

Hidden Data essentially relies on two forms: i) non-physical; and ii) physical (see Berghel et al, 2006). The former is associated with Cryptography and Steganography, whereas the latter is associated with finding undetected storage locations within the file system. Huebner (Huebner et al, 2006) defines effective hiding techniques as those meeting the following criteria:

- Standard file system check should not return any errors.
- Hidden data will not be overwritten, or the possibility of data being overwritten is low.
- Hidden data will not be revealed when using standard GUI file system interfaces.
- A reasonable amount of hidden data can be stored.

The first definition above does not include the modifications of VBR as hidden data, since a simple "chkdsk" would reveal there is something wrong with the volume; at this point most investigators would apply a partition recovery tool and retrieve the data. Boot sector modifications are quite common - most viruses developed during the 80's and 90's rely on boot sector modifications (Cohen, 1994). While most anti-virus software detects and eliminates such viruses, there exists software to repair damage boot partitions, alas, these were not designed for Forensic Computing and only work on live devices, not images, and therefore such use would risk contamination of digital evidence.

There are two problems: First, how to alter the boot sector for the recovery of the data; and the second how to recover the data without compromising the integrity of the image – *the formal logic aims to prove that no data tampering occurred during the modification of the boot sector.* The structure of this paper is as follows: Section 2 will give the background theory behind boot sectors; section 3 will provide guidelines on how to recover images; section 4 introduces the notation for a formal logic for Digital Forensic Experiments; section 5 argues how the authentication of the evidence remains intact and how the formal logic is extended to Digital Investigations; and, finally, section 6 makes conclusions.

2. File Systems and the BIOS Parameter Block, BPB.

This section gives a brief overview of the BPB under FAT16 and NTFS, respectively.

2.1. File Allocation Table, FAT16.

Figure 2.1 is a description of BPB and the associated values, taken and adapted from (Carrier, 2006; Microsoft, 2000).

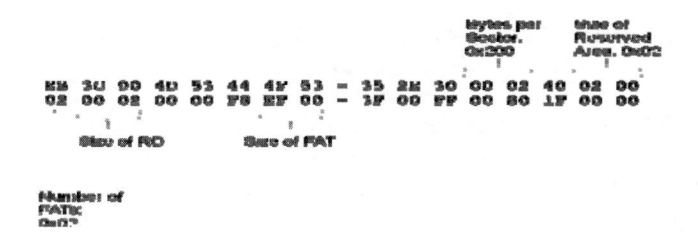

Figure 2.1: BPB values showing location, associated values and representation.

From Figure 2.1 the FAT structure can be calculated and is represented in Figure 2.2. Cluster 2 is derived from Equation 2.1 and shows that an increase in the values in the Reserved Area will result in an increase in value for Cluster 2.

Cluster 2 = Reserved Area + (Number of FATs * FAT size) + Size of Root Directory
(2.1)

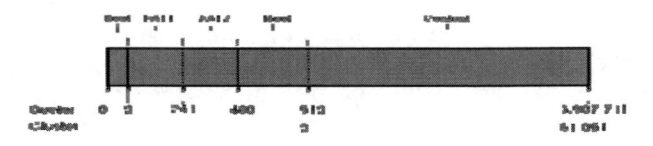

Figure 2.2: Schema of FAT structure derived from values in Figure 2.1, not to scale.

Modifying the BPB, e.g. the values of the bytes representing the size of the reserved area from 0x02 to 0xFF, results in the structure of the file system being shifted right without modifying any of the data stored in the content area. The file system does not adapt to the changes and becomes corrupted, leading to the file system being unrecognisable and unreadable and hence no access to the data. This process is reversible and resetting the parameters back to their original settings will result in the recovery of the drive.

2.2. New Technology File System, NTFS.

NTFS key feature is the Master File Table, MFT. Location of the MFT is stored in the boot sector as shown in Figure 2.3. Bytes 0x30-0x37 represent the Logical Cluster Number, LCN, of the MFT and the value of the offset is 0x4F80A, or 325,642 in decimal.

0	1	2	3	4	5	6	7	8	9	A	B	C	D	E	F
EB	52	90	4E	54	46	53	20	20	20	20	00	02	04	00	0C
00	00	00	00	00	F8	00	00	3F	00	FF	00	80	1F	00	0C
00	00	00	00	80	00	00	00	7F	A0	3B	00	00	00	00	0C
0A	F8	04	00	00	00	00	00	04	00	00	00	00	00	00	0C
F6	00	00	00	02	00	00	00	9C	93	44	A8	A9	44	A8	8C
00	00	00	00	FA	33	C0	8E	D0	BC	00	7C	FB	68	C0	07

Figure 2.3: Boot sector of NTFS partition. Highlighted bytes show the offset, in clusters, to the MFT.

Therefore the location of the $MFT is dependent on bytes 0x30-0x37 in the BPB and any changes to this value will result in the partition not being able to find the MFT; there is only one value it should not be, and that is the MFT Mirror, since if the boot sector pointed to the MFT Mirror the partition would still be readable.

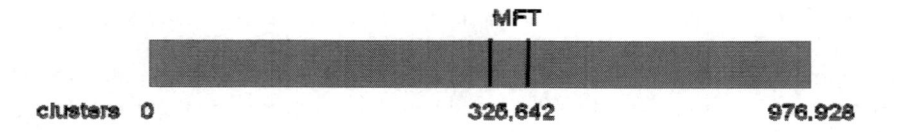

Figure 2.4: Schema of NTFS structure showing location of Master File Table, MFT, derived using values from Figure 2.3 (not to scale).

2.3. Summary

Experiment 1 will modify the values for the Reserved Area on a FAT16 device and render the partition unreadable. Experiment 2 will modify the values for Logical Cluster Number, LCN, for the MFT on a NTFS device and render the partition unreadable - an interview with Senior Forensic Computer Analysts of 7 years, revealed that such modifications would go undetected. The experiments have made two assumptions: i) changing these bytes has no effect elsewhere on the disk; and ii) reversing these changes recovers the data. By applying the formal logic to the experiment it can be proved that the recovery process above does not tamper the data. All methods that require altering evidence should be accompanied with explanatory/contemporaneous notes and there needs to be a method of identifying and correcting the problems detailed in sections 2.1 and 2.2. This will be investigated in the next section.

3. Analysis

The problem is given an image where it is suspected that there has been some boot sector tampering, then how is the process reversed if the default values are not known *a priori*? Some guidelines are given to reverse the process and return it to its original settings; this section will provide the theory behind steps taken to derive values independently of the boot sector, since it has become unreliable.

3.1. FAT Structure.

As mentioned in Section 2 the FAT structure is dependent on the Reserved Area. This analysis is restricted to restoring the value of the Reserved Area and independent of the values in the BPB. Table 3.1 outlines the parameters required to calculate the location of cluster 2.

Description	Acronym
Bytes Per Sector, located in boot sector; bytes 0x0B-0x0C.	BPS
Sectors Per Cluster, located in boot sector; byte 0x0D	SPC
Reserved Area, located in boot sector; bytes 0x0E-0x0F.	RES
Total Sectors in File System, located in boot sector bytes 0x20-0x23.	Partition_Sectors
Offset to partition, located in Partition table in MBR.	Partition_Offset
Size of Image, number of bytes allocated to image file. This can be derived from looking at the properties of the image.	SoI
Number of Sectors in Physical device.	Physical_Sectors

Table 3.1: Parameters used to calculate BPB values.

3.1.1. Data Acquisition.

Using a write-blocker image the MBR and the relevant logical partition; ensure that during data acquisition hashing algorithms have been employed and verified. Return the device. Use the MBR to determine the following:

1. **BPS**: Assume there are 512 Bytes Per Sector.

2. **Physical_Sectors:** Use mmls command from TSK (The Sleuth Kit, 2010) to calculate the size, in sectors, of the device.

3. **SoI**: Size of Image is equal to the product of **BPS** and **Physical_Sectors**.

4. If **SoI=BPS*Physical_Sectors** then move to next section; else then **BPS**=2***BPS** and goto 3. Repeat Until true.

3.1.2. **RES**:Size of Reserved Area on Logical Partition, bytes 14-15.

Bytes 14-15 represent the value of the number of reserved sectors that exist before FAT1. FAT1 will occur at the beginning of a new sector; therefore, using the value of BPS calculated in section 3.1.1 increment in steps of BPS through the document in a Hex Editor. Recognising FAT is non-deterministic, however, there are two markers that may help. First the end-of-file marker represented by the value, 0x0FFF FFFF and 0xFFFF in FAT32 and FAT16, respectively. Second are contiguous cluster chains that will have entries one value greater than the cluster they are representing, e.g. the 8th cluster would point to the 9th cluster and have a value of 0x09. The first two clusters have different values that cannot always be relied on between different devices, however, the two points of cluster chains and end-of-file markers are very good indicators of FAT1. The beginning of FAT1's offset address is a factor of **BPS** and **RES**, therefore once the offset for FAT1 is discovered then it is simply divided by **BPB** to give **RES**.

At this point, the recovery process is complete for our experiment and the reversal process of restoring the values will begin. When making changes to images, keeping contemporaneous notes updated is an important part of the process to ensure reproducibility. After the alterations the image should be run through a hashing algorithm. This process is explained in a later section.

3.2. NTFS Structure.

Section 2 showed that NTFS partitions are dependent on finding the location of the MFT. This analysis is restricted to restoring the value of the LCN and independently of the logical boot sector calculating the original value of the LCN. Repeat the stages in sub-section 3.1.1 to complete the Data Acquisition phase and the calculation of bytes per sector.

3.2.1. Logical Cluster Number, LCN.

For every file included on the partition there is a corresponding MFT Entry. The MFT itself is a file, $MFT, and is the first entry in the MFT; thus the MFT has a reference to itself. This self reference can be used to find the location of the MFT and ultimately the original values of the LCN.

The $MFT file can be found by a simple string search, e.g. search of "FILE0" and $MFT, should result in addresses in the same sector. Record this figure as **LCNOffset**. Open the image in a hex editor and go to the offset of the MFT. Figure 3.1 shows a hex-dump of the image. The **LCNOffset (0x27FF5000)** needs confirming as outline in Equation 3.1.

$$\text{LCNOffset} = ((LCN*SPC) + \text{Partition\_offset}) *BPS \qquad (3.1)$$

Navigate to the Data Attribute in the MFT Entry, for more details on NTFS Data structures see Chapter 11 in (Carrier, 2006). Check that the non-resident flag is set true, see byte 264 in bold in Figure 3.1. The content of the Data Attribute contains the VCN run list for the file, i.e the location of the file. In this case it is **0x3280000A F804**. The VCN run list has two parts the length and the location in clusters. The low 4-bits of the first byte represent the number of bytes to represent the length, **0x8000**, and the high 4-bits of the first byte represent the number of bytes to represent the location, **0x0AF804**. Transform this value to big endian notation, 0x04F80A and enter the values in Equation 3.1

```
( (0x04F80A * 0x04) + 0x1F80) * 0x200 = 0x27FF5000

  0    46494C45 30000300 FE224000 00000000  FILE 0... ."@. ....
 16    01000100 38000100 A0010000 00040000  .... 8... .... ....
 32    00000000 00000000 06000000 00000000  .... .... .... ....
 48    02000000 00000000 10000000 60000000  .... .... .... `...
:
144    00000000 00000000 30000000 68000000  .... .... 0... h...
:
256    80000000 48000000 01004000 00000100  .... H... ..@. ....
272    00000000 00000000 7F000000 00000000  .... .... .... ....
288    40000000 00000000 00000400 00000000  @... .... .... ....
304    00000400 00000000 00000400 00000000  .... .... .... ....
320    3280000A F80400A6 B0000000 50000000  2... .... .... P...
:
400    e8000100 0030a98a ffffffff 00000000  .... .0.. .... ....
```

Figure 3.1: Hex-dump of MFT entry of MFT. At offset 256 shows the beginning of the Data Attribute that contains the VCN of the MFT itself.

4. Formal logic for Digital Forensic Experiment.

Following the analysis in the previous sections the observation of two experiments on a NTFS and FAT partition are completed. These experiments cannot represent all the possible changes and different instances that can be made, but are merely a demonstration of applying the Formal logic to a Digital Forensic Experiment and primarily to see if the hypothesis that the reversal process recovers the data is correct.

4.1. Notation

Table 4.1 introduces the notation to represent physical devices and images as I, and hashing and copying as functions H and D, respectively.

I_n ,	where I represents images, $n=0,1,2,3,...,N$ is the identification of the image e.g. I_2 represents Image 2 with no modifications and I'_2 represents Image 2 with a modification.
$H_k(I_n)$,	where H represents a hashing algorithm identified by k, e.g. $H_{md5}(I_2)$ employs the hashing algorithm md5 to Image I_2 .
$D(I_n)$,	where D represents duplication $D(I_n) \rightarrow I_{n+1}$ and $H_{md5}(I_n) = H_{md5}(I_{n+1})$. The duplication of I'_n will produce an image I_{n+1}, e.g. $D(I'_n) \rightarrow I_{n+1}$ and $H_{md5}(I'_n) = H_{md5}(I_{n+1})$. However, $H_{md5}(I'_n) \neq H_{md5}(I_n)$ since I'_n is a modification of I_n .

Table 4.1: Formal Logic Notation for Data Acquisition in Forensic Computing.

4.2. Method

The experiment is to image the physical device, record the MD5 and SHA hash values and ensure they are verified. Then make changes to the device, image the physical device, record the MD5 and SHA hash values and ensure they are verified. The aim of both experiments is to return the image of the device to its original state and see if the hash values match that of the original device. This will prove that the changes made to the evidence have not altered the data in any way and were necessary. Using the notation in Table 4.1 the experiments can be formalised in the enumerated list below:

1. Image I_0 . $D(I_0) = I_1$; (imaging of device).
2. Record and verify Hash the values, $H_k(I_0) = H_k(I_1)$
3. Image I_1 . $D(I_1) = I_2$
4. Record and verify the hash values. $H_k(I_1) = H_k(I_2)$.
5. Make relevant changes to the partition boot sector on the original device, I'_2, ie make it unreadable.
6. Image I'_2. $D(I'_2) = I_3$
7. Record and verify the hash values. $H_k(I'_2) = H_k(I_3)$.
8. Reverse the changes, as noted in section 3, I'_3, ie make it readable.
9. Record the hash values of I_1 and I'_3 i.e. $H_k(I_1) = H_k(I'_3)$.

List 4.1 Formal logic for Experiments – to be completed with contemporaneous notes – specific to Experiments 1 and 2.

In general there are two stages to the experiment: forward and backward chain of events. These are reflected in List 4.2 that should be applied to general experiments. By looking at the change between associated iterations can reveal where further research by the investigator is required.

Forward and Backward Chain of events
1. Image device, $D(I_0) = I_1$
2. Record and verify the hash values. $H_R(I_0) = H_R(I_1)$.
3. Time, $t=1$;
4. Document and make any changes to I_t to yield I'_t
5. Duplicate I'_t. $D(I'_t) = I_{t+1}$;
6. Record and verify the hash values, $H_R(I'_t) = H_R(I_{t+1})$.
7. Time, $t=t+1$;
8. Repeat stages 4 – 7 until no more modifications are required.

Check $H_R(I_0) = H_R(I_t)$, if these are correct then the experiment is a success.

Listing 4.2 Formal logic for Digital Investigation Experiments, FDIE.

4.3. Results.

Two 2GByte USB Memory sticks, each formatted with a single logical partition as FAT16 and NTFS, where used in the experiment. After formatting, 35 digital images of various sizes were copied to the device. The hash values are documented for each experiment in Table 4.2. The experiments show that changes can be recorded at intermediate stages and that a third independent party when following these instructions will also yield the same result. Table 4.2 shows that the hash values in stage 9 are identical. Hence the image has returned to its former state, without changing the data in the content area. Also, Table 4.2 shows that the image is identical to the original state and therefore the 35 digital images can be retrieved. Stages 1-9 were developed to maintain the integrity of the experiment and ensure that no evidence spoliation occurred. In the next section these stages are adapted and proposed as a set of guidelines for Forensic Computing Practitioners when it is necessary to make changes to the image.

5. Evidential Integrity.

McKemmish (McKemmish, 1999) mentions "... the examiner has a responsibility to correctly identify and document any change...." and comments further "During the forensic examination this point may seem insignificant, but it becomes a critical issue when the examiner is presenting their findings during judicial proceedings. Whilst the evidence may be sound, questions regarding the examiner's skills and knowledge can affect their credibility as well as the reliability of the process employed".

	Experiment 1 – FAT16	Experiment 2 – NTFS
2	$H_k(I_0)$=d6655334452c5ce811867a0941c6eec0	$H_k(I_0)$=fdeecf171e38c7928fdcbb6753f87ab7
	$H_k(I_1)$=d6655334452c5ce811867a0941c6eec0	$H_k(I_1)$=fdeecf171e38c7928fdcbb6753f87ab7
4	$H_k(I_1)$=d6655334452c5ce811867a0941c6eec0	$H_k(I_1)$=fdeecf171e38c7928fdcbb6753f87ab7
	$H_k(I'_1)$=d6655334452c5ce811867a0941c6eec0	$H_k(I'_1)$=fdeecf171e38c7928fdcbb6753f87ab7
7	$H_k(I'_1)$=107ca1f93083cd434542ee8dff0d7e4c	$H_k(I'_1)$=1eb2fe26df606a6bffc58de059639dc9
	$H_k(I_2)$=107ca1f93083cd434542ee8dff0d7e4c	$H_k(I_2)$=1eb2fe26df606a6bffc58de059639dc9
9	$H_k(I'_2)$=d6655334452c5ce811867a0941c6eec0	$H_k(I'_2)$=fdeecf171e38c7928fdcbb6753f87ab7
	$H_k(I_4)$=d6655334452c5ce811867a0941c6eec0	$H_k(I_4)$=fdeecf171e38c7928fdcbb6753f87ab7

Table 4.2. Table documenting results for experiment. Hashing algorithm, k, is MD5. Numbers in left hand-hand column relate to steps in section 4.2. The final stage in both experiments matched and all 35 images were recovered.

McKemmish makes two important points: "*document any change*"; and "*reliability of the process*". The 9 stages in section 4.2 combined with contemporaneous notes ensure these two important factors when handling digital evidence in the experiments in section 4.3. This allows independent third parties to follow steps above and verify that no other alterations have contaminated the data; only modifications documented in contemporaneous notes have been made. However the 9 stages in section 4.2 cover an experiment and have been refined for a digital investigation where it is necessary to modify the image:

1. Image device, $D(I_0) = I_1$
2. Record and verify the hash values. $H_k(I_0) = H_k(I_1)$.
3. Time, $t=1$;
4. Document and make any changes to I_t to yield I'_t
5. Duplicate I'_t. $D(I'_t) = I_{t+1}$;
6. Record and verify the hash values, $H_k(I'_t) = H_k(I_{t+1})$.
7. Time, $t=t+1$;
8. Repeat stages 4 – 7 until no more modifications are required.

List 5.1 Formal Logic for Digital Investigation (FDI) – to be completed with contemporaneous notes.

The proposed formal logic above not only documents the changes but also verifies the changes, by applying a hashing algorithm after each iteration, and thus assuring that independent third parties can reproduce identical results.

6. Conclusions.

The experiment shows that the proposed Formal Logic works, and the contributions are:
- Disabling partitions using BPB modifications; section 2 gives examples of how partitions can be modified and hence, all data cannot be read.
- Formal Logic Notation for Digital Investigations (section 4.1).
- Formal Logic for Digital Investigation Experiments involving Evidence Tampering, provided in section 4.2.
- Formal Logic for Digital Investigations involving Evidence Tampering, provided in section 5.

This experimental formal logic was extended to Digital Investigations. Documenting change and using hashing algorithms of the image to allow independent third parties to achieve identical results.

If assumptions are made about proprietary systems, then apply DFIE to see if these assumptions can be corroborated by comparing hash numbers in the forward and backward chain processes.

Finally, if during a digital investigation modifications are required in order to read the data then apply FDI. When third parties are required to reproduce results independently following FDI iterations and contemporaneous notes made will identify at which stage, by different hashes, and thus limit the scrutiny and cost of such an investigation.

7. References

Berghel, H., Hoelzer, D. And Sthultz, M. 2006. "Data Hiding Tactics for Windows and Unix File Systems". http://www.berghel.net/publications/data_hiding /data _hiding.php [accessed February 2010].

Bowen, J, P., and Hinchey, M. J., 2006. "Ten Commandments of Formal Methods: Ten Years on....". IEEE Computer Soceity, January issue.

Carrier, B. 2006. "File System Forensic Analysis". Addison-Wesley.

Cohen, F. 1994. "A Short Course on Computer Viruses". Wiley.

Huebner, E., Bem, D., and Cheong K-W. 2006. "Data Hiding in the NTFS file system." Journal of Digital Investigation. Vol 3.

Microsoft. 2000. "FAT: General overview of On-Disk Format". Hardware White Paper.

McKemmish, R,. 1999. "What is Forensic Computing?". Australian Institute of Criminology. http://www.aic.gov.au

The Sleuth Kit. 2010. The Sleuth Kit, TSK downloaded from www.sleuthkit.org.

Reconstructive Steganalysis by Source Bytes Lead Digit Distribution Examination

A. Zaharis[1], A. Martini[2], T. Tryfonas[3], C. Illioudis[4] and G Pangalos[5]

[1]University of Thessaly, Greece
[2]SIEMENS SA, Greece
[3]University of Bristol, UK
[4]ATEI of Thessaloniki, Greece
[5]Aristotle University of Thessaloniki, Greece
e-mail: alexzaharis@gmail.com, dimart@gmail.com, theo.tryfonas@bristol.ac.uk, iliou@it.teithe.gr; pangalos@auth.gr

Abstract

This paper presents a novel method of JPEG image steganalysis. Our approach is driven by the need for a quick and accurate identification of stego-carriers from a collection of files of different formats, where there is no knowledge of the steganography algorithm used, nor previous database of suspect carrier files created. The suspicious image is analysed in order to identify the encoding algorithm while various meta-data is retrieved. An image file is then reconstructed in order to be used as a measure of comparison. A generalisation of the basic principles of Benford's Law distribution is applied on both the suspicious and the reconstructed image file in order to decide whether the target is a stego-carrier. We demonstrate the effectiveness of our technique with a steganalytic tool that can blindly detect the use of JPHide/JPseek/JPHSWin, Camouflage and Invisible Secrets. Experimental results show that our steganalysis scheme is able to efficiently detect the use of different steganography algorithms without the use of a time consuming training step, even if the embedding data rate is very low. The accuracy of our detector is independent of the payload. The method described can be generalised in order to be used for the detection of different type images which act as stego-carriers.

Keywords

Steganalysis, Image Reconstruction, JPEG, Benford's Law, lead digit distribution.

1. Introduction

Data hiding has always been a major part of Computer Forensics, as many cases have been solved because of hidden data retrieved by experts. Data hiding in an information system can be performed for various reasons including potential malware attacks, hiding data for later use in a compromised environment by an attacker, exchanging secret information via the Internet, or when an offender hides useful information in his personal computer.

There are numerous methods that can be used in order to hide data from potential interception. One of them is steganography (Anderson et al. 1998; Kessler 2004) on image files, which is a common technique among personal computer users. This technique has been well described, and is well known to forensic investigators. Different tools have been developed to computerize the process of locating suspect carrier files of different file types using visual, protocol compatibility or statistic analysis attacks (Fridrich and Goljan 2002). Most of these techniques concentrate and actually work against specific steganography algorithms/tools. While others that are used for universal blind steganalysis need a training step for agents to be more efficient in locating statistic anomalies on carrier files (Barbier et al. 2007) These techniques are of great performance when the training step includes a large number of true positive carrier files to be examined but can be very time consuming. On the other hand the above techniques mentioned have low hit rate for no training step.

In order to speed up the process of steganalysis without sacrificing high detection rates, we are going to present a less common technique of detecting image steganography carrier files. Our method concentrates on reconstructing (Nosratinia 2001) a reconstructed 'original' image in order to use it as a comparison measure against the original possibly stego-carrier file.

This paper deals with:

- Benford's Law, along with the reasons of choosing this kind of metric as a detection schema.
- The presentation of the process of creating a reconstructed image, resembling the data structure of the original image file before embedding any hidden data in it.
- The design and usage of a forensic tool utilizing the above mentioned technique to blindly detect image carrier files via a single comparison of file structure and not via a time-consuming training step of a decision agent.
- Finally, hit ratio results are presented along with time analysis of the detection process in order to prove the unique use of this steganalytic tool.

The contribution of this paper to the Forensics community concentrates on the presentation of an out of the box steganalytic technique that minimizes computation time along with the creation of forensic tool that implements a well known statistical analysis method (Benford 1938). This tool can be extended in order to be applicable to other image file types while complying with the known computer forensic policies.

2. Steganography Concepts and Tools

We selected a variety of steganography algorithms and tool implementations that hide information inside different parts of JPEG image files. In particular we focus on JPHSWin's (Latham 1999) Least Significant Bit (LSB) option, Invisible Secrets' Fuse method (2011) as well as Camouflage's Fuse method (2011), in order to examine our approach's ability to detect suspicious files in different hiding locations inside the JPEG format.

In our work we are going to distinguish four types of image files:

- The original file, which in our case would be a JPEG image file created/saved with MS Paint.
- The carrier file, which in our case is going to be the result of steganography applied on the original file with either, JPHSWin, Camouflage or Invisible Secrets.
- The reconstructed original file, which in our case is going to be generated by our tool in order to simulate the original MS Paint JPEG file.
- The suspect file, which can be either an Original file or a Carrier file. Our purpose is to identify its exact type.

A crucial point of this work is to generate a reconstructed image file as similar as possible to the original file. To do so, we initially have to identify the software or encoding algorithm of the suspect JPEG image (EXIF Make). We are therefore going to use an open source image analysis tool, namely "JPEGSnoop" (2011), which can determine the various settings that were used by the digital camera when taking the photo (EXIF metadata, IPTC), but can also extract information that indicates the quality and nature of the JPEG image compression used by the camera while saving the file.

Moreover, one of the features of JPEGsnoop, is an internal database that compares an image against a large number of compression signatures. JPEGsnoop reports what digital camera or software was likely used to generate the image. This is extremely useful in determining whether or not a photo has been edited / tampered in any way. This type of feature is sometimes referred to as Digital Image Ballistics / Forensics.

In our efforts to recreate a JPEG encoding algorithm (JPEG 2011, JPEGClub 2011) we chose to simulate the MS Paint software algorithm using JAVA. Thus a tool has been created that acted partially as an Ms Paint Simulator to use as our cloning machine in an attempt to recreate an almost identical original file (reconstructed file) when given a suspect file. This software can be easily extended in order to simulate different types of JPEG encoding implementations.

3. Benford's Law

Benford's law, also known as the first digit law or significant digit law, is an empirical law. It was first discovered by Newcomb in 1881 and rediscovered by Benford in 1938. It states that the probability distribution of the first digits, x (x = 1, 2,..., 9), in a set of natural numbers is logarithmic. More specifically, if a data set satisfies Benford's law, its significant digits will have the following distribution:

$$p(x) = \log 10 \ (1 + 1/x), x = 1,2,\ldots,9 \qquad (1)$$

Where p(x) stands for probability of x.

Although counterintuitive, validity of Benford's law has been demonstrated in various domains. While the naturally generated data obey the Benford's law well, deliberately altered data and random guess data do not follow this law in general. This property has been widely used in fraud detection in accounting area (Buck et al. 1993, Nigrini, 1996). However, the applications of Benford's law in the image processing field have only recently been explored. The most common reason to use Benford's Law in digital image Forensics is for identifying whether the most significant digits of the block-DCT coefficients follow Benford's law and determine possible carrier files (Hernandez et al. 2000; Jolion 2001; Acebo & Sbert 2005; Perez-Gonzalez et al. 2007). We, on the other hand, are going to use a Generalisation of Benford's Law basic principles ("GBL") against byte array statistics of the file examined.

4. A Generalisation of Benford's Law

Steganography on a JPEG image can cause major alteration throughout the byte array structure of the file depending on the steganography algorithm used. Therefore an initial idea was to use Benford's Law to detect such alterations on byte values of a suspect file. We found however that Bendford's Law cannot be applied conclusively on the byte arrays of a file and no safe conclusions can be made as far as a suspect file is a stego-carrier.

We noted however that on a byte array sequence of a file, it is important to detect changes on the least and most significant digit of each byte, as those are mostly affected by popular methods of steganography. Differences on the rest of the digits are of minor importance and can be omitted. We are going to use this generalisation of Benford's Law (GBL) in an algorithm to detect deliberate modifications due to steganography. This method can differentiate between bit alteration as resulted through the purposeful process of Steganography and unavoidable bit alteration resulted by image reconstruction.

4.1. Proposed Algorithm

Given a Suspect Image file F:

1. Calculate its byte array sequence F[file.length()].
2. Calculate the probability x=1,2,...,9 of the first and the last digit of the byte array sequence F[file.length()] for the Suspect File.
3. Calculate the probability x=1,2,...,9 of the first and the last digit of the byte array sequence F[file.length()] for the reconstructed 'original' file.
4. Compare the results of step 2-3 and using a predefined threshold, decide whether the suspect file is a carrier file or not.

The procedure of the determination of the similarity threshold, used in step 4 is in described in detail in Section V (Detection Algorithm Section).

It was observed that by applying GBL on the byte arrays of a suspect and a reconstructed file the GBL results are crucially different if examining a true stego-carrier and its reconstructed file as opposed to examining an original file and its reconstructed file. Thus GBL can be a valuable metric to detect such anomalies leading to determining if a file is a true stego-carrier.

4.2. Advantages against other Detection Algorithms

The advantages of the applying GBL as a steganography detection algorithm are:

- High detection rate (Par VII, Figure 8)
- Fast detection, only needed digits of a byte array sequence are examined minimizing detection time. No previous database of suspicious files, or training step is needed.
- Extensible algorithm, the GBL algorithm can be used in order to detect steganography inside different image formats other than JPEG. GBL is not a format-dependent steganography detection algorithm as described on Section VI.

5. Reconstruction of Original JPEG Image

In order to design a quick and efficient way of reconstructing an original JPEG image from a suspicious one, the use of known image processing tools along with Java image libraries were utilized. For the purposes of our research, original JPEG images were created with MS Paint and were used to prove the concept of our method.

The process of steganalysis that is going to be described deals with suspect files, about which the steganalyst:

1. Doesn't know whether the file is a stego-carrier file or not.

2. Has no information about the hidden message or file type or the steganography algorithm used to embed that message, provided the file is a stego-carrier file.

5.1. Step 1 – JPEGSnoop

Given a suspect file < S >, the process of reconstruction begins by obtaining useful information about the file after examining it with the JPEGSnoop tool. The information obtained by JPEGSnoop is:

1. The Quantization Table (Quality Factor)
2. The "EXIF Make" or Software Signature that created the picture examined.

It is important to highlight the fact that all three steganography tools examined (JPHSWin, Camouflage, Invisible Secrets) do not re-encode the JPEG image. Parts of the image are altered in order to embed information but the EXIF Make or Software Signature does not change at all. Taking the above mentioned aspect into consideration, one can safely use the JPEGSnoop tool to identify the software that created the original File even if the only file in hand was the suspect file. Knowing the software that created the original file helps in deciding on how to alter the encoding algorithm in order to create a recinstructed file that resembles the original file as close as possible.

```
Precision=8 bits
Destination ID=0 (Luminance)
    DQT, Row #0:    8   6   5   8  12  20  26  31
    DQT, Row #1:    6   6   7  10  13  29  30  28
    DQT, Row #2:    7   7   8  12  20  29  35  28
    DQT, Row #3:    7   9  11  15  26  44  40  31
    DQT, Row #4:    9  11  19  28  34  55  52  39
    DQT, Row #5:   12  18  28  32  41  52  57  46
    DQT, Row #6:   25  32  39  44  52  61  60  51
    DQT, Row #7:   36  46  48  49  56  50  52  50
    Approx quality factor = 74.75 (scaling=50.51 variance=0.81)
```

Figure 1: Luminance Quality Factor

```
Precision=8 bits
Destination ID=1 (Chrominance)
    DQT, Row #0:    9   9  12  24  50  50  50  50
    DQT, Row #1:    9  11  13  33  50  50  50  50
    DQT, Row #2:   12  13  28  50  50  50  50  50
    DQT, Row #3:   24  33  50  50  50  50  50  50
    DQT, Row #4:   50  50  50  50  50  50  50  50
    DQT, Row #5:   50  50  50  50  50  50  50  50
    DQT, Row #6:   50  50  50  50  50  50  50  50
    DQT, Row #7:   50  50  50  50  50  50  50  50
    Approx quality factor = 74.74 (scaling=50.52 variance=0.19)
```

Figure 2: Chrominance Quality Factor

```
*** Searching Compression Signatures ***

    Signature:            0182408A81A4ABF04D4A34A8A5E98C58
    Signature (Rotated):  012D821C6AB210E2A753BE053B8F55D0
```

Figure 3: The MS Paint Signature

When the Software Signature (in our case MS Paint) and quantization table are extracted, we proceed to step 2.

5.2. Step 2 – Reconstructive Image Encoding

In this step our goal is to achieve a simulation of the software JPEG encoding system (MS Paint) extracted on Step 1. We have already specified on the previous step the quantization tables used and we can assume that the Huffman tables and header syntax are specific for every JPEG file created by specific software. The only other part missing is the actual source / image RGB / YCC values which are going to be used as an input to our JPEG encoding system.

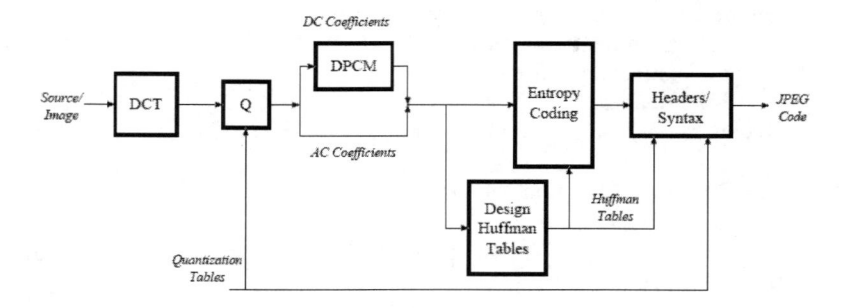

Figure 4: The JPEG Encoding System (Nosratinia 2001)

Different methods have been developed in order to retrieve RGB / YCC values (MATLAB 2011) with the best possible precision in order for the reconstruction to be lossless. We are going to use a less accurate method of Image RGB / YCC data retrieval by utilizing the JAVA Advance Imaging API (JAI). By using standard methods one can retrieve the wanted RGB /YCC values with great precision and minimum time loss.

Using those data as an input to our Dynamic JPEG encoding system, also programmed using JAVA, a reconstructed 'original' JPEG image <P> is created. Step 2 concludes the process of a reconstructed image construction. The output of this process will be used in our GBL in order to detect whether the suspect file used on Step 1 is actually a carrier file.

6. Proposed Steganalysis Method and Detection Algorithm

6.1. The Steganalysis Method

Given a Suspect file <S> :

Step 1 – Data Retrieval

1. The quantization table (quality factor) is extracted from <S>.
2. The "EXIF Make" or Software Signature that created the picture is identified.
3. Headers are extracted from <S>.
4. RGB / YCC values are extracted from <S> using JAVA Advanced Imaging API.

Step 2 – Image Reconstruction

1. Retrieved software signature of Section 1 is used in order to specify the structure of the image file to be reconstructed.
2. According to the structure identified above the following dynamic parameters of JPEG encoding system are set :
    1. Quantization tables
    2. Huffman tables
    3. Headers
3. Reconstructed image file <P> is encoded.

Step 3 – The Detection Algorithm

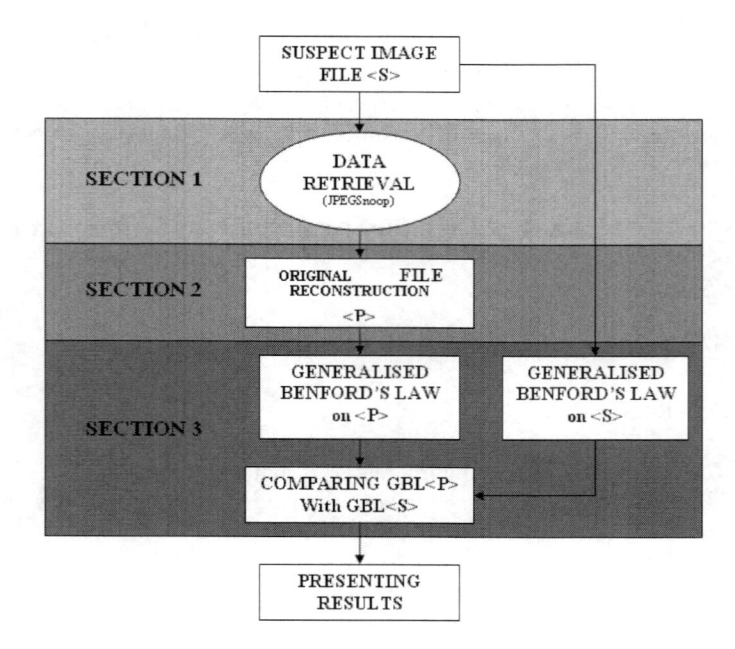

1. Generalised Benford's Law is applied on Image <S> as described on paragraph III.
2. Image size and hash value of Image <S> is calculated.
3. Generalised Benford's Law is applied on Image <P> as described on paragraph III.
4. Image size and hash value of Image <P> is calculated.
5. Comparing results of Steps 1 & 3 Section 3, updating similarity factor.
6. Comparing results of Steps 2 & 4 Section 3, updating similarity factor.
7. ```
if   (similarity_factor>   similarity_   threshold){
"Suspect File <S> is not Carrier File" }   else
{"Suspect File <S> is Carrier File" }
```

**Figure 5: Three Steps of the Proposed Steganalysis Method.**
```

Similarity Factor is a parameter that indicates how similar two files are. Similarity Factor values range from zero (0) to nine (9) which is the highest degree of similarity. Its value is calculated by the following algorithm for LSB steganography:

```
Similarity_factor=0;
for (int i=1;i<=9;i++){
if(Math.abs(<S>GBL(i) - <P>GBL(i))<=2.5)
Similarity_factor++;
}

if(Math.abs(<S>.size()-<P>.size())<=800){
Similarity_factor++;
}
```

While for Fuse steganography the following algorithm is used:

```
Similarity_factor=9;
Size_dif=Math.abs(<S>.size()-<P>.size());

for (int i=1;i<=9;i++){
if(Math.abs(<S>GBLp(i) - <P>GBLp(i))<=15)
Similarity_factor++;
  }

if(Math.abs(<S>.size()-<P>.size())<=800){
Similarity_factor++;
}
```

<S>GBL(x) stands for Generalized Benford's Law on file data distribution for the first digit and last digit with value x where x = 1,2...9.

<S>GBLp(x) stands for Generalized Benford's Law on part of the file data distribution for the first digit and last digit with value x where x = 1,2...9. The size of the part examined is equal to: Size_dif=Math.abs(<S>.size()-<P>.size());

Similarity Threshold is a predefined constant value that has been calculated after applying Generalised Benford's Law on large number of Reconstructed Files created by the previously stated process applied on original image files. This value is encoding specific, so MS Paint has a certain Similarity Threshold while Photoshop 9 has a different one.

After thorough examination of a large number of JPEG image files it has been identified that the Similarity Threshold for MS Paint has a value ~five (~5). The following table depicts the experimental results in scale of 1500 JPEG image files of different dimensions and size.

JPEG Image Size	320 x 240	600 x 320	800 x 600
Number of Original Image Files used	500	500	500
Average similarity factor	7.86	6.98	5.66
Minimum/Maximum	6 / 9	5 / 9	5 / 9
Number of Carrier Image Files used	1500	1500	1500
Average similarity factor	1.23	3.25	4.57
Minimum/Maximum	0 / 3	1 / 4	2 / 5

Figure 6: Statistics of Average / Minimum / Maximum Similarity Factor.

Stego-Carrier Files were divided into three different groups of five hundred (total 1500) Original Files each. For each group JPHSWin, Camouflage and Invisible Secrets were used in order to embed the smallest in size, file possible (1kb ASCII .txt file). As it is depicted in Figure 6, a similarity factor of five (5) can be considered as a similarity threshold.

An amount of 1.5% false positive stego-carrier files was identified but this percentage decreased when the embedded file became larger (5KB ASCII .txt file).Further techniques to minimize the false positive identifications is discussed in Section VI.

The proposed method can be extended in order to detect steganography not only on JPEG image files, as described above, but also on a variety of other common image formats (BMP, TIFF, PNG).

7. A GBL STEGANALYSIS TOOL

The GBL Steganalysis Tool is going to utilize the above mentioned detection algorithm along with some Stego-tool specific detection methods in order to achieve high hit rate in minimum time. This steganalysis tool is formally named Ben-4D.

The diagram of figure 7 displays the basic methods implemented by BEN-4D tool. The core of the detection procedure used is the actual steganalysis method presented on Paragraph V. Once the suspect file has been identified as a stego-carrier file extra detection methods are applied in order to specify the steganography algorithm used. Ben-4D searches for specific patterns and signatures used by each individual steganography algorithm.

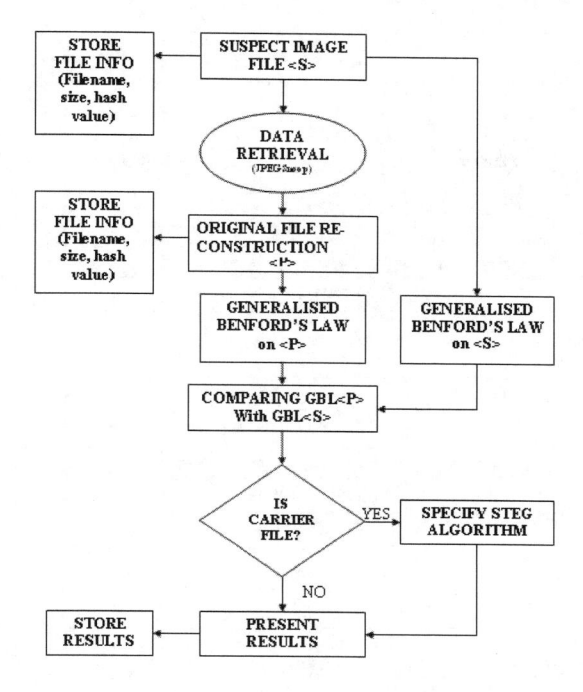

Figure 7: BEN-4D's execution flow diagram.

Stego-only attack: Only the stego-object is available for analysis. For example, only the stego-carrier and hidden information are available.

Example Steg- Algorithm specific Detection

Some detection fingerprints used to identify the existence of a specific steganography algorithm are:

1. No standard Huffman tables used (JPHSWin).
2. Noticeable difference in size, between Carrier file and Reconstructed file (Camouflage,Invisible Secrets).
3. Not standard headers (Invisible Secrets).
4. Altered bits following a specific pattern.
5. Not proprietary file termination (Camouflage).

A combination of the Generalized Benford's Law detection along with some of the detection fingerprints stated above can increase the detection hit rate of carrier files as well as decrease the False – Positive detection, mentioned on a previous paragraph, from an average 15% to 0.1 %.

Figure 8, represents the hit rates obtained using only Generalized Benford's Law detection algorithm in a comparison to using a combination of Generalized Benford's Law and other detection fingerprints.

JPEG Image Dimensions	320 x 240				600 x 320				800 x 600			
File Type	Original	JPHSWin	Camouflage	Invisible Secrets	Original	JPHSWin	Camouflage	Invisible Secrets	Original	JPHSWin	Camouflage	Invisible Secrets
Number of Files	500	500	500	500	500	500	500	500	500	500	500	500
Average Size (kb)	30	34	31	31	100	104	101	101	200	205	201	201
GBL Hit rate	89%	89.1%	99.6%	99.7%	88.5%	86.7%	99.6%	99.7%	88%	82.2%	99.6%	99.7%
False Positive Steg. Detection	10%				15%				20%			
Scan time (sec) per item	~1	~2	~1	~1	~1	~2	~1	~1	~1	~2	~1	~1
Total time (min)	8.3	16.6	8.3	8.3	8.3	16.6	8.3	8.3	8.3	16.6	8.3	8.3
GBL + Sig. Hit rate	99.9%	99.8%	100%	100%	99.9%	98.1%	100%	100%	99.9%	97.4%	100%	100%
False Positive Steg. Detection	0.1%				0.1%				0.1%			
Scan time (sec) per item	~2	~3	~2	~2	~2	~3	~2	~2	~3	~4	~3	~3
Total time (min)	16.6	25	16.6	16.6	16.6	25	16.6	16.6	25	33.3	25	25

Figure 8: BEN-4D's Hit Rate Statistics (1kb hidden data)

Figure 8 also demonstrates how the larger in dimension and size the image is, the smaller the GBL hit rate becomes. This can be explained due to the fact that the overall alteration of the byte array structure is statistically smaller thus more difficult to detect. Section 1, Step 4, YCC/RGB values are copied with a loss. The bigger the size of the embedded medium the higher the hit rates. Thus the results illustrated on Figure 8 are the worst case scenario.

Finally, scanning time is almost doubled when utilizing the full steganalysis algorithm in comparison to simply utilizing GBL. This fact will be used as a feature to give BEN-4D's user the opportunity to choose between two different scan modes a fast one and a full one.

8. CONCLUSIONS AND FUTURE WORK

Steganalysis is a serious concern within the field of Computer Forensics, as a number of cases exist that have been solved due to hidden data retrieved by experts. This paper's contribution to this is a novel method of steganalysis using Generalized Benford's Law on Reconstructed Cover Image Stego-Carrier Files.

We designed and develop a user-friendly tool with a Graphical User Interface (GUI) in order to simplify the process of steganalysis and aid the average investigator user.

Experimental statistical results presented in this paper, demonstrate that using our proposed method high rate, effective and quick detection of the given steganography algorithms can be achieved.

Consequently, taking into account the potential impact of malicious use of steganography, it is essential to develop a general purpose software tool that will not only effectively locate all kinds of JPEG steganography, including double encoding algorithms such as Outguess or F5 that are not yet supported, but it will also be able to detect steganography on any possible image carrier file.

As an enhancement of our theoretical work:

1. Data loss during the reconstruction process can be diminished by using enhanced algorithms. This will result in almost identical Reconstructed Files to the Original ones or what is known as lossless transcoding (Sanchez 2006).
2. The use of more complex steganography algorithms, such as Outguess or F5, can be detected by adding new steps to the developed algorithm. These algorithms re-encode the original image in order to produce a carrier File. The encoding procedure is standard for every one of these algorithms, producing unique "EXIF Make" or Software Signature. This can be a starting point for further investigation of the suspect file.

As an improvement to the tool designed:

1. More steganography algorithms have to be detected, including the ones that re –encode the Carrier file.
2. More JPEG encoding algorithms need to be supported.
3. More image formats have to be supported including BMP, TIFF and PNG.
4. Cryptanalysis of the verified stego-carrier files can be added, in order to export the hidden information.

By both improving the method and the software implementing it, a new powerful detection tool will be produced assisting in the recovery of hidden files of potential evidential value.

9. References

Acebo, E.D. and Sbert, M. (2005), "Benford's law for natural and synthetic images," in Proc. of the First Workshop on Computational Aesthetics in Graphics, Visualization and Imaging, L. Neumann, M. Sbert, B. Gooch, and W. Purgathofer, Eds., Girona, Spain, pp. 169–176.

Anderson, R., Fabien A., Petitcolas, P. (1998), "On the limits of steganography", IEEE Journal of Selected Areas in Communications

Barbier, J., Filiol, E., Mayoura,K. (2007), "Universal Detection of JPEG Steganography", Journal of Multimedia, Vol. 2 no 2, pp. 1-9.

Benford, F. (1938), "The law of anomalous numbers," Proc. of the American Philosophical Society, vol. 78, pp. 551–572.

Buck, B., Merchant, A., Perez, S. (1993), "An illustration of benford's first digit law usinbg alpha decay half lives," European Journal of Physics, vol. 14, pp. 59–63.

Camouflage website, http://camouflage.unfiction.com/ (last accessed June 2011)

Fridrich, J., Goljan, M. "Practical Steganalysis of Digital Images – State of the Art", In Proceedings of SPIE

Hernandez, J.R., Amado, M., Perez-Gonzalez, F. (2000), "DCT domain watermarking techniques for still images: Detector performance analysis and a new structure," IEEE Trans. on Image Processing, vol. 9, no. 1, pp. 55–68.

Independent JPEG Group - http://www.ijg.org/ (last accessed June 2011)

Invisible Secrets website, http://www.invisiblesecrets.com/ (last accessed June 2011)

Jolion, J.M. "Images and benford's law" (2001), Journal of Mathematical Imaging and Vision, vol. 14, no. 1, pp. 73–81.

JPEGClub - http://jpegclub.org/ (last accessed June 2011)

JPEGSnoop, http://www.impulseadventure.com/photo/jpeg-snoop.html (last accessed June 2011)

Kessler, G. (2004), "Null Ciphers: An Overview of Steganography for the Computer Forensics Examiner", FBI's Forensic Science Communications.

Latham, A. (1999), "Steganography: JPHIDE and JPSEEK", http://linux01.gwdg.de/~alatham/stego.html (last accessed June 2011)

MATLAB JPEG Toolbox by Phillip Sallee http://redwood.ucdavis.edu/phil/demos/jpegtbx/jpegtbx.htm (last accessed June 2011)

Nigrini, M. (1996), "A taxpayer compliance application of Benford's law", Journal of the American Taxation Association, vol. 1, pp. 72–91.

Nosratinia, A. (2001), "Enhancement of JPEG-Compressed Images by Re-application of JPEG", JOURNAL OF VLSI SIGNAL PROCESSING SYSTEMS FOR SIGNAL IMAGE AND VIDEO TECHNOLOGY, Vol. 27 No 1/2, pp. 69-80.

Pérez-González, F., Heileman, G., Abdallah, C.T. (2007) "Benford's law in image processing", in IEEE International Conference on Image Processing, San Antonio, TX, USA.

Sanchez, D. (2006), "Lossless JPEG transcoding", ECE 533 Project Report.

Combating Information Hiding Using Forensic Methodology

C. Balan, D.S. Vidyadharan, S. Dija and K.L. Thomas

Centre for Development of Advanced Computing, Trivandrum, India
e-mail: cbalan@cdactvm.in, divyasv@cdactvm.in, dija@cdactvm.in,
thomaskl@cdactvm.in

Abstract

Advancement in disk technology led to the development of hard disks of terra byte sizes. Users have the option to divide the storage into a number of partitions based on the nature of uses. In case of Master Boot Record partitioning scheme, whenever a partition is created, the complete track containing MBR/EMBR of the storage media is reserved to store boot information and partition table information. But this information requires only the first sector of the track. The remaining sectors in that track cannot be used for any other purpose, as the file system cannot access these free sectors and hence, the chances of overwriting these sectors are very low. So, this area can be used to hide any critical information. The user will get a large amount of storage space for hiding data depending on the number of partitions. This area becomes an important area in Forensics Analysis. In this paper, first we describe the details of data hiding in unused areas, which cannot be easily overwritten by the Operating Systems and how it can be analysed using standard cyber forensics software. Analysing such areas using cyber forensics tools may give lot of valuable information and also will lead to reduce the criminals in hiding information.

Keywords

Data hiding, MBR, EMBR

1. Introduction

Certain kind of users are interested in storing data in a hidden manner. This may be to protect crucial information from intentional access by others. Data can be made hidden in a number of ways without entering any information into the data structures of the file system. For example, data can be hidden inside unused bits of an image file (Hal Berghel, 2007). Data can be stored inside the free area of a cluster used by an ordinary file. But all these methods have its own flaws. For example, the data stored in free space of clusters can be overwritten as more data is added to original file.

In a disk, there is an area that is not considered as part of the partition and hence invisible to the file system. This area constitutes the sectors reserved for storing the master boot record. Boot record needs only one sector space. The remaining sectors in the track can be used for data hiding. The file system and most of the currently available tools are not capable of accessing the information stored in this area. So a chance of overwriting this area is very less. Thus these free sectors become a very valuable location to keep important information from external access.

2. Disk and Partitions

Hard disk drives are the popular digital storage media used in desktop systems. It comes with different capacities. Nowadays, commonly available capacity ranges from 160 GB to 2 TB. As on July 2010 the highest capacity available is 3 TB. The hard disk drives are divided into tracks and tracks are further divided into sectors (Brian Carrier, 2005). Recently, sector size in a hard disk has changed from 512 bytes to 4096 bytes (Seagate Corporation Web Site, 2011). But the most of the application are still considering a sector as 512 bytes. Built-in emulator inside the hard disk handles the necessary conversions. Here, for explaining data hiding areas, we are taking a sector as a 512 byte sized unit.

Storage space of the disk can be further divided into partitions. Partitions can be either primary or extended. Fig. 1 shows an example of 80GB disk, divided into five partitions with one primary partition. First, the total space is divided into a primary partition and an extended partition. The extended partition is further divided into four logical partitions.

Bytes	Data
0-445	Boot Code
446-509	Partition Information
510-511	Signature (0x55AA)

Table 1: MBR Structure

Boot code and partition information is held in the Master Boot Record (MBR). MBR is the very first sector in the disk and the structure is as shown in Table 1 (Chad Steel, 2006). In a sector of size 512 bytes, the first 446 bytes is the boot code and the next 64 bytes contains information about 4 partitions, each with 16 bytes and ends with signature of 2 bytes. The MBR can hold a maximum of four numbers of partitions, 3 primary and one extended; or four primary partitions. It allows only one extended partition and it can be further divided into logical partitions. The partition table information of 16 bytes length gives the size, starting sector of the partition, number of sectors and the file system of the partition. Fig. 2 shows the boot sector of a disk, with the partition table information highlighted.

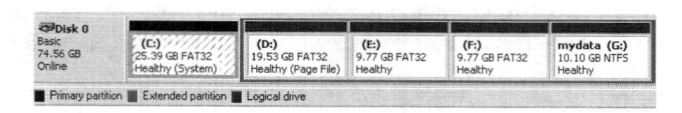

Figure 1: Disk 0 is divided to five partitions

3. Extended Master Boot Record (EMBR)

Extended master boot record (EMBR) is the first sector of the extended partition. The logical partitions in the extended partitions are created as primary partitions in the EMBR. The structure of EMBR is same as MBR but it can hold only one primary and one extended partition. So every logical partition makes a chain of primary and extended partitions.

MBR comes only in the first sector of a track. The remaining sectors in the track containing MBR is free and cannot be used by the partition for any other purpose. So these sectors are completely unused. The EMBR also uses only the first sector from the track assigned to it. So there will be free sectors in each of these logical partitions.

Since the partition cannot start from the second sector of the track, the sectors other than the first sector allocated for MBR/EMBR is not used for any other purpose by the operating system. Normally these sectors in the MBR/EMBR tracks remain unused. Within the EMBR sector, 32 bytes are used to store the information of two partitions and 2 bytes for the signature. The remaining 478 bytes are free since there is not boot code inside the EMBR. So, in the case of EMBRs we have free sectors plus 478 free bytes. This is the area where users can hold or hide secret information of any kind. Again, tools that can retrieve the contents of sectors can show the hidden data. So, the data has to be stored in an encrypted form.

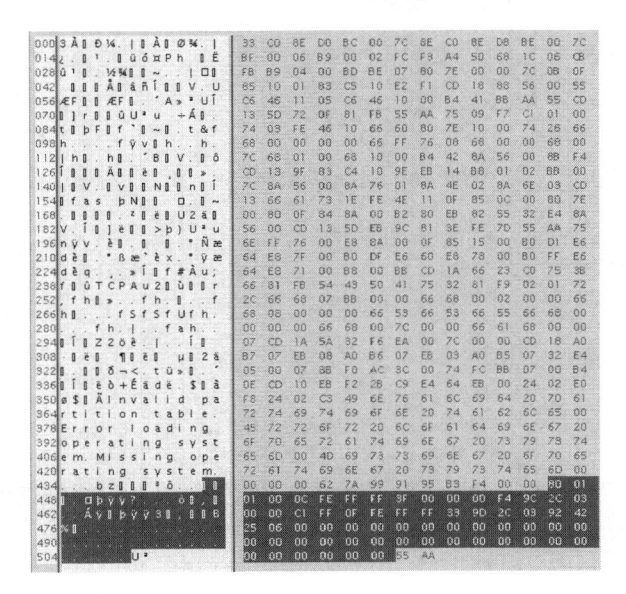

Figure 2: The Boot sector with Partition information highlighted.

It is clear that as the number of partitions in the hard disk increases, the percentage of unused sectors in the disk also grows. This wasted area can be used for storing any important information, which is to be hidden because of any reason.

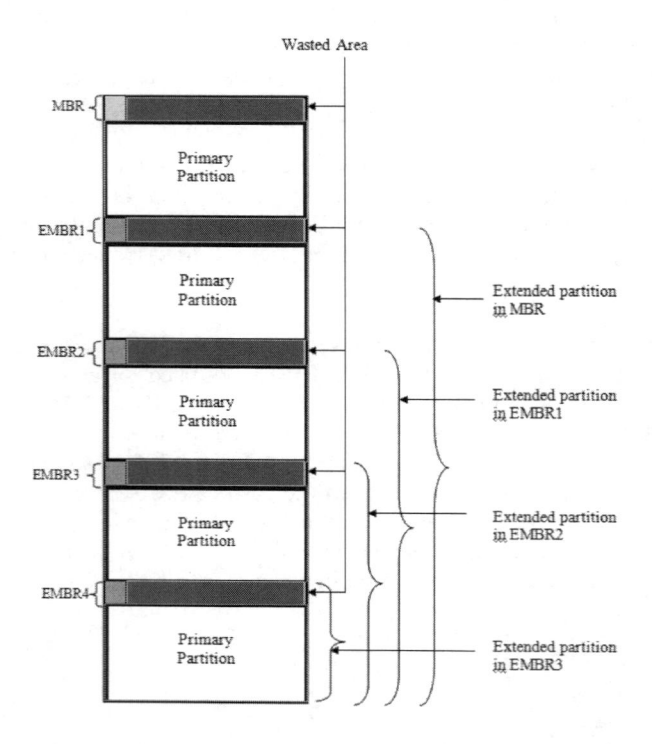

Figure 3: EMBR and the slack space inside a single track

Since this space cannot be accessed by the file system, there is no way to recover the hidden data from these sectors. Fig. 3 shows MBR and EMBR along with the wasted space inside track allocated for storing boot record.

4. Other Slacks

The unused space inside the track allocated for the MBR is called MBR slack and the wasted space inside the EMBR is called EMBR slack. Other than these MBR and EMBR slacks, there are a number of unused spaces or slacks in a hard disk.

4.1. Disk Slack

The sectors those are left after dividing the total space in to a number of partitions are called disk slack. So these are the unpartitioned sectors inside the disk. Normally file system cannot access this area and so this area can be used for information hiding.

4.2. Partition Slack

Cluster is the basic data allocation unit within a partition. The partition size may not be a multiple of the cluster size. So there will be a number of free sectors within the partition. These sectors are known as partition slack. Data hidden in this area will never be overwritten until formatting or repartitioning is done.

4.3. File Slack

In windows file systems, a file or folder takes at least one cluster for storing the data. Cluster size can vary from 512 bytes to 64 KB. File size can be of any size limited by the file system attributes. Since the file size cannot be multiples of cluster size always, there may be free space in the last cluster of the file. This is named as a file slack. Briefly it can be defined as space from the end of the file to the end of the last sector allocated to that cluster. Space from end of the file to the end of containing sector is called RAM Slack. RAM Slack will always be less than the size of a sector.

The partition slack and disk slack can be used for information hiding where there is less chance of overwriting the data without formatting the disk. But in the case file slack and RAM slack, the space may get overwritten at any time by modifying the file content.

5. Writing Data

Before writing the data that is to be hidden, first calculate the sectors or bytes that are free in the disk. Fig. 4 shows a flow chart for computing the MBR/EMBR slack inside a hard disk. After this, we can use a hexadecimal editor tool for writing the required content to these sectors. The advantage here is that no file system or forensic tool will show this as a file while inspecting the disk.

6. Advantages

The main advantage of using MBR Slack, EMBR Slack, Partition Slack and Disk slack for information hiding is that, nobody can easily overwrite the content since these sectors are not accessible by the file system. In the case of RAM Slack or file slack the data may be simply overwritten while deleting the files or modifying the files. L. Shu-fen et al. use a mechanism to mark the sectors that are used for data hiding as Bad Sectors (Shu-fen L. et al., 2009). But here, there is no point in marking the sectors as bad sectors as the file system will never access these sectors. So this information hiding methodology offers high flexibility and low risk. The MBR slack data cannot be over written even by re-partitioning.

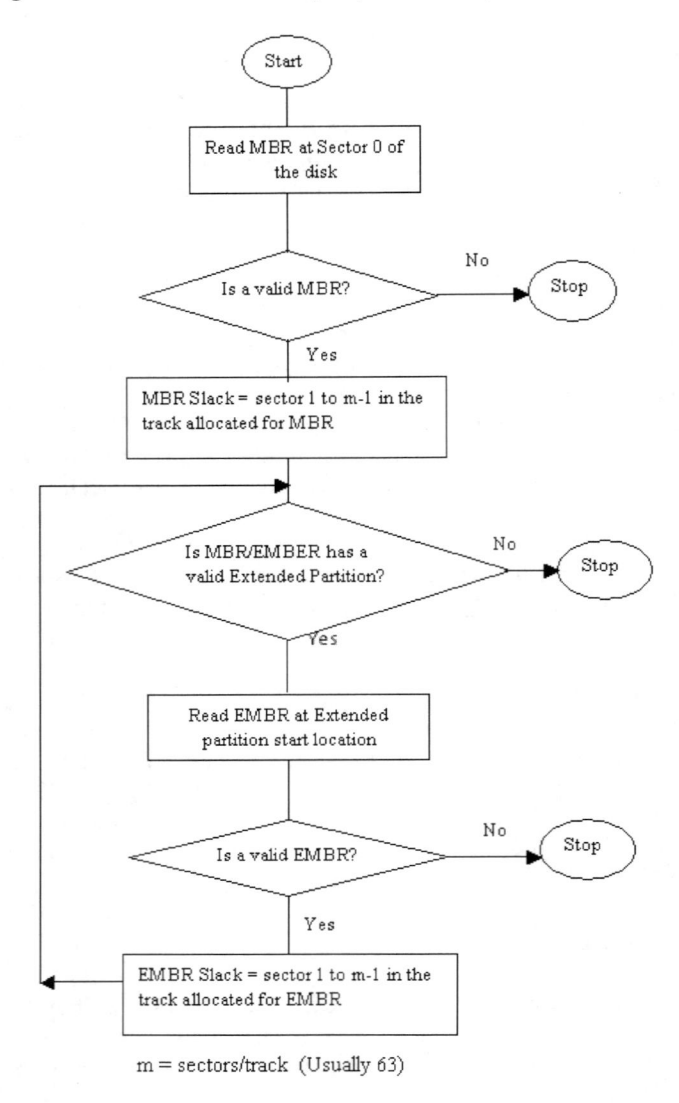

Figure 4: Flowchart for computing MBR/EMBR slack.

So we can use the MBR/EMBR slack for hiding important data for a long term. Also, this method is secure and the complexity is low. Another major advantage is that, we can hide large chunk of data, that requires more than one EMBR slack, can be stored as fragmented in different EMBR slacks in the same hard disk. It enables the user to hide big files inside the hard disk without much risk. If we are storing the data in an encrypted form then it will not be directly readable using a hex editor. These features make this method of data hiding very useful for a wide range of information hiding applications.

7. Hidden Data Recovery

We have seen different areas within a hard disk that can be utilized for intentional data hiding by criminals. Cyber crime analysts are interested in finding hidden data as they may give very crucial hints for proving crimes. Cyber forensic analysis starts with the acquisition of digital evidence without the support of operating system and file system. In the case of hard disk, a bit stream copy commonly known as disk image of the hard disk is acquired and further analysis is carried out in this copy. In this disk image, all the sectors are available and so the analyst can access every location including MBR/EMBR slack. The analyst should give special attention to the contents residing in the slack.

8. Conclusion

We have discussed how criminals can hide data inside a hard disk without the intervention of file system. As this is a safe method of hiding data without the fear of being overwritten by other files, there are chances that this fact can be misused by anti-social elements. So depending on the purpose for which the hidden data is stored, we have to devise methods for quick recovery of data stored in MBR/EMBR slack of large hard disks with numerous partitions. Standard Cyber Forensics Tools can analyse data hidden in these areas and can provide protection from these antisocial activities.

9. References

Carrier, B. (2005), *File System Forensic Analysis,* Addison Wesley Professional, US.

Steel, C. (2006), *Windows Forensics: The Field Guide for Corporate Computer Investigations*, John Wiley & Sons, Indiana.

Berghel, H. (April 2007), "Hiding Data, Forensics and Anti-Forensics", *Communications of the ACM*, vol. 50, No.4, pp15-20.

Shu-fen L., Sheng P., Xing-yan H., Lu T. (2009), "File hiding based on FAT file system", *IT in Medicine & Education*, vol. 1, pp1198-1201.

Seagate Corporation Web Site (2011), "The Transition to Advanced Format 4K Sector Hard Drives", www.seagate.com/docs/pdf/whitepaper/tp613_transition_to_4k_sectors.pdf, (Accessed 31 May 2011)

Forensic Analysis of Navman GPS Devices

D. Jones

e-mail: daniel.jameson.jones@gmail.com

Abstract

Navman devices can provide a wealth of information to forensic investigators and could prove to be vital to an investigation. In this paper we focus on one Navman device, including what information is left behind on the device and how that information can be interpreted into meaningful data that can be used by a forensic investigator.

Keywords

Navman, GPS

1. Introduction

Navman devices are some of the more common personal navigation devices around, and can be found on sale in most electronic stores and even in some supermarket chains.

With the availability of such devices, the chances of a forensic investigator encountering one of these devices as part of their investigation is likely. Therefore it pays that an investigator has an understanding of what these devices can store and how useful that information can be in an investigation.

In this paper we focus on the analysis of the Navman iCN320.

Each section of the paper will cover the details of the device, as well as the various files of interest and what information is contained within these files, followed by a conclusion.

2. Specifications of the Navman iCN320

The Navman iCN320 consists of the following hardware specifications outlined in table 1. Note that it appears that the data storage for the device is located on an SD memory card attached to the device; no other storage was identified on the device.

The operating system within the device does not appear to be a Windows CE OS (NavmanUnlocked Wiki (2011)), but may be a variation of a Linux OS as these devices have been modified to operate under a Linux operating system (duff.dk Website (2011)).

Processor:	Intel® PXA-255 300MHz Applications Processor
Memory:	32MB SDRAM
Screen:	2.83" (71.1mm) landscape TFT LCD colour display
Power:	5V DC, 1A
GPS Receiver:	SiRFstarII™
GPS update rate:	Typically every second once fix established
GPS accuracy:	Fix to 5 metres 95% of the time
Hard Drive:	No

Table 1: Technical Specifications of Navman iCN320 (Navman Website (2010))

3. Acquisition of the Navman iCN320

As the SD memory card contained the only known storage from the device it was the only component that could be acquired for further analysis.

The SD memory card was acquired with the use of a write blocked multimedia card adaptor (an Addonics AESDD12U2WP) and FTK Imager (v3.0.0.1443). The result of the acquisition produced a forensic copy (image) of the SD memory card in an EnCase E01 format.

Analysis of the forensic copy was conducted within EnCase v6.16.2.

4. Files of interest within the Navman iCN320

The following files of interest were identified within the 'root' directory of the SD memory card image; the information has been presented in a table containing the name of the file and its purpose.

File Name:	Purpose:
RECENT.DAT	Contains the recently entered destinations.
FAVVER4.DAT	Contains user saved favourite locations.
ROUTE.DAT	Contains the last recorded route entered from the device

Table 2: Details on files of interest from a Navman iCN320

The next sections of the paper cover the analysis of the data structure of each of the identified files.

5. Data analysis of the file 'RECENT.DAT'

The file 'RECENT.DAT' consists of record entries containing the address, latitude and longitude of that record entry. Examination of the file identified no file header or footer associated with the file. The record entries appear to begin at the start of the file.

Each record entry is 520 bytes in length; the first byte seems to be a marker that indicates the type of record entry (possibly how the record was entered into the device, such as a record that was saved from a point on the map or a point of interest (POI) or saved from a location that was manually entered by the user).

The record then contains the name and address of the location, which is stored as plain text, this location appears to be 431 bytes in length.

The record entry then contains some information for a length of 75 bytes; the purpose of this information is unknown.

The next portion of information is the longitude and latitude coordinates, which are 8 bytes in length within the record entry with 4 bytes allocated to the longitude and latitude coordinates respectively; the coordinates are stored as 32-bit signed integers.

Following on from the longitude and latitude coordinates are four bytes containing unknown information, followed by a byte denoting the end of the record entry.

Below is a table containing the details of the structure of a single record entry with the file 'RECENT.DAT':

Offset (Bytes):	Length (Bytes):	Description:
0	1	Marker (possibly identifying the entry type).
1	431	Free text – containing the name and address of the record entry.
432	75	Unknown
507	4	Longitude Coordinate stored as a 32bit signed integer.
511	4	Latitude Coordinate stored as a 32bit signed integer.
515	4	Unknown
519	1	End of record marker (denoted by 0x00)

Table 3: Table containing layout of a single record entry within the file 'RECENT.DAT'

6. Data analysis of the file 'FAVVER4.DAT'

The file 'FAVVER4.DAT' consists of record entries containing the address, latitude and longitude of that record entry. Examination of the file identified no file header or footer associated with the file the record entries appear to begin at the start of the file.

Each record entry is 1508 bytes in length; with the name of the location stored as plain text starting at the beginning of the record and continuing for 280 bytes in length.

The record entry then contains some information for a length of 72 bytes; the purpose of this information is unknown.

The next portion of information is the longitude and latitude coordinates, which are 8 bytes in length within the record entry with 4 bytes allocated to the longitude and latitude coordinates respectively; the coordinates are stored as 32-bit signed integers. These are stored in the same manner as with the file 'RECENT.DAT'.

Following on from the longitude and latitude coordinates are some mixed data that is unknown and null bytes for 1148 bytes to denoted record length of 1508 bytes.

Below is a table containing the details of the structure of a single record entry with the file 'FAVVER4.DAT':

Offset (Bytes):	Length (Bytes):	Description:
0	280	Free text – containing the name and address of the record entry.
280	72	Unknown
352	4	Longitude Coordinate stored as a 32bit signed integer.
356	4	Latitude Coordinate stored as a 32bit signed integer.
360	1148	Unknown

Table 4: Table containing layout of a single record entry within the file 'FAVVER4.DAT'

7. Data analysis of the file 'ROUTE.DAT'

The file 'ROUTE.DAT' consists of only one record entry containing the address, latitude and longitude of that record entry.

Examination of the file identified a file header consisting of 5 null bytes (0x00). No file footer was identified.

Each record entry is 532 bytes in length; with the name of the location stored as plain text starting at the beginning of the record and continuing for 432 bytes in length.

The record entry then contains some information for a length of 75 bytes; the purpose of this information is unknown.

The next portion of information is the longitude and latitude coordinates, which are 8 bytes in length within the record entry with 4 bytes allocated to the longitude and latitude coordinates respectively; the coordinates are stored as 32-bit signed integers. These are stored in the same manner as with the file 'RECENT.DAT' and 'FAVVER4.DAT'.

Following on from the longitude and latitude coordinates are sixteen (16) bytes containing unknown information, followed by a byte denoting the end of the record entry.

Below is a table containing the details of the structure of the single record entry with the file 'ROUTE.DAT':

Offset (Bytes):	Length (Bytes):	Description:
5	432	Free text – containing the name and address of the record entry.
437	75	Unknown
512	4	Longitude Coordinate stored as a 32bit signed integer.
516	4	Latitude Coordinate stored as a 32bit signed integer.
520	16	Unknown
536	1	End of record marker (denoted by 0xFF)

Table 5: Table containing layout of a single record entry within the file 'ROUTE.DAT'

8. Conclusion

The basic principles and understandings of the information that can be retrieved from these devices can allow an investigator to enhance their investigation and provide a much greater depth of detail in any investigation involving these types of devices.

Further research can be made into identifying some of the unknown sections of the files identified by the author. From further work tools can be developed to automate the process of analysing these types of devices and better equip an investigator when dealing with such devices and make the process of analysing and reporting these devices that much easier.

9. References

Navman Website (2010), "iCN 320 - Tech Specs", http://www.navman.com/in-car/europe/uk/Products/66739/3431/3435/, (Accessed 30 May 2011)

NavmanUnlocked Wiki (2011), "NavmanUnlocked Wiki - Unlock", http://navmanunlocked.wikispaces.com/Unlock, (Accessed 30 May 2011)

duff.dk Website (2011), "Navman iCN 330 - now with linux", http://duff.dk/navman/, (Accessed 30 May 2011)

Active Detection and Prevention of Sophisticated ARP-Poisoning Man-in-the-Middle Attacks on Switched Ethernet LANs

K. Kalajdzic[1,2] and A. Patel[2,3]

[1] Center for Computing Education - CCED, Alipasina 2/1, 71000 Sarajevo, Bosnia and Herzegovina
[2] Department of Computer Science, Faculty of Information Science and Technology, Universiti Kebangsaan Malaysia, 43600 UKM Bangi, Selangor, Malaysia
[3] Faculty of Computing Information Systems and Mathematics, Kingston University, Penrhyn Road, Kingston upon Thames KT1 2EE, United Kingdom
e-mail: kenan@unix.ba, whinchat2010@gmail.com

Abstract

In this paper we describe two novel methods for active detection and prevention of ARP-poisoning-based Man-in-the-Middle (MitM) attacks on switched Ethernet LANs. As a stateless and inherently insecure protocol, ARP has been used as a relatively simple means to launch Denial-of-Service (DoS) and MitM attacks on local networks and multiple solutions have been proposed to detect and prevent these types of attacks. MitM attacks are particularly dangerous, because they allow an attacker to monitor network traffic and break the integrity of data being sent over the network. We introduce backward compatible techniques to prevent ARP poisoning and deal with sophisticated stealth MitM programs.

Keywords

ARP, ARP Poisoning, Man-in-the-Middle Attacks, Intrusion Prevention, LAN

1. Introduction

Address Resolution Protocol (ARP) (Plummer, 1982) is an essential component of communication in an Ethernet LAN environment. It provides a mechanism to translate logical network addresses into physical (MAC) addresses which are required for the exchange of packets on a local network.

ARP is a stateless protocol designed without security in mind, which makes it an ideal means for launching DoS and MitM attacks on a LAN. By sending spoofed MAC addresses in ARP reply packets, a malicious host can poison the ARP cache of other hosts on the local network and thereby easily redirect network traffic.

To mitigate the danger of ARP-based attacks on local networks, multiple techniques have been proposed to detect and prevent attacks by malicious hosts. Detection of ARP poisoning is usually performed by specialized network tools, such as `arpwatch` (LBNL Network Research Group, n.d.), or Intrusion Detection Systems.

In (Carnut & Gondim, 2003) and (Trabelsi & Shuaib, 2007) the authors propose delegating the detection to specialized detection or test stations.

For prevention of ARP-based attacks, a simple solution consists of using static ARP entries in the ARP cache. This solution, however, doesn't scale well especially in heterogeneous networks with dynamic IP addressing. Other solutions include use of cryptography for authenticating ARP replies (Bruschi et al., 2003), (Goyal & Tripathy, 2005), (Lootah et al., 2007), artificial intelligence (Trabelsi & El-Hajj, 2007), or hardware support for dynamic ARP inspection (Cisco Systems, 2009).

We have developed two methods for detection and prevention of ARP-poisoning-based MitM attacks. For simplicity and convenience, we call these Method 1 and Method 2, respectively. Our motivation was to find ways to cope with increasingly sophisticated MitM attack tools, while still maintaining backward compatibility with existing ARP implementations. We avoided the use of specialized computers as helpers in the attack detection process, in contrast with several of the aforementioned methods which require the use of such computers (e.g. a test station or a CA server).

Method 1, described in Section 2, uses certain techniques proposed in (Trabelsi & Shuaib, 2007), but brings several improvements in the approach to detection. Instead of relying on a test host to detect potential attacks, each host performs detection by itself. This eliminates the need for a test host, which is a single point of failure, and makes it possible to extend Method 1 to perform distributed and coordinated detection with multiple hosts. Moreover, with Method 1 detection is triggered by a reception of one or more ARP replies and targets only the hosts who send these replies, instead of scanning the whole network in the search of potential attackers.

Method 2, introduced in Section 3, addresses limitations of Method 1 in dealing with sophisticated MitM attack tools. It relies on a novel technique for detection of MitM attacks on switched Ethernet LANs through modification of the switch CAM table in a way which makes the detection transparent to the MitM host.

2. Method 1 – Reverse ARP poisoning with active IP probing

Method 1 consists of the following two steps:

1. **Reverse ARP poisoning** – A host implementing reverse ARP poisoning sends an ARP reply as a response to every ARP reply it receives from other hosts. The purpose of this reverse ARP reply is to poison the ARP cache of attacking hosts.

2. **Active IP probing** – Active IP probing is then used to differentiate between legitimate hosts and MitM hosts. This step consists of sending a single IP packet to the host from which the initial ARP reply was received and analyzing the response. For simplicity, in this document we use probe packets containing simple ICMP echo requests, even though it may generally be more reliable to use TCP or UDP instead of ICMP.

The best way to illustrate the workings of Method 1 is to see it in action. For this purpose, we use two common scenarios.

In the first scenario, we analyze the packet exchange in the case of a legitimate host sending an ARP reply. The second scenario will then show how Method 1 behaves when a MitM host attempts to carry out an ARP poisoning attack.

Figure 1 is used as a reference for both scenarios. We assume that all three hosts, HostA, HostB and HostX, are on the same Ethernet LAN. Furthermore, HostA and HostB are legitimate hosts and HostX is a MitM attacker. Also, HostA uses a regular implementation of ARP, as found in modern operating systems. HostB, on the other hand, implements Method 1, and thus handles ARP traffic in a different way, as will be described shortly.

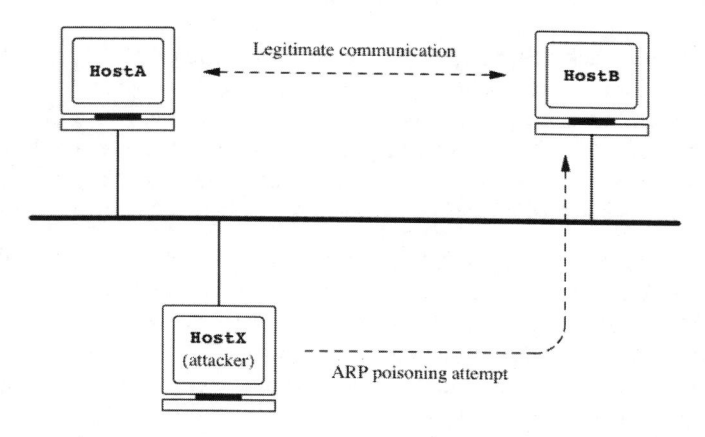

Figure 1: An ARP poisoning attack on a switched LAN

2.1. Scenario 1 – Legitimate ARP reply

In this scenario, HostA sends a legitimate ARP reply to HostB. We can follow the exchange of packets generated as Method 1 is employed:

1. HostA sends an ARP reply packet to HostB. Since this is a legitimate ARP reply, it contains the mapping between HostA_IP and HostA_MAC.

2. HostB executes the first step of Method 1, and immediately sends an ARP reply back to HostA attempting to poison its ARP cache. In this ARP reply HostB maps HostA_IP to HostB_MAC. Since, however, HostA is the owner of HostA_IP, it simply drops this ARP reply with the invalid mapping.

3. HostB then continues to the second step of Method 1 and sends an ICMP echo request packet addressed to HostA_IP with HostA_MAC as the destination MAC address in the Ethernet frame header.

4. `HostA` receives the ICMP echo request and responds to `HostB` with an ICMP echo reply. For `HostB` this is an indicator that the reverse ARP poisoning attempt was unsuccessful and that the ARP reply sent by `HostA` is a legitimate one.

   5. As a result, `HostB` stores the mapping `HostA_IP` ↔ `HostA_MAC` in its ARP cache.

2.2. Scenario 2 – ARP poisoning attempt

In this scenario the attacking host `HostX` attempts to poison the ARP cache of `HostB` in order to impersonate `HostA`. This should allow the attacker to hijack all traffic going from `HostB` to `HostA`. Since `HostB` implements Method 1, the exchange of packets in this case will be as follows:

   1. The first packet is an ARP reply sent from `HostX` to `HostB`. This ARP reply contains the mapping between `HostA_IP` and `HostX_MAC`. If `HostB` had a regular implementation of ARP, it would accept this ARP reply and store the incorrect mapping in its ARP cache. From that point on, `HostB` would deliver all network traffic destined to `HostA_IP` to `HostX`'s network interface.

   2. Nevertheless, `HostB` handles ARP traffic in compliance with Method 1, so instead of blindly accepting the ARP reply from `HostX`, `HostB` begins the detection procedure by sending a reverse ARP reply to `HostX`. This ARP reply contains the mapping between `HostA_IP` and `HostB_MAC`. Assuming that the attacking host (i.e. `HostX`) uses an unmodified implementation of ARP, the reply sent by `HostB` will poison its ARP cache.

   3. `HostB` proceeds with the MitM detection by delivering an ICMP echo request packet, destined to `HostA_IP`, to `HostX`'s network interface (by using `HostX_MAC` as the destination in the Ethernet frame header).

   4. `HostX` is acting as a MitM attacker, so it attempts to forward this ICMP echo request packet to `HostA`. However, since `HostX`'s ARP cache has previously been poisoned by `HostB`, `HostX` delivers the probe packet to `HostB`'s MAC address. This effectively means that the same packet sent in the previous step by `HostB` will be returned to it by `HostX`. The detection of a duplicate packet is a clear indicator for `HostB` that reverse ARP poisoning was successful and that `HostX` is a MitM attacker.

   5. `HostB` thus drops the initial ARP reply sent by `HostX`. Since at this point an intrusion attempt has been detected, `HostB` can generate a real-time intrusion alert and log the intrusion attempt for the purpose of a future forensic investigation.

3. Method 2 – IP probing with CAM table poisoning

Method 1, described in Section 2, works well for detection of MitM computer systems which rely on the operating system built-in routing and ARP functions. There are, however, much more sophisticated MitM programs, which take full control over packet forwarding. This allows these programs to disguise themselves very well in order to evade detection. One popular program which falls into this category is the well-known *Cain & Abel* (Montoro, n.d.).

Cain & Abel doesn't rely on the ARP and routing functions of the operating system, but instead maintains its own mappings between IP addresses and MAC addresses. The program utilizes these private mappings when forwarding frames between hosts on the network. This makes it insusceptible to reverse ARP poisoning, which is the basis of Method 1.

In order to be able to detect any MitM host, regardless of the way it handles routing of packets between other hosts in the network, we need to influence flow of packets in a way which is beyond control of the MitM host.

In the following paragraphs, we describe one method to achieve this, which we call Method 2 for brevity and simplicity. Figure 2 will serve as a reference for our description of Method 2.

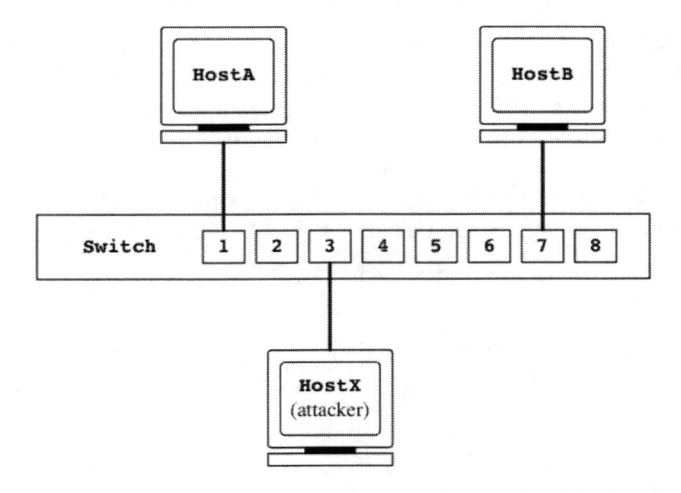

Figure 2: Physical connection of hosts in our LAN

During normal operation of the switch, its CAM (in order to minimize switching latency, Ethernet switches store the mappings between MAC addresses and switch ports in a table inside a special Content-Addressable Memory) table contains the mappings shown in Table 1.

MAC Address	Port
HostA_MAC	1
HostB_MAC	7
HostX_MAC	3

Table 1: Switch CAM table during normal operation

We again assume that HostX wants to redirect traffic between HostA and HostB through the use of ARP poisoning. HostA uses a regular implementation of TCP/IP, including ARP, and HostB employs Method 2. We can now follow the use of Method 2 through the following flow of events:

1. HostX sends an ARP reply to HostB. This ARP reply contains the mapping between HostX_MAC and HostA_IP.

2. Before entering this mapping into its ARP cache, HostB begins executing Method 2, whose first step is broadcasting of an ARP request for HostA_IP.

3. As a result of this ARP request, HostB receives two replies with two different MAC address mappings for HostA_IP: one reply comes from HostA with HostA_MAC and the other is from the attacker with HostX_MAC. Method 2 doesn't require these two replies to reach HostB in any particular order.

4. The reception of two different MAC addresses for a single IP address is a first indicator for HostB that one of them comes from a MitM attacker. Thus, HostB continues with the next step of Method 2, which is sending multiple ICMP echo request packets out its network interface. All these packets carry HostB_IP as the source IP address and HostA_IP as the destination IP address in their IP header. However, their Ethernet frame header may contain one of the following two combinations of MAC addresses:

    (a) HostX_MAC is the destination MAC address and HostA_MAC is the source MAC address,

    (b) HostA_MAC is the destination MAC address and HostX_MAC is the source MAC address.

5. To understand the purpose of using these two MAC address combinations, let us analyze what happens when HostB sends two ICMP echo request packets addressed as in 4a and 4b, respectively:

    (a) The frame, addressed as specified in 4a leaves HostB and enters the switch through port #7. Based on the entries in its CAM table (see Table 1), the switch forwards the frame to HostX through port #3. Meanwhile, since the frame with source MAC address HostA_MAC entered the switch through port #7, the switch updates its CAM table with a new mapping for HostA_MAC so the CAM table now has the contents shown in Table 2. HostX receives the frame, looks up the destination IP address, and forwards the frame immediately towards `HostA`, specifying `HostA_MAC` as the destination MAC address. Once this frame reaches the switch, two possibilities exist:

  i. If the switch CAM table still contains the mapping between `HostA_MAC` and port #7, the switch will forward the frame out through port #7. `HostB` receives its own ICMP echo request packet, which is an indicator that `HostX` attempted to forward this frame to `HostA`. This means that `HostX` is not the real owner of `HostA_IP`, but a MitM attacker.

  ii. If, in the meantime, `HostA` sent some network traffic through switch port #1, the original mapping of `HostA_MAC` to port #1 in the CAM table of the switch will have been restored. In this case, the switch forwards the ICMP echo request through port #1 to `HostA`, and `HostA` responds by sending an ICMP echo reply packet back to `HostB`. In this case `HostB` cannot conclude with certainty that `HostX` forwarded the frame to `HostA`.

(b) The frame, addressed as specified in 4b enters the switch through port #7, and switch forwards it through port #1 to `HostA`. Since the source MAC address of this frame is `HostX_MAC`, the switch maps `HostX_MAC` to port #7 in its CAM table. Table 3 shows the new mapping. When `HostA` receives the ICMP echo request packet, it builds a response in form of an ICMP echo reply packet with source IP address `HostA_IP` and destination IP address `HostB_IP`.

  i. Assuming that `HostA`'s ARP cache has been previously poisoned by `HostX`, the response packet will be sent in a frame addressed to `HostX_MAC`. If the contents of the CAM table haven't been modified in the meantime (i.e. they are still as shown in Table 3), the switch will deliver this frame through port #7 to `HostB`. If, on the other hand, `HostX` generated some network traffic while `HostA` was preparing the response, the CAM table will have returned to its original state (see Table 1). Thus, the switch will send the response packet from `HostA` to `HostX` through port #3. Because `HostX` is a MitM host, it will forward the response to `HostB`.

  ii. If the ARP cache of `HostA` hasn't been modified, it will contain a correct mapping between `HostB_IP` and `HostB_MAC`. Therefore, the ICMP reply packet from `HostA` will be sent to `HostB_MAC` and delivered by the switch through port #7 to `HostB`.

We see that, in either case, using the MAC address combination given in 4b results in an ICMP echo reply packet being sent to `HostB`. In other words, it can not happen that in the given scenario an ICMP echo request packet with source MAC address `HostX_MAC` and destination MAC address `HostA_MAC` gets delivered back to `HostB`.

MAC Address	Port
HostA_MAC	7
HostB_MAC	7
HostX_MAC	3

Table 2: Switch CAM table after HostB sends a frame from HostA MAC to HostX MAC through port #7

MAC Address	Port
HostA_MAC	1
HostB_MAC	7
HostX_MAC	7

Table 3: Switch CAM table after HostB sends a frame from HostX MAC to HostA MAC through port #7

When, on the other hand, the combination of source and destination MAC addresses is specified as in 4a, it is possible for the original ICMP echo request packet to be delivered back to HostB (see 5(a)i), though it may also happen that HostB receives an ICMP echo reply from HostA (see 5(a)ii). The latter case cannot generally be distinguished from the case described in 5b, which uses frames addressed as in 4b.

Therefore, we must ensure that a host implementing Method 2 (in our case, HostB) quickly sends multiple ICMP echo request packets with both combinations of source and destination MAC addresses given in 4a and 4b. To identify the MitM host it suffices for HostB to receive only one of its own ICMP echo request packets back through its network interface.

Method 2 alters the CAM table of the switch so that some frames destined to HostA are delivered to HostB (see Table 2). To restore the original mapping of HostA_MAC to port #1 (see Table 1), HostB may broadcast an ARP request for HostA_IP. This would force HostA to send back an ARP reply and thereby help switch *reassociate* its MAC address with port #1.

Notice that, for Method 2 to work, HostB's network card must be put into *promiscuous mode* (when a network card operates in promiscuous mode, it accepts all traffic and passes it to the central processing unit, even if this traffic is not addressed to that particular network card), so it can collect the hijacked frame which HostX attempts to forward to HostA. Another important assumption is that HostA was not subject to a DoS attack, so it was able to respond to our ARP requests.

4. Results

We ran multiple tests on a switched Ethernet LAN to test the effectiveness of Method 1 and Method 2 in detecting ARP-poisoning-based MitM attacks. In all these tests our setup was as depicted by Figure 2. HostA and HostB were running *Windows XP* and *Linux* respectively, and the operating system of HostX changed as required by the tests. Using several common tools, we performed MitM attacks from HostX, attempting to poison the ARP cache of HostA and HostB. The role of HostB was to detect these attack attempts by employing Method 1 and Method 2.

4.1. Detecting `Ettercap` and `dsniff` with Method 1

In the first test HostX (running *Backtrack Linux*) performed attacks against ARP cache of HostA and HostB using two mainstream attack tools, Ettercap (Ornaghi & Valleri, n.d.) and arpspoof with dsniff (Song, n.d.).

HostB was set up to perform attack detection with Method 1. Since Ettercap and dsniff rely on the operating system built-in ARP and routing functions, we were able to successfully perform reverse ARP poisoning and detect all the attacks through active IP probing (i.e. Method 1) with 100% accuracy.

4.2. Detecting *Cain & Abel* with Method 1

For the purpose of this test we booted HostX into *Windows XP* and launched multiple MitM attacks against HostA and HostB using *Cain & Abel*. This time, however, HostB failed to detect any of our attacks. Knowing that *Cain & Abel* uses its own IP-to-MAC address mappings when forwarding packets, this was expected.

4.3. Detecting *Cain & Abel* with Method 2

As we know from Section 3, when using Method 2 HostB poisons the CAM table of the switch in order to capture the frame which HostX attempts to forward towards HostA. This is not a big problem when HostA is idle. If, however, HostA is actively communicating, this creates a race between HostA and HostB. Depending on the rate at which HostA sends out packets into the network, it may be more or less difficult for HostB to win the race and hijack the packet required for detection of the MitM attack.

To test the effectiveness of Method 2, we set up HostA to send many thousands of packets per second into the network and measured the attack detection ratio, whereby

$$Detection\ ratio = \frac{Number\ of\ successful\ detections}{Total\ number\ of\ probes\ sent}$$

During these tests, HostB was sending either single probe packets or series of 3, 5 or 7 packets per probe. The results of our measurements are summarized in Figure 3.

We notice that the success of detection depends on the number of packets sent in a single probe. The rather low detection ratio of 30% for single-packet probes was doubled by sending three packets in each probe. Further increases in number of packets per probe to five and seven raised the detection ratio to 80% and 90% respectively.

It is also obvious that the detection ratio doesn't depend on the rate at which HostA sends packets into the network. If we neglect the variations in the value of the detection ratio, which exist due to a stochastic nature of real-time network communication, we can consider all four curves in Figure 3 as constants.

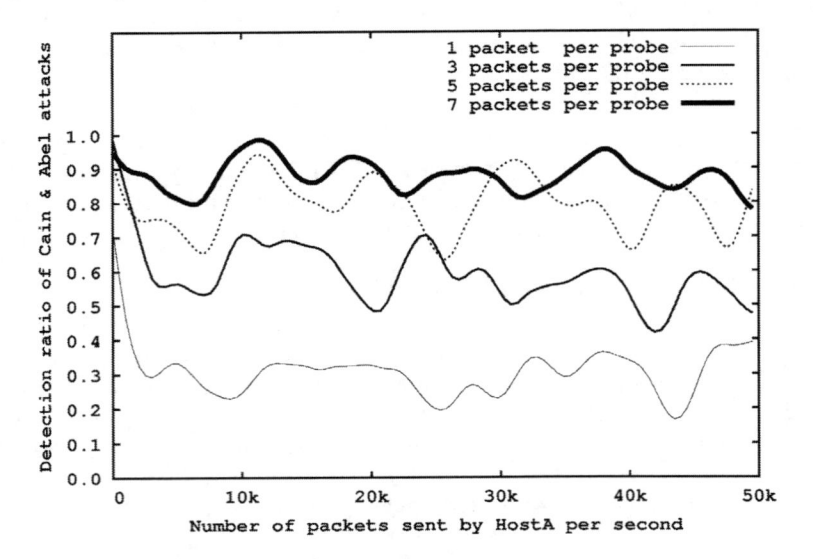

Figure 3: Success in detection of *Cain & Abel* with Method 2

5. Limitations of Method 1 and 2

Both the theoretical discussion and results of our experiments have revealed certain limitations of both proposed methods.

As we know from Sections 2 and 4.2, the biggest limitation of Method 1 is its inability to handle detection of MitM attack tools which use their own IP-to-MAC address mappings for forwarding packets (e.g. *Cain & Abel*). Even though Method 2 solved this problem, other factors exist which may limit its effectiveness.

In the third step of the detection process with Method 2, we assumed that HostB receives ARP replies for HostA_IP from both HostA and HostX. While this is generally the case, HostX might as well launch a DoS attack against HostA, preventing it from successfully delivering its ARP reply to HostB. This way only HostX's ARP reply would reach HostB, rendering Method 2 useless.

The results of our experiments in Section 4.3 have shown that the effectiveness of Method 2 depends on the number of packets sent in a single probe. Sending too many probe packets, however, may cause disruption in traffic flow towards HostA, due to the fact that HostB temporarily hijacks all LAN traffic destined to HostA_MAC. This problem may be solved by storing the hijacked packets in a queue on HostB and delivering them back to HostA after the probe.

6. Conclusion

In this paper we have described two novel methods for detection and prevention of ARP-based MitM attacks on switched Ethernet LANs. Both methods work as extensions to the ARP protocol and don't interfere with normal ARP operation. Therefore, both these methods can co-exist on the same LAN with regular ARP implementations and are thus suitable for incremental deployment. We have seen examples of such co-existence in experiments in which one host (`HostB`) used either Method 1 or Method 2, while another host (`HostA`) used default implementation of ARP as provided by the operating system.

Even though both our methods can be used to identify and prevent ARP poisoning attacks, an ultimate solution to the problem of ARP insecurity can only be provided through an improved version of the ARP protocol, which would be backwards compatible and would allow for an incremental implementation. In (Abad and Bonilla, 2007) the authors have given a definition of an ideal solution for prevention of ARP-based attacks, which may be the first step towards reaching this goal.

7. References

Abad, C. & Bonilla, R. (2007), "An analysis on the schemes for detecting and preventing ARP cache poisoning attacks", in *Distributed Computing Systems Workshops, 2007. ICDCSW'07. 27th International Conference on Distributed Computing Systems Workshops*, IEEE, p. 60.

Bruschi, D., Ornaghi, A. & Rosti, E. (2003), "S-ARP: a secure address resolution protocol", in *Proceedings of the 19th Annual Computer Security Applications Conference, 2003. ACSAC'03.*

Carnut, M. & Gondim, J. (2003), "ARP spoofing detection on switched Ethernet networks: A feasibility study", in *Proceedings of the 5th Symposium on Security in Informatics*.

Cisco Systems (2009), "Configuring Dynamic ARP Inspection", in *Catalyst 6500 Series Switch Cisco IOS Software Configuration Guide, Release 12.2(18) SXF and Rebuilds and Earlier Releases*, San Jose, CA, USA: Cisco Systems, 38:1–38:22.

Goyal, V. & Tripathy, R. (2005), "An efficient solution to the ARP cache poisoning problem", in *Information Security and Privacy*, Springer: pp. 40–51.

LBNL Network Research Group. `arpwatch`: the Ethernet monitor program; for keeping track of Ethernet/IP address pairings (online) available at ftp://ftp.ee.lbl.gov/ arpwatch.tar.gz.

Lootah, W., Enck, W. & McDaniel, P. (2007), "TARP: Ticket-based address resolution protocol", *Computer Networks 51(15)*, 4322–4337.

Montoro, M. Cain & Abel (online) available at http://www.oxid.it/cain.html.

Ornaghi, A. & Valleri, M. Ettercap (online) available at http://ettercap.sourceforge.net/.

Plummer, D. (1982), "RFC-826: An Ethernet Address Resolution Protocol", Network Working Group.

Song, D. dsniff (online) available at http://monkey.org/~dugsong/dsniff/.

Trabelsi, Z. & El-Hajj, W. (2007), "Preventing ARP Attacks Using a Fuzzy-Based Stateful ARP Cache", in *Communications, 2007. ICC'07. IEEE International Conference on Communications 2007*, IEEE: pp. 1355–1360.

Trabelsi, Z. & Shuaib, K. (2007), "NIS04-4: Man in the Middle Intrusion Detection", in *Global Telecommunications Conference, 2006. GLOBECOM'06.* IEEE: pp. 1–6.

Towards a Forensically Ready Cloud Storage Service

T. Spyridopoulos and V. Katos

Information Security and Incident Response Unit,
Democritus University of Thrace, Greece
e-mail: {theospyr,vkatos}@ee.duth.gr

Abstract

In this paper we examine the feasibility of developing a forensic acquisition tool in a distributed file system. Using GFS as a vehicle and through representative scenarios we develop forensic acquisition processes and examine both the requirements of the tool and the distributed file system must meet in order to facilitate the acquisition. We conclude that cloud storage has features that could be leveraged to perform acquisition (such as redundancy and replication triggers) but also maintains a complexity, which is higher than traditional storage systems leading to a need for forensic-readiness-by-design.

Keywords

Distributed storage forensics, remote acquisition, jurisdiction.

1. Introduction

The imperative need for forensic readiness within an organization can be established not only from the need to incorporate forensic acquisition capabilities within security best practices (Grobler & Louwrens, 2007), but from the fact that "ongoing and proactive computer investigations are now a mandatory component of the IS enterprise" (Patzakis, 2003). However the marketing momentum surrounding Cloud oriented solutions reminds us the late 1990s e-commerce unprecedented growth, where security amongst other important facets of an Information System was not within the strategic priorities of a newly formed dot com. Within the last 15 years there has been a significant change in culture and information security is nowadays seen as means to help an organization succeed.

Yet it seems that although a bottom-up approach to security is followed during the design phase of a cloud infrastructure, forensic capabilities have not received enough attention. Considering that a user's actions could lead to litigation and as such his/her files – deleted or not – would need to be retrieved from the cloud, there need to be processes in place to support forensic readiness. Forensic acquisition of virtual disks should also be carried out in a way that shared space belonging to legitimate users will not be harvested in order to protect their privacy. This constraint together with jurisdiction introduces interesting challenges and calls for both technical and non-technical approaches when developing a "cloud-dd" tool.

2. Background

The term cloud refers to an infrastructure that enables convenient, on-demand network access to a shared pool of resources (e.g. storage, networks, servers, applications and services) that can be rapidly provisioned and released (Mell and Grance, 2009). Cloud systems essentially compose a network of distributed clusters forming a pool of resources ready to be used from clients. The physical distance between the location of each cluster varies from some meters in one data center to thousands of kilometers between data centers located in different countries or even different continents. Thus, when someone uses a cloud, her data are distributed in a network of clusters around the world. To achieve distribution of data, cloud systems make use of a distributed file system (Thanh *et al.*, 2008). Such distributed file systems include Google File System (GFS) (Ghemawat *et al.*, 2003), Hadoop Distributed File System (HDFS) (Hadoop, n.d.), Cloudstore (formerly Kosmos File System) (Cloudstore, n.d.), Sector (Gu & Grossman, 2009) and Ceph (Weil *et al.*, 2006).

Digital forensics in traditional computational environments is a subject thoroughly examined in the last decade. The procedures followed in order to gather digital evidence with ensured admissibility in court, are described in standard operating procedures documentation such as the ACPO guidelines (ACPO, 2008). In addition, a variety of forensics acquisition tools has been developed (e.g. the Forensic Toolkit (FTK), EnCase and Foremost) which can automate the collection and analysis – to some extent – of evidence.

However, data distribution and resource pooling in a cloud make the investigator's work much more challenging than in a traditional computational environment as existing digital forensics tools seem inappropriate.

In addition, every country is governed by its own privacy policies and laws. Thus, gathering digital evidence from a cloud's server that is located in a foreign country, outside of our jurisdiction area, could result in violating the country's privacy protection legislation (Taylor *et al.*,2010; Garrison *et al.*, 2010). Still, the legal procedure to gain access to evidence held in a public cloud may lead in acquiring wrong data and result into privacy violations. Grobauer and Schreck (2010) present incident handling issues in the cloud.

3. Challenges in Forensics Data Acquisition in Cloud Systems

A cloud system poses many obstacles to forensic data acquisition. These obstacles involve both technical setbacks and legal restrictions. The conjunction of these two factors can raise serious challenges in cloud forensics. A coarse classification is shown in Table 1.

The terminology used in this paper is clarified below:

- Live data mainly refer to the data that belong to the cloud's user/suspect and still have not been deleted (or have not been permanently deleted). In this point it is obvious that the user/suspect still uses the cloud.
- Permanently deleted data refer to the data that the suspect has permanently deleted.
- By jurisdiction we refer to whether we have the right to access the data (servers are inside jurisdiction) or not (servers are outside jurisdiction).

State of data / Jurisdiction	Live	Permanently Deleted
Within	(almost) traditional forensics	Metadata acquisition - Lack of knowledge about the data owner
Outside	Transfer data within jurisdiction area and treat as traditional forensics	Metadata acquisition - Privacy violation - Lack of knowledge about the data owner

Table 1: Challenges

In general, a distributed file system architecture comprises of a master control server (in many cloud distributions it is referred as namenode or master) and several storage servers (also known as datanodes or slaves). Masters maintain the metadata of the data that reside in the cloud and are also responsible for the delegation of data to slaves. Slaves are used to store the actual data.

4. GFS Architecture

As described earlier, like any distributed file system, GFS comprises of a master server, and multiple slaves, and is accessed by multiple users as shown in Figure 1.

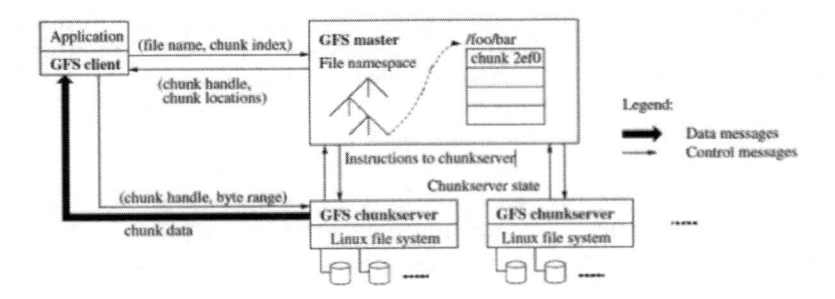

Figure 1: GFS structure (*source:* Ghemawat *et al.*, 2003).

According to Ghemawat *et al.* (2003), user files in a GFS are divided by the master into fixed-size chunks (Figure 1). Each chunk is identified by an immutable and globally unique 64-bit chunk handle assigned by the master at the time of chunk creation. Files and chunks are all uniquely and eternally identified by the logical times at which they were created.

Slaves (or chunkservers) do not store whole files, instead they store chunks on local disks, according to their local file system (e.g. ext3), and read or write chunk data specified by a chunk handle and byte range. Furthermore, a file's chunks can be distributed in more than one slave. For fault tolerance, each chunk is replicated more than once (preferably three times), in different slaves. As a result, each replica is stored as a plain file in the slave's local file system.

The master maintains all file system metadata. This includes file and chunk namespaces, access control information (in sector/sphere access control information is stored in a different server), the mapping from files to chunks and the current location of the chunks. All metadata is kept in master's memory. However, namespaces, along with access control and mapping information are also kept persistent by logging mutations to an operation log stored on the master's local disk and replicated on remote machines. Chunk location is not stored persistently.

When a file is deleted, the master logs the deletion instantly and eventually, after an interval of time during which the file can be recovered in case of an accidental delete (this interval is three days, but can be configurable), all its metadata (both file's and chunks') are deleted from the master's memory. In addition, all its chunks and their replicas are also deleted from the slaves. After the deletion, the space that the chunks used to hold is considered as free.

5. Forensic acquisition scenarios

In the traditional IT infrastructure, it is relatively easy to gather evidence from digital storage devices. This is typically achieved by performing a bit-stream, exact copy of the suspect's hard drive. However in a cloud system the situation is more complicated as we cannot have direct access to the hardware and sometimes investigation can face legal impediments. Our methodology commences by developing four scenarios showing then challenges that arise when attempting to retrieve data from a cloud (Table 1). We then use these scenarios to draw the requirements and develop algorithms to enable forensic acquisition.

5.1. Scenario 1: Live Data - Within Jurisdiction

In the first scenario, we examine the situation in which the state of the suspect's data is still live (files have not been deleted) and the slaves where files' chunks are held are within jurisdiction area (Figure 2a.). In this situation there are not any particularly problems for the investigator to gather the data, as she can acquire them through the suspect's computer or just by having access to the master server. In the second case, the investigator must be able to recognise suspect's files among other users' files inside the master in order to maintain the privacy of the non-suspect users. After the distinction has been done, it is relatively straightforward to access those files. Well known standard operating procedures can be applied in this case for live acquisition similar to internet-based evidence gathering (Shipley, 2009a;2009b).

5.2. Scenario 2 Live data – Outside jurisdiction

In this scenario the data are still available to the end user, but unlike the first scenario the investigator cannot access either them or their copies. This implication comes when the location of the slaves that maintain the chunks of these data is out of our jurisdiction area, perhaps in another country with different legislation. Thus, legal arrangements and agreements have to be done between involved countries for such situations. However, it would be much more preferable, in terms of timeliness and bureaucracy, if we had the possibility to avoid involvement of a foreign country.

In this case we can leverage the cloud's functionality to transfer the files, or more specifically the chunks of the file, within our jurisdiction area without manually obtaining them. An approach of transferring suspect's data within jurisdiction area is to activate the cloud's inherent mechanism of redundancy by introducing failures (Figure 2b.). When the master detects that one of the file's copies, or even the file itself, is unavailable due to a failure, it tries to make a new replica of it. The new replica's chunks are stored in a slave (or multiple slaves) according to the mechanism the cloud uses. Thus, by deliberately deleting one of the file's replicas or just by deleting its metadata in the master we can force the cloud to make another replica. Manipulating the cloud's mechanism in order to store the replica's chunks in a slave (or slaves) within our jurisdiction area we have achieved our goal. From this point on, data are considered to be within jurisdiction and as in Scenario 1 the investigator can easily obtain them.

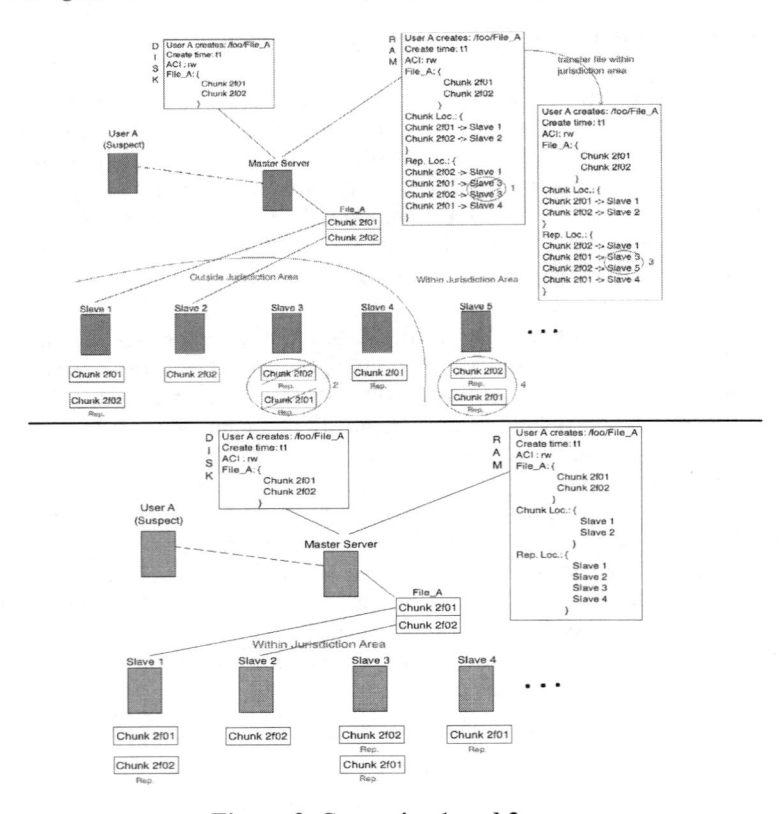

Figure 2: Scenarios 1 and 2

5.3. Scenario 3 Permanently Deleted – Within Jurisdiction

As we described above for the GFS, upon file deletion GFS does not immediately reclaim the available physical storage either in master's memory or is slaves' disks. That means that neither the metadata of the file nor the chunks that compose it are deleted. This happens to improve reliability in an event of an accidental delete. Thus, the file is not completely lost, it is just renamed to a hidden name and can be read under its new name or recovered simply by renaming it back to normal (this functionality is similar to the conventional operating systems recycling bin). This mechanism would be very helpful in the case of a digital forensics investigation. However, both metadata and chunks after a file's deletion do not remain in the system forever. More specifically, after the interval of three days has elapsed, the hidden file is removed from the namespace, its in-memory metadata are erased and slave's storage space, in which the deleted file's chunks used to reside, is freed. From this point on, the investigator is not capable of acquiring the deleted file directly.

At a first level, from a forensic readiness and compliance perspective certain regulations requiring deleted data to be retained for a period comparable to telecoms industry would partially address the problem. These regulations should be implemented in the existing legislation on digital data retention, such us European Union's Data Retention Directive (2006) and Electronic Evidence Compliance by the U.S. Internet Service Provider Association (2003).

However, in a cloud system the amount of data stored in it is significantly large and what is more it is constantly growing. Thus, retention of data can be a rather resource consuming and expensive process. As such, the period in which deleted data can be retained may not meet the expectations and needs of the investigator. Another way for deleted data acquisition is required.

After the expiration of the period during which a deleted file is preserved, the state of the deleted file and its chunks in the system is as follows:

A. From the master's perspective:
- File namespace: Stored permanently in master's disk in a log file
- Chunk namespace: Stored permanently in master's disk in a log file
- Mapping file to chunks: Stored permanently in master's disk in a log file
- Location of the chunks: Lost. Not logged.

B. From the slaves' perspective:
- Chunk deletion follows the normal deletion of a file in the slave's local file system, since every chunk is considered as a unique file.
- Deleted chunks retain their position on the disk as long as they are not overwritten by other chunks.
- Chunk metadata in the local file system are retained as long as they are not deleted by other metadata.

As it is shown, even though the file has been deleted from the master, along with its chunks from the slaves', not all of the information is lost. In fact, information that link chunks' names to a file is persistently preserved (Figure 3).

Filename

Chunk 2ef0
Chunk 2ef1
Chunk 2ef2

Figure 3: A File consisting of three chunks

In addition, these chunks that compose the deleted file along with their local metadata still exist somewhere in the cloud, at least as long as they are not overwritten by other chunks and metadata respectively. Moreover, the fact that multiple copies of the file's chunks exist, the possibility for them to be found before they get overwritten can be non-negligent. However, unlike common file systems it is not easy to determine whether these chunks belong to the suspect's deleted file. A slave server accommodates data, which belong to more than one user. Furthermore, we do not have any indication on where to look for these chunks, since the location of each chunk is not logged by the master. Thus trying to harvest data from a crop of slaves might lead to privacy issues. As such, a straightforward dd application on the slave would not be a suitable, legal option.

For example, let us suppose that user_A (our suspect) creates a file (File_A), which is comprised of chunk_1234, and chunk_1235 located on slave 1 and slave 2 respectively. Their replicas are distributed into the slaves as shown in Figure 4a.

Later on the suspect deletes her file. As we can see in Figure 4b, all respective metadata in master's volatile memory are destroyed. Also the space in the slaves' local file systems where the chunks and their metadata resided is now considered free and ready to be used by other data.

At this point, although the suspect has deleted her file, its contents still exist in the cloud, but the location is not known since the master does not keep any information about the respective chunk locations. A brute force search approach involving every slave, using their names as a keyword would require excessive amount of time and resources. Therefore a first requirement emerging from this scenario would be the need for the master to store the chunk locations on its disk in the form of a log file, as it does with the other metadata. By maintaining a location history log file the recovery would be considerably more efficient than exhaustive search, whenever of course recovery would be possible.

In the meantime another user, userB, uses the cloud to store his data (let us say that he wants to store file_B). As he creates the file in the cloud and chunks are being created, three distinct alternatives can take place, as it is shown in Figure 5a:
1. Chunks that belong to file_B can overwrite chunks that belonged to the deleted file_A.
2. Metadata of the chunks that belong to file_B can overwrite metadata of the chunks that belonged to file_A.
3. Chunks of file_B and their metadata leave chunks of file_A and their metadata unaffected.

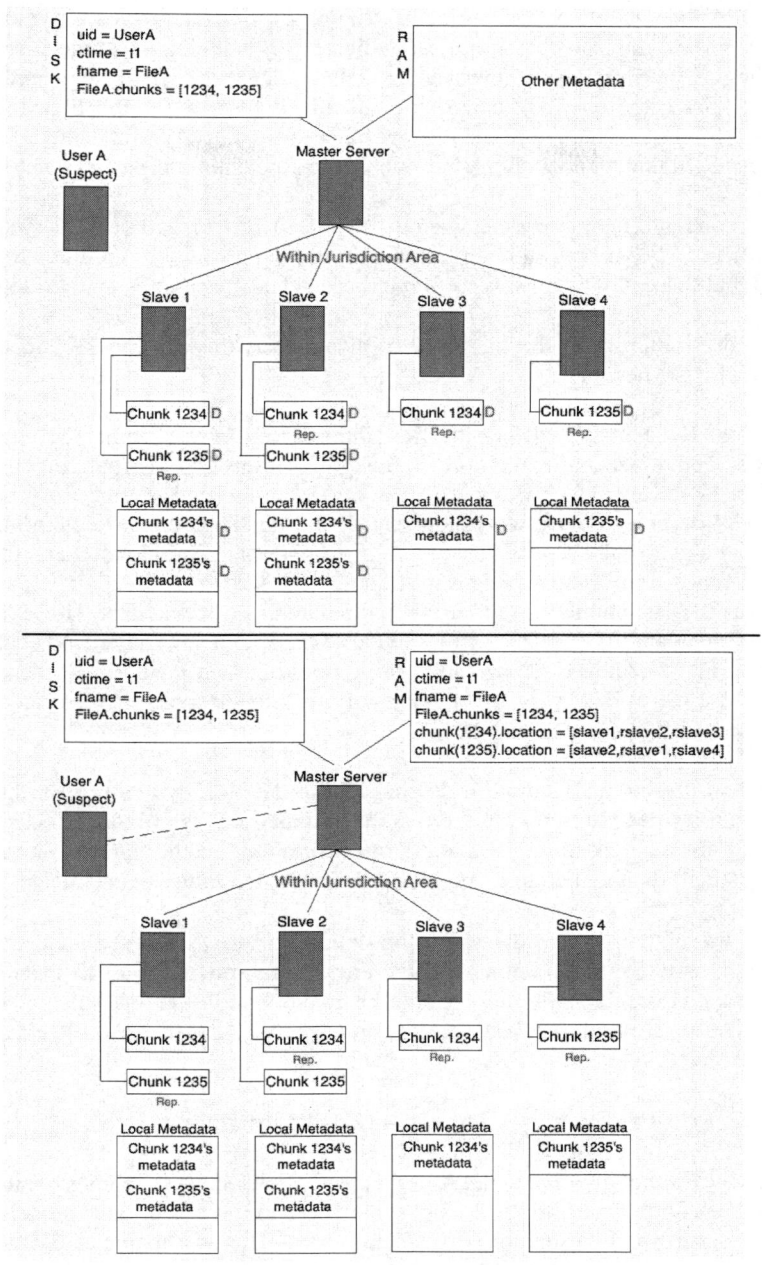

Figure 4 File creation and deletion

According to the first alternative, Chunk_1236 of file_B overwrites Chunk_1235. However, metadata of Chunk_1235, though deleted they still exist. This is due to the slave's local file system (for example ext3). Acquisition of

File_A chunks would be performed by reading the deleted metadata from the local file system of the slave (slave1) as indicated by the master's metadata (since according to our proposed approach the chunk locations are also stored on the master's disk), followed by examining the block bitmap for the blocks that are indicated by the metadata, only to discover that those blocks are allocated. From this it is concluded that another chunk has overwritten the chunk of file_A.

In the second alternative, the metadata of Chunk_1237 of file_B overwrite those of Chunk_1235 of file_A. In this case, Chunk_1235 will continue to exist in slave 4, but there will be no way to find it, because its metadata is overwritten.

For the third alternative there is no complication, as the old chunks and metadata coexist with the new ones.

Lastly, userB decides to delete his file (Figure 5b). At this point, the alternatives described above become even more challenging. In the first alternative both deleted metadata of Chunk_1235 and Chunk_1236 point at the same position in the slave. Unlike before, now we cannot check the block bitmap to determine if this chunk belongs to the suspect's file_A. At a fisrt stage we cloud check the chunk deletion times from their metadata in the local file system and decide which one of them was the last chunk written in this particular space of the disk. However, if the deleted metadata of Chunk_1236 were overwritten by other metadata, only metadata of Chunk_1235 would survive pointing at a position on the disk that Chunk_1236 resides. This could eventually lead to gathering wrong evidence and violating the privacy of userB.

In order to present an accurate reflection of file deletion dynamics in a distributed file system we need to highlight the fact that chunk consists of many blocks and it is not likely for a chunk to be completely overwritten by another chunk. Therefore we should rather talk about chunk blocks being overwritten rather than chunks.

Against the above we are driven to the conclusion that evidence acquisition in a cloud is mostly based on chunk blocks. For this reason, in order to examine each block of a chunk separately there should be a "block to last chunk's name" mapping mechanism where each block should be connected with the name of the chunk that it lastly belonged to.

5.4. Scenario 4 Permanently Deleted – Outside jurisdiction

In this scenario not only the data are permanently deleted, and the investigator cannot obtain them directly (if they still exist somewhere in the cloud), but the deleted data are also out of the investigator's jurisdiction area. This is a major challenge for the investigator as the process of gathering data is the most complicated of all scenarios.

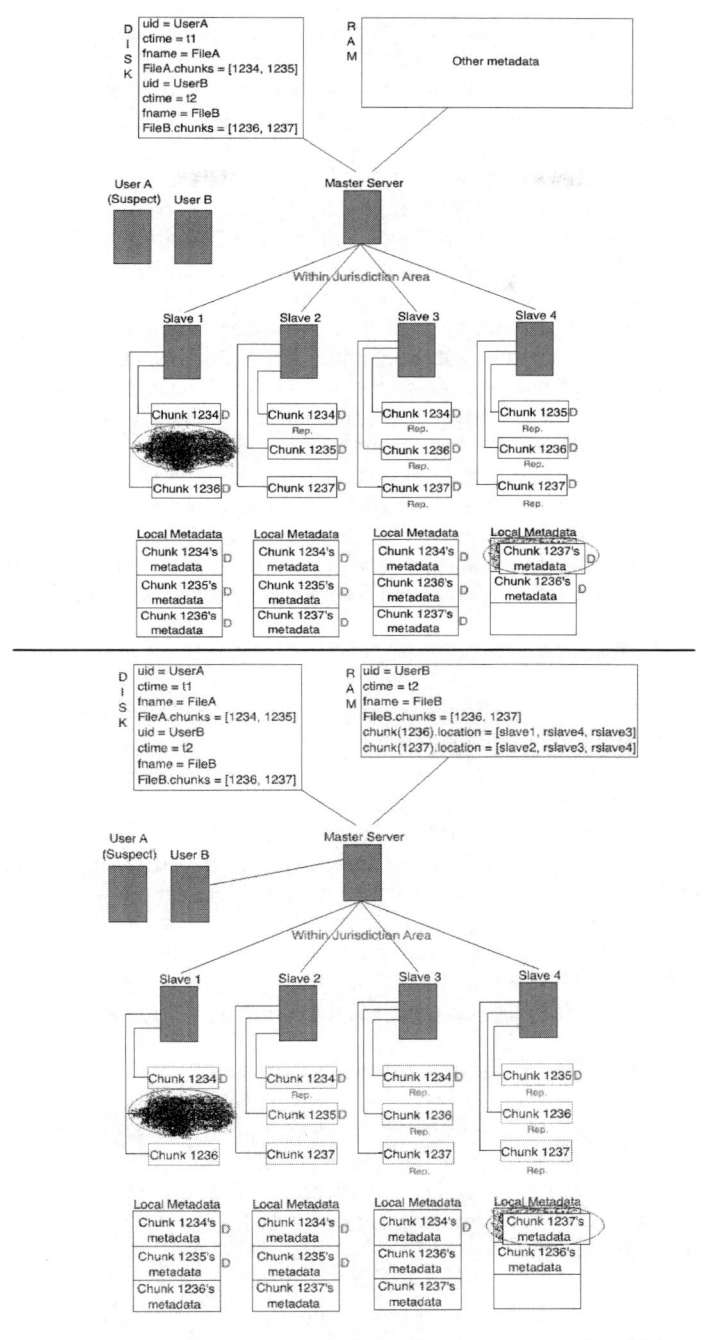

Figure 5: UserA and userB delete their respective files

In this scenario, the acquisition of evidence cannot be conducted unless a legal agreement (such as the Mutual Legal Assistance Treaty) has been established between involved countries. This comes as a result to the fact that the cloud's inherent mechanism of redundancy does not work for deleted files.

Similar to the third scenario, using the "block to last chunk's name" mapping mechanism we introduced, we can easily determine which blocks belong to the chunks that compose the suspect's file(s). At this point, in order to simplify the work that needs to be done by the other countries where slaves are located, we formally request the respective parties through a mutual assistance treaty to "resurrect" (undelete) these blocks, by setting their bits in the block bitmap, under the chunk's metadata. Note that because some of the chunk blocks may have had been overwritten by another user's chunk blocks, the chunk may now be smaller than before (this can be checked by examining the "block to last chunk's name" map we previously introduced). If so, modifications to the chunk's metadata should be performed to reflect the smaller chunk length in order to partially recover the chunk (i.e. the part that belongs to the suspect user). In the meantime, we copy the metadata regarding the file from the master's disk into the master's memory. Eventually, we can recover the whole file, or part of it. Bringing those files within the area of our jurisdiction involves the procedures described in the second scenario.

5.5. Gap analysis summary

Summarising what we have introduced in the above scenarios in order a cloud storage system to be forensically ready the following gaps need to be filled:

1. Legal arrangements and agreements have to be established between involved countries in order to avoid illegal privacy violations.
2. Regulations regarding cloud's digital data retention when they are deleted should be implemented in the current related legislation.
3. From a technical point of view, the "block to last chunk name" mapping mechanism should be implemented in the cloud's structure.
4. Lastly the master server should persistently store the chunk locations along with the rest metadata described earlier on disk, in file records.

5.6. Requirements for a cloud forensics acquisition tool

NIST's Digital Data Acquisition Tool Specification (NIST, 2004) defines requirements for digital media acquisition tools used in computer forensics investigations. According to this specification and taking into account the characteristics of a cloud system, acquisition tools for cloud forensics should meet the following requirements:

- The tool shall be able to acquire a digital source using access to the master server and the suspect's machine, the only access interfaces visible to the tool.

- The tool shall be able to cause the activation of the cloud's inherent feature of redundancy.
- The tool shall be able to create either a clone of a digital source, or an image of a digital source, or provide the capability for the user to select and then create either a clone or an image of a digital source.
- The tool shall operate in at least one execution environment and shall be able to acquire digital sources regardless to the user's, master's or slaves' local execution environment.
- The tool shall completely acquire all visible data sectors from the indicated by the master's metadata area in the slaves.
- The tool shall completely acquire all hidden data sectors from the indicated by the master's metadata area in the slaves.
- All data sectors acquired by the tool from the slaves shall be accurately acquired.
- If there are unresolved errors reading from a slave then the tool shall notify the user of the error type and the error location.
- If there are unresolved errors reading from a slave then the tool shall use a benign fill in the destination object in place of the inaccessible data.

The tool, except from mandatory features described above, may also offer additional features, according to the NIST specification.

6. Concluding remarks

Despite the advantages the introduction of a cloud infrastructure may bring into a corporate network, the additional layer of complexity will create further challenges and issues that the first responder and forensic analyst will need to address during the digital evidence acquisition phase. In this paper we considered a coarse distinction between deleted and undeleted data as well as within and outside jurisdiction. The need for revising the technical, procedural and legal requirements was realised. Forensic readiness should not be an afterthought as a security incident involving litigation is likely to become commonplace. As such, a forensically ready cloud storage is important for the sustainability, success and adoption of cloud services.

7. Acknowledgements

The research leading to these results has received funding from the European Community's Seventh Framework Programme ((FP7/2007-2013_FP7-REGPOT-2010-1, SP4 Capacities, Coordination and Support Actions) under grant agreement no. 264226 (project title: Space Internetworking Center-SPICE). This paper reflects only the author's views and the Union is not liable for any use the may be made of the information contained therein.

8. References

ACPO, "Good Practice Guide for Computer-Based Electronic Evidence", 2008

Cloudstore, http://kosmosfs.sourceforge.net

EC, "Directive 2006/24/ec of the european parliament and of the council of 15 March 2006 on the retention of data generated or processed in connection with the provision of publicly available electronic communications services or of public communications networks and amending Directive 2002/58/EC", Official Journal of the European Union, 13/04/2006.

"Electronic Evidence Compliance – A Guide for Internet Service Providers", 18 Berkeley Tech. L.J. 945, 947 (2003) (Prepared by the U.S. Internet Service Provider Association).

Garrison, C, Schiller, C., Steele, J. "Digital Forensics for Network, Internet, and Cloud Computing", Syngress Media, 2010

Ghemawat, S. Gobioff, H., Leung, S. "The Google file system", 19th ACM symposium on Operating systems principles, October 19-22, 2003, Bolton Landing, NY, USA

Grobauer, B. and Schreck, T., "Towards Incident Handling in the Cloud: Challenges and Approaches", Proceedings of the 2010 ACM workshop on Cloud computing security workshop.

Grobler, T. and Louwrens, B., 2007, in IFIP International Federation for Information Processing, Volume 232, New Approaches for Security, Privacy and Trust in Complex Environments, eds. Venter, H., Eloff, M., Labuschagne, L., Eloff, von Solms. R., (Boston: Springer), pp. 13–24.

Gu, Y, and Grossman, R. "Sector and Sphere: the design and implementation of a high-performance data cloud", Phil Trans R Soc A 367, 2009, pp. 2429-2445.

Hadoop File System, http://hadoop.apache.org/hdfs

Mell, P. and Grance, T. "The NIST Definition of Cloud Computing", National Institute of Standards and Technology, 2009.

National Institute of Standards and Technology, "Digital Data Acquisition Tool Specification", 2004.

Patzakis J., Computer Forensics as an Integral Component of Information Security Enterprise, Guidance Software, Available from: http://www1.stpt.usf.edu/gkearns/Articles_Fraud/computerforensics.pdf, 2003

Shipley, T. "Collection of evidence from the Internet: Part 1. A basic methodology", Digital Forensic Investigator, http://www.dfinews.com/article/ collection-evidence-internet-part-1, 2009a

Shipley, T. "Collection of evidence from the Internet, Part 2: The cloud", Digital Forensic Investigator, http://www.dfinews.com/article/collection-evidence-internet-part-2, 2009b.

Taylor, M., Haggerty, J., Gresty, D., Hegarty, R. "Digital evidence in cloud computing systems", Computer Law & Security Review, Volume 26, Issue 3, 2010, pp. 304-308

Thanh, T. Mohan, S. Choi, E. Kim, S., Kim, P. "A Taxonomy and Survey on Distributed File Systems," Fourth International Conference on Networked Computing and Advanced Information Management, vol. 1, pp.144-149, 2008

Weil, S, Brandt, S., Miller, E. Long, D., Maltzahn, C. "Ceph: a scalable, high-performance distributed file system", 7th symposium on Operating systems design and implementation, November 06-08, 2006, Seattle, Washington

9. Appendix

Algorithm 1: Transfer live files inside jurisdiction area	Algorithm 2: Acquire permanently deleted, inside jurisdiction area files through master

Input: user's filenames
Output: user's filenames
 	
B={b_j | b_j=(fname, state, chunks(),
      chunks.location(),
...)}
For j=1..|B|
    If b_j.state == live
    If chunks.location() != wslave()
        // wslave() = slaves within jurisdiction
        For k=1..|chunks|
            del chunks(k).location(n)
            // n = a number between 1 and m
            // m = number of a chunk's replicas + 1
        End For
        create new replica in wslave()
    End If
    End if
End for
	Input: user's filenames
	Output: user's files
	
	B={bj | bj=(fname, state, chunks(),
	      chunks.location(), ...)}
	For j=1..|B|
	  Acquire chunks.location.metadata()
	  For each unique chunk
	    For k=1..|chunks.location.metadata.blocks()|
	      Check block to last chunk's name map
	      If last chunk's name != fname.chunk(of unique chunk)
	        break
	      else
	        Acquire block(k)
	        Chunkfile(k) = block(k)
	      End if
	    End for
	    File = File + Chunkfile(of unique chunk)
	  End for
	End for

Proceedings of the Sixth International
Workshop on Digital Forensics & Incident Analysis (WDFIA 2011)

Requirements for Wireless Sensor Networks in Order to Achieve Digital Forensic Readiness

F. Mouton and H.S. Venter

Information and Computer Security Architecture, University of Pretoria
e-mail: moutonf@gmail.com

Abstract

The field of wireless sensor networking is a new and upcoming one and unfortunately still lacking as far as digital forensics is concerned. All communications between different nodes (also known as *motes*) are sent out in a broadcast fashion. These broadcasts make it quite difficult to capture data packets forensically whilst retaining their integrity and authenticity. This paper examines the differences between IEEE 802.15.4 wireless sensor networks and IEEE 802.11x wireless networks when it comes to implementing digital forensic readiness within the network environment. It focuses on the differences in the communication protocol, proof of authenticity and integrity, time stamping, modification of the network after deployment and other differences between IEEE 802.15.4 wireless sensor networks and IEEE 802.11x wireless networks. Each of these elements is discussed, after which a table is provided that shows the specific requirements to be taken into account when proposing digital forensic readiness in a wireless sensor network environment.

Keywords

Forensic readiness, digital forensics, wireless sensor networks

1. Introduction

Our pursuit of a better lifestyle has led to a vast improvement in the technology to which we have access in today's world. The concept of a wireless sensor network (WSN) is just another technology developed to improve our ability to better accomplish our daily tasks. The implementation of security protocols on WSNs has not received much attention to date, and, even more so, very little consideration has been given to digital forensics within a WSN environment.

The problem is that currently there is no formal set of requirements for achieving digital forensic readiness in wireless sensor networks. The purpose of this paper is to determine how IEEE 802.15.4 wireless sensor networks differ from IEEE 802.11x wireless networks when it comes to implementing digital forensic readiness.

The remainder of the paper is structured as follows: The second section provides some background information about WSNs and digital forensic readiness. Section 3 discusses the differences between IEEE 802.11x wireless networks and IEEE 802.15.4 wireless sensor networks with regard to digital forensic readiness. Section 4 proposes a set of requirements that need to be adhered to when implementing digital forensic readiness for wireless sensor networks. Finally, a summary is provided of the forensic readiness requirements that are proposed and of future work to be done in this field.

2. Background

Wireless sensor networks still constitute a relatively new area of research in computer science and the first papers on WSNs were only published in the last decade (Chong & Kumar, 2003; Mouton & Venter, 2009). Much of the research on WSNs has been dedicated to new areas of application aimed at supporting our modern lifestyle. Some background information for a better understanding of WSNs is provided next, before strategies for the achievement of digital forensic readiness for WSNs are suggested.

2.1. Wireless Sensor Networks

WSNs belong to the general family of sensor networks that use multiple distributed sensors to retrieve data from various environments of interest. Chong and Kumar (2003) provide a history of previous accomplishments of WSNs and show how they have evolved in terms of sensing, communication and computing. WSNs consist of wireless nodes with embedded processors and ad hoc networks (Estrin et al., 2001), and involve wireless communication (Ye, Heidemann & Estrin, 2002). Mouton and Venter (2009) define a WSN as an ad hoc network that consists of tiny and resilient computing nodes known as *motes* or sensors. These *motes* are extremely efficient with regard to power consumption and can collaborate effectively with other *motes* in their vicinity. A graphical representation of a wireless sensor network is provided in Figure 1, while in Table 1 the functions of each of the components are subsequently summarised briefly (Mouton & Venter, 2009; Heinzelman, Kulik & Balakrishnan, 1999; Sohrabi et al., 2000).

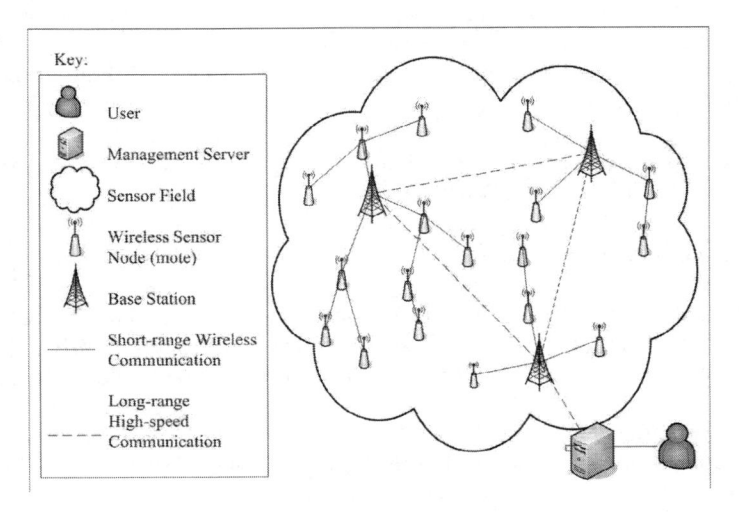

Figure 1: A graphical representation of a wireless sensor network (Mouton & Venter, 2009).

WSN component	Functions of each component
User	The user can interact with the WSN through the management server.
Management Server	The management server serves as an interface console for the WSN.
Sensor Field	The sensor field denotes the physical boundaries of the WSN.
Wireless Sensor Node (*mote*)	Each *mote* contains a small subset of the various sensors. *Motes* in the network can also act as repeaters for packets that need to reach the base station.
Base Station	A base station serves as a gateway node through which the information of the *motes* has to travel to reach the management server.
Short-range Wireless Communication	Short-range wireless communication links are established between neighbouring *motes* and the neighbouring base stations.
Long-range High-speed Communication	Long-range high-speed communication links are established between further-ranged base stations and the management server.

Table 1: Brief summary of functions of the components of a wireless sensor network (Mouton & Venter, 2009).

WSNs can be used in many environments. Their *motes* may consist of many different types of sensors, such as thermal, visual, infrared, radar or acoustic. These motes can monitor a wide variety of ambient conditions, including humidity, pressure, sound, noise levels, temperature, lightning conditions and objects moving through a designated area (Elson & Estrin, 2001; Kahn, Katz & Pister, 1999).

Some applications of WSNs include military applications such as the tracking of moving objects and battlefield surveillance (Zhao, Shin & Reich, 2002); environmental applications such as habitat monitoring, forest fire detection and flood detection (Mainwaring et al., 2002); and health applications such as the tracking and monitoring of doctors and patients in hospitals, as well as of drug administration in hospitals (Lu et al., 2002). Finally, WSNs can also be used for home and building automation applications.

The next subsection focuses on providing the reader with a workable definition of digital forensic readiness in a WSN context.

2.2. Digital Forensic Readiness

To achieve digital forensic readiness in any type of environment, it is essential to first establish an acceptable definition for it. However, since it is a fairly new concept and the subject of divergent opinions, consensus must still be reached in this regard.

In defining digital forensic readiness, Tan (2001) identifies two objectives that have to be balanced carefully: maximising the ability to collect credible digital evidence, and minimising the cost of performing a digital forensic investigation. Tan also argues that several steps need to be taken to ensure that an environment is ready as far as digital forensics is concerned. Rowlingson (2004), on the other hand, suggests ten steps that describe the key activities in implementing a digital forensic readiness programme. Because Rowlingson's steps have actually been designed to create a business process model for digital forensic readiness, this paper gives preference to Tan's objectives for meeting the requirements of digital forensic readiness in a WSN environment.

Even though Tan's two objectives provide a very good definition of digital forensic readiness, it is important to refine them somewhat to make the definition more specific to a WSN environment. For the purpose of this paper, digital forensic readiness is defined as the notion to perform a digital forensic investigation in the shortest amount of time with the least amount of cost and without having to disrupt the original network that has to perform mission-critical tasks. This definition is set as the main goal for achieving digital forensic readiness on WSNs.

The next section discusses the differences between IEEE 802.15.4 wireless sensor networks and IEEE 802.11x wireless networks when it comes to implementing digital forensic readiness.

3. Differences between WSNs and WLANs

WSNs have special needs compared to IEEE 802.11x wireless networks and hence have more specialised requirements than would apply to wireless networks (also known as wireless local area networks or WLANs). There are many important factors that make a WSN unique and distinguish it from a WLAN. The factors that are addressed in this paper are the following:

- Communication protocol
- Proof of authenticity and integrity
- Time stamping
- Modification of the network after deployment
- Protocol data packets
- Radio frequencies
- Power supply
- Network overhead
- Data integrity

The factors listed above are the main ones that differentiate WSN environments from WLAN environments. The reasoning behind the choice of these factors will become apparent in the coming subsections, where each factor is addressed individually. It is, however, important to remember that the core of the argument about the importance of these factors concerns the manner in which they influence the design decision of how to implement a digital forensic readiness application for WSNs.

While examining each of these factors, it is important to note that the authors assume that no modification to the original WSN (hence forward referred to as *oWSN*) is allowed and thus a secondary independent forensic WSN (hence forward referred to as *fWSN*) would be used for the digital forensic readiness implementation of the *oWSN*.

The discussions in each subsection below briefly focus on how these factors differ from WLAN to WSN, and subsequently our focus shifts to how to address them in WSNs.

3.1. Communication Protocol

All communication within a WSN occurs in a broadcast fashion and thus a *mote* never really knows which of its neighbouring *motes* actually receives the packet (Akyildiz et al., 2002; Tseng, Ni & Shih, 2003). The default functioning of a *mote* in the sensor field is to receive all packets – upon receipt of a packet it then has to analyse if the packet was meant for it or not. This analysis requires some processing that drains the battery of the *mote*, which is an important consideration in WSN communication.

The broadcasting technique used in WSNs is very different from the communication techniques used in an IEEE 802.11x wireless network. In the WLAN environment, one can determine if a packet has arrived at its destination by monitoring the network, since acknowledgement packets are sent to confirm the receipt of packets (Xylomenos & Polyzos, 1999; Xylomenos et al., 2001). This is not the case in a WSN environment.

Due to the broadcasting fashion in which WSNs communicate, the *mote* that broadcasts packets will never be completely sure whether the packet was received by the *mote* for which the packet was intended. This uncertainty could be overcome by introducing a communication protocol that allows the receiving *mote* to reply with a receipt acknowledgement packet. However, because this would require extra transmissions that can lead to a greater battery drain, this procedure cannot simply be implemented in all WSNs. The suggested technique also has several other disadvantages. If a flooding attack is launched against the *oWSN*, it would compel the *oWSN* to reply to each flooding attempt with receipt acknowledgement messages, which would then flood the entire *oWSN*.

Considering that a protocol founded on receipt acknowledgement packets can have such a severe impact on a WSN environment, it seems quite impractical to use such a protocol in this environment. Hence the authors have agreed to accept that most WSN *motes* will be uncertain as to whether or not packets have actually arrived at their destination. This causes severe problems in terms of forensic monitoring with a secondary network. It could likely be the case that the packets received by the *oWSN* base station might differ from those received by the *fWSN* base station in the case that some of the packets are dropped in either of the two WSNs. In the case of the *fWSN*, however, this problem could be avoided by implementing a protocol that uses receipt acknowledgement packets, because it is in the nature of a forensic network to always be sure that the information received at either point of the communication line contains some degree of authenticity and integrity. In order to achieve sound digital forensic readiness, it is crucial to prove the authenticity and integrity of the data packets that have been received. The next subsection focuses on defining what the authors see as authenticity and integrity. The differences between maintaining the authenticity and integrity from a WLAN and a WSN perspective are also discussed, as well as possible ways of maintaining authenticity and integrity within a WSN environment.

3.2. Proof of Authenticity and Integrity

Authenticity and integrity first need to be defined as there could be different opinions on precisely what each of them means. In the context of this paper, authenticity is defined as the certainty that the origin and destination of the data packet are kept intact throughout its whole lifetime. The lifetime of a data packet runs from the time that it is sent from the first *mote* up to the time when it is received and processed by the base station. Next, integrity is defined as the certainty that the correctness of the data within the data packet is kept intact throughout the lifetime of the data packet.

Numerous techniques for proving the authenticity and integrity of packets in an IEEE 802.11x wireless network have already been published (Chen, Jiang & Liu, 2005; Komori & Saito, 2004; (Guizani & Raju, 2005). Firewalls, Intrusion Detection Systems, Wireless Routers and Wireless Network Interface Cards are all examples of equipment you would find in an IEEE 802.11x wireless network and most of these devices have the ability to generate a log or some other way of showing which data packets have passed through the network. Most of these abilities are fairly simple techniques that are performed by the device itself. In most cases where a log file is generated, it is safe to assume that the information reflected in the log file is actually the true pattern of traffic that has passed through the device. However, this is only the case when it is certain that the device is not defective or that the log file has not been tampered with. This single log file can also be backed up by looking at all the other devices through which this single packet has travelled, as most devices in an IEEE 802.11x environment should have some form of logging. In a WSN environment, however, very little or no logging is done on the *motes* in the sensor field, due to various reasons. These reasons can include the limited power source and the limited storage space that these devices have. WSN equipment, by default, only does logging at the base station and if logging were to be required at every *mote,* one would have to go and implement this yourself. This obviously raises another issue, namely as to the trustworthiness of the code with which one does the logging. Tried and tested techniques for logging are generally more trustworthy than one's own attempts at implementing logging. It is easier to defend the authenticity and integrity of a well-known logging technique than that of a self-developed technique. In the case where a self-developed technique is used, it must be based on some solid theory as to why it can provide authenticity and integrity. Because WSNs differ so significantly from WLANs, the authors have decided to propose a form of logging that is based on the Casey Certainty Scale (Casey, 2002).

Fortunately, in a WSN environment, multiple *motes* tend to be able to each capture the same data packet simply because they are all in range of a particular broadcasted packet. This is a feature of WSNs, which is not the case in IEEE 802.11x networks. Most devices in WLANs will ignore packets that are not meant for them and do not even attempt to log these packets. The opposite is true for WSNs, where motes attempt to capture every data packet within range. This feature of WSNs can be successfully exploited in an attempt to prove the authenticity and integrity of packets in the WSN. All the packets captured by each independent *fWSN mote* could be forwarded to the base station, as a central point of analysis, in an effort to prove the authenticity and integrity of the data packet according to the Casey Certainty Scale (Casey, 2002).

According to Casey (2002), the integrity and authenticity of information is more certain if this information was recorded by different independent sources. Each *mote* can, in essence, be seen as an independent source. Thus, the authenticity and integrity of each packet can be determined based on the number of *motes* in the network that have received the same broadcasted packet. This paper therefore assumes that, in accordance with the Casey Certainty Scale (Casey, 2002), a packet that has been seen by a larger number of *motes* has far greater authenticity and integrity than a packet that has only been seen by a few forensic *motes* in the network.

The above technique constitutes only one of several ways to determine the authenticity and integrity of the packets in a WSN. Time stamping and the sequence of packets can also be used for this purpose. However, time stamping in a WSN is a tedious task. The next subsection is nevertheless devoted to it.

3.3. Time stamping

Time stamping in a WLAN environment is a fairly easy task, since all the devices in a WLAN would under normal conditions either have access to a time server or have been set with the correct time. Thus, time stamping in the logs for a WLAN would under most conditions be correct, provided that the device has not been tampered with or is not faulty. In the case of a WSN, however, only the management server (which is connected to the base station) has a sense of time. The *motes* in a WSN environment have no sense of physical world time and the only measurement they can use is their own sense of time, which is the time that has elapsed since they were switched on (Sundararaman, Buy & Kshemkalyani, 2005; Su & Akyildiz, 2005; Sun, Ning & Wang, 2006). Such elapsed time can be measured on WSN devices in terms of ticks, where each tick represents 100 nanoseconds (Sundararaman, Buy & Kshemkalyani, 2005). This uptime, although fairly accurate, is a poor indication of time, because each *mote* in the entire network has to be switched on simultaneously and the time should also be synchronised by transmitting their uptime along with their data packets. It is impractical to switch on *motes* simultaneously and synchronisation is not feasible due to resource restrictions.

When tests were conducted concerning the time stamping of WSNs, the authors noted that it takes at most one second to capture any data packet and transmit it to the *fWSN* base station. This nevertheless introduced a time delay between capturing a packet and receiving it at the base station. The time delay also differed according to the distance of the *fWSN* mote from the base station in terms of hops and physical distance. Thus the time stamps at the base station are not an accurate reflection of when the packet was initially captured, as the base station is the only device that can assign an accurate time stamp if it is connected to the management server. (The reason for this is that only the management server has access to a time server (Sundararaman, Buy & Kshemkalyani, 2005; Su & Akyildiz, 2005).) It is also important to note that each *fWSN* mote captures packets sequentially, in the order that the *oWSN* motes transmit their data packets. This proves to be a vital piece of information, because one would then be able to claim that even if the time stamps are altered, the sequence would still be intact. The order in which they arrive at the *fWSN* will stay intact even if the time stamps are slightly delayed. This allows one to assume that the time delay between capturing the packet and sending it to the forensic base station would not really affect the authenticity and integrity of the packets, as the sequence of packets can be used to determine their authenticity and integrity.

The trustworthiness of log time stamps is an issue that many digital forensics researchers have queried and investigated (Schatz, Mohay & Clark, 2006; Schneier & Kelsey, 1999). The dilemma faced by the fWSN is merely intensified. It becomes a more severe issue to trust the time stamps as the limitation as having no access to a centralised time server for WSNs might prevent them from reflecting the correct time. However, since the sequence of the data packets is not altered, this (rather than the time stamps) could be used to verify the authenticity and integrity of the data packets. This paper therefore assumes that the fixed sequence of the data packets is more important than the precise time at which they were transmitted. More information can be gathered by looking at the sequence of the data packets than by looking at their time of transmission.

It is therefore sufficient to capture the data packets and merely provide a time stamp for them as soon as they arrive at the *fWSN* base station. In the event that this is done, one would admittedly create a time stamp error. The time stamp error would nonetheless be a constant error for each *oWSN* mote respectively, as it would reflect the time the data packet was first transmitted together with the added time it took for this data packet to reach the *fWSN* base station. The *fWSN* base station, which is connected to a time server, assigns a time stamp to each data packet upon its arrival there. This allows the order of the packets to be kept intact and records a one-second error on the time stamp of each packet due to the fact that the base station assigns the time stamps and not the forensic *mote* that captured the packet initially. The time stamp error stays constant for all the packets received from a specific *mote* in the sensor field and thus it is still possible to guarantee the authenticity and integrity of a packet. This constant error could be measured, if needed, by comparing the time stamps at the *oWSN* base station and the *fWSN* base station. The time stamp, combined with the sequence of the data packets, would then be sufficient to be used in a forensic investigation.

Another issue that the authors have considered while examining the differences between WLANs and WSNs is the feasibility of modifying the network after it has been deployed. This matter is discussed in the following subsection.

3.4. Modification of the network after deployment

Being able to modify the network after deployment is the only factor that was found to be fairly similar between WLANs and WSNs, as it is always possible to modify code on a device by retracting it from the field, redeveloping it and then redeploying it back into the field. However, the practicality of altering *oWSN* devices after deployment must be taken into consideration. It is important to remember that *oWSN motes* are usually scattered in an area and to alter them, one would have to go and collect the entire network and redeploy it. Hence, it seems essential that the *oWSN* should not be modified to accommodate an *fWSN* solution. This is the very reason why the authors have opted to add an overlaying *fWSN* to the *oWSN* in order to do all the forensic monitoring. The overlaying *fWSN* would consist of a separate set of WSN *motes* that does not affect the *oWSN* and also requires no modification of the *oWSN*.

The difficulty and impracticality of modifying the *oWSN* has led the authors to believe that this should also be seen as a specific requirement when attempting to provide forensic readiness to a WSN environment. Considering that we cannot easily alter the *oWSN*, we must ensure that the *fWSN* should be able to handle any type of protocol headers and footers that could originate from the *oWSN*. Against this background, the next subsection focuses on the protocol data packets that are used by WSN devices and the reasons why it is important to take this into consideration when implementing an overlaying *fWSN*.

3.5. Protocol Data Packets

The *oWSN* can have many different types of communication protocols in its normal operation. For example, the data packets can include packets to determine the routing protocol, sensory packets, encrypted packets or even malformed packets. In order to ensure that all of the possible protocols used in WSNs are encapsulated in this approach, it has been assumed that the *oWSN* uses an address-free protocol. This protocol generates the largest amount of network overhead in WSNs, as it would cause data to be sent from a source *mote* in the network to every other *mote* in the network on each data transmission (Dunkels, Osterlind & Zhitao, 2007). The most commonly used address-free protocols are data dissemination protocols, where neither the sender *mote* nor any of the other motes in the network knows the address of the receiving *mote*. If the *fWSN* is able to successfully log this communication of an address-free protocol in a way that ensures authenticity and integrity, one could assume that the name-based WSN protocols would effortlessly be accounted for, as they have much less network overhead (Dunkels, Osterlind & Zhitao, 2007).

As is also the case in WLANs, the *motes* in the *fWSN* should listen in promiscuous mode and should be able to handle any type of packet that is transmitted or received by the *oWSN*. The authors define promiscuous mode to be a configuration of the WSN *mote* in which all traffic within the WSN *mote*'s frequency range and wireless range will be received by the WSN *mote*. Thus, if an attacker uses a foreign *mote* to inject data into the *oWSN*, the *fWSN* should also be able to listen in on this data. This requirement should be fairly simple to adhere to, because if the *fWSN* is implemented on the same type of equipment, it should be possible to intercept all communication.

Lastly, the *fWSN* should be using a name-based WSN protocol for communication between other *fWSN motes* as it is more optimal in terms of network overhead than address-free protocols. In name-based protocols the source *mote* knows the address of the receiving *mote* and the *motes* between the sender and receiver know the path to the receiving *mote* (Dunkels, Osterlind & Zhitao, 2007).

All the major differences between WSNs and WLANs have now been discussed. Due to space constraints, discussions on radio frequencies, power supply, network overhead and data integrity have been omitted. However, the following section is devoted to arranging all these factors, including the ones that have been excluded from the discussion, into a single workable list of requirements that need to be adhered to when implementing digital forensic readiness in a WSN environment.

4. Forensic Readiness Requirements for WSNs

The previous sections identified the factors that differentiate between WLANs and WSNs in terms of digital forensic readiness. These factors were simply broad overviews of issues to be considered in the WSN environment (most of which do not exist in a WLAN environment).

The authors consequently propose a broad, yet detailed set of the important requirements to be adhered to in order to successfully implement digital forensic readiness in a WSN environment. This list of requirements (see Table 2) could serve as a good starting point for anyone working on digital forensic readiness and makes it easier for an individual to implement digital forensic readiness within a WSN environment. Most other researchers focus mainly on one or two of these requirements by going into more detail on them in their research papers, but many other requirements are usually not mentioned, regardless of their importance.

Table 2 therefore gives a quick but comprehensive overview and summarises *all* the important requirements that need to be taken into account in order to achieve digital forensic readiness in an IEEE 802.15.4 WSN environment.

Factors	Detailed requirement list
Communication Protocol	1. The *fWSN* should use a receipt acknowledgement packet protocol to ensure that all data packets captured by the *motes* in the field do indeed reach the base station.
	2. The broadcasted communication from the *oWSN* should be intercepted in a manner that ensures that the data packets are not altered in any fashion.
	3. The *fWSN* should be able to capture all possible types of communication that can be sent from the *oWSN*.
Proof of Authenticity and Integrity	4. The authenticity and integrity of all the data packets should remain intact while being captured on the *fWSN*.
	5. The data packets that are captured in the *fWSN* should be stored in such a way that their authenticity and integrity are not compromised.
	6. It should be possible to verify the authenticity and integrity of all the data packets in case a digital investigation takes place.
Time Stamping	7. The data packets should have a time stamp assigned to them that does not violate their authenticity and integrity.
	8. The sequence of the packets captured should reflect the true sequence in which they were transmitted from the original network.
Modification of the network after deployment	9. It should be possible to implement the *fWSN* without any modification of the *oWSN*.
Protocol Data Packets	10. The *fWSN* should be designed in such a manner that the network topology or the routing protocol used by the *oWSN* does not influence the *fWSN*'s operation.
Radio Frequencies	11. The *fWSN* should be able to communicate on the same radio frequencies that are available to the *oWSN*.
	12. All communication within the *fWSN* should occur on a frequency not utilised in the *oWSN*.
	13. If an intruder WSN is in the area and communicates on a frequency that influences the *oWSN*, then the *fWSN* should be able to forensically capture these data packets.
Power Supply	14. The *fWSN* should not increase power consumption in the *oWSN* and the *fWSN* should have at least the same or a longer network lifetime than the *oWSN* in terms of battery power.
Network Overhead	15. While intercepting communication, there should be no extra network overhead on the *oWSN*.
Data Integrity	16. The *fWSN* should by no means be able to influence the *oWSN* or influence any sensory data transmitted within the *oWSN*.

Table 2: Requirements in order to achieve digital forensic readiness in a IEEE 802.15.4 WSN environment

The list in table 2 provides a sound basis to start from when attempting to achieve digital forensic readiness in a WSN environment. The following section concludes this paper and proposes future work.

5. Conclusion

Wireless sensor networks constitute a type of network that makes any type of digital forensic analysis very difficult due to the nature of the network. This paper therefore proposed a list of requirements that need to be taken into consideration when implementing digital forensic readiness for an IEEE 802.15.4 wireless sensor network.

The main aim of this paper was to establish the differences between IEEE 802.15.4 wireless sensor networks and IEEE 802.11x wireless networks from a digital forensic readiness point of view. The problem was that currently there is no formal set of requirements for successfully implementing digital forensic readiness in wireless sensor networks. This problem was addressed by focusing on the special needs WSNs have for digital forensic readiness and providing a list of requirements that need to be taken into account when implementing digital forensic readiness in WSNs.

In future research, the authors intend to explore this list of requirements in greater detail and develop a digital forensic readiness prototype for wireless sensor networks. The focus of the research will be to develop the prototype in such a way that it proves to be robust enough to function in most types of WSNs.

6. References

Akyildiz, I.F., Su, W., Sankarasubramaniam, Y. and Cayirci, E. (2002) 'Wireless sensor networks: a survey', *Computer Networks*, vol. 38, no. 4, pp. 393-422.

Casey, E. (2002) 'Error, Uncertainty and Loss in Digital Evidence', *Internation Journal of Digital Evidence*, vol. 1, no. 2, Summer.

Chen, J., Jiang, M. and Liu, Y. (2005) 'Wireless LAN security and IEEE 802.11i', *Wireless Communications, IEEE*, vol. 12, no. 1, February, pp. 27-36.

Chong, C. and Kumar, S.P. (2003) 'Sensor networks: evolution, opportunities, and challenges', *Proceedings of the IEEE*, vol. 91, no. 8, pp. 1247-1256.

Crossbow Technology Inc (2007) *Imote2 Hardware Reference Manual*, Revision A edition, San Jose: Crossbow Technology Inc.

Doufexi, A., Armour, S., Butler, M., Nix, A., Bull, D., McGeehan, J. and Karlsson, P. (2002) 'A comparision of the HIPERLAN/2 and IEEE 802.11a wireless LAN standards', *IEEE Communications Magazine*, vol. 40, no. 5, May, pp. 172-180.

Dunkels, A., Osterlind, F. and Zhitao, H. (2007) 'An adaptive communication architecture for wireless sensor networks', Proceedings of the 5th international conference on Embedded networked sensor systems, Sydney, Australia, 335-349.

Elson, J. and Estrin, D. (2001) 'Time synchronization for wireless sensor networks', Proceedings of the 15th International Symposium on Parallel and Distributed Processing, 1965-1970.

Estrin, D., Girod, L., Pottie, G. and Srivastava, M. (2001) 'Instrumenting the world with wireless sensor networks', Proceedings of the 2001 IEEE International Conference on Acoustics, Speech and Signal Processing, 2033-2036.

Guizani, M. and Raju, A. (2005) 'Wireless Networks and Communications Security', in Xiao, Y., Li, J. and Pan, Y. (ed.) *Security and Routing in Wireless Networks*, 3rd edition, New York: Nova Science Publishers.

Heinzelman, W.R., Kulik, J. and Balakrishnan, H. (1999) 'Adaptive protocols for information dissemination in wireless sensor networks', In Proceedings of the 5th Annual ACM/IEEE International Conference on Mobile Computing and Networking, Seattle, 174-185.

Kahn, J.M., Katz, R.H. and Pister, K.S. (1999) 'Next century challenges: mobile networking for "Smart Dust"', In Proceedings of the 5th Annaul ACM/IEEE International Conference on Mobile Computing and Networking, New York, 271-278.

Komori, T. and Saito, T. (2004) 'A secure wireless LAN system retaining privacy', 18th International Conference on Advanced Information Networking and Applications, Kanagawa, 370-375.

Lu, C., Blum, B.M., Abdelzaher, T.F., Stankovic, J.A. and He, T. (2002) 'RAP: a real-time communication architecture for large-scale wireless sensor networks', Proceedings of the 8th IEEE International Workshop on Real-Time and Embedded Technology and Applications Symposium, 55-66.

Mainwaring, A., Culler, D., Polastre, J., Szewczyk, R. and Anderson, J. (2002) 'Wireless sensor networks for habitat monitoring', In Proceedings of the 1st ACM International Workshop on Wireless Sensor Networks and Applications, New York, 88-97.

Mouton, F. and Venter, H.S. (2009) 'A Secure Communication Protocol for Wireless Sensor Networks', Proceedings of the Annual Security Conference "Security Assurance and Privacy: organizational challenges", Las Vegas.

Polastre, J., Hill, J. and Culler, D. (2004) 'Versatile low power media access for wireless sensor networks', Proceedings of the 2nd international conference on Embedded networked sensor systems, Baltimore, 95-107.

Rowlingson, R. (2004) 'A Ten Step Process for Forensic Readiness', *International Journal of Digital Evidence*, vol. 2, no. 3.

Schatz, B., Mohay, G. and Clark, A. (2006) 'A correlation method for establishing provenance of timestamps in digital evidence', Proceedings of the 6th Annual Digital Forensics Research Workshop, 98-107.

Schneier, B. and Kelsey, J. (1999) 'Secure audit logs to support computer forensics', *ACM Transactions Information System Security*, vol. 2, no. 2, May, pp. 159-176.

Shnayder, V., Hempstead, M., Chen, B., Allen, G.W. and Welsh, M. (2004) 'Simulating the power consumption of large-scale sensor network applications', In Proceedings of the 2nd international Conference on Embedded Network Sensor Systems, Baltimore, 188-200.

Slijepcevic, S. and Potkonjak, M. (2001) 'Power efficient organization of wireless sensor networks', In IEEE International Conference on Communications, 472-476.

Sohrabi, K., Gao, J., Ailawadhi, V. and Pottie, G.J. (2000) 'Protocols for self-organization of a wireless sensor network', *Personal Communications, IEEE Wireless communications*, vol. 7, no. 5, October, pp. 16-27.

Su, W. and Akyildiz, I.F. (2005) 'Time-diffusion synchronization protocol for wireless sensor networks', *IEEE/ACM Transactions on Networking*, vol. 13, no. 2, pp. 384-397.

Sundararaman, B., Buy, U. and Kshemkalyani, A.D. (2005) 'Clock synchronization for wireless sensor networks: a survey', *Ad Hoc Networks*, vol. 3, no. 3, pp. 281-323.

Sun, K., Ning, P. and Wang, C. (2006) 'TinySerSync: secure and resilient time synchornization in wireless sensor networks', Proceedings of the 13th ACM conference on Computer and communications security, Alexandria, 264-277.

Tan, J. (2001) *Forensic Readiness*, Technical Report edition, Cambridge: @Stake.

Tseng, Y., Ni, S. and Shih, E. (2003) 'Adaptive Approaches to Relieving Broadcast Storms in a Wireless Multihop Mobile Ad Hoc Network', *IEEE Transactions on Computers*, vol. 52, no. 5, pp. 545-557.

Wander, A.S., Gura, N., Eberle, H., Gupta, V. and Shantz, S.C. (2005) 'Energy analysis of public-key cryptography for wireless sensor networks', Third IEEE International Conference on Prevasive Computing and Communications, 324-328.

Xylomenos, G. and Polyzos, G. (1999) 'TCP and UDP Performance over a Wireless LAN', In Proceeedings of the IEEE INFOCOM.

Xylomenos, G., Polyzos, G., Mahonen, P. and Saaranen, M. (2001) 'TCP performance issues over wireless links', *IEEE Communications Magazine*, vol. 39, no. 4, pp. 52-58.

Ye, W., Heidemann, J. and Estrin, D. (2002) 'An energy-efficient MAC Protocol for wireless sensor networks', Proceedings of the 21st Annual Joint Conference of the IEEE Computer and Communication Societies, 1567-1576.

Zhao, F., Shin, J. and Reich, J. (2002) 'Information-driven dynamic sensor collaboration for tracking applications', *IEEE Signal Processing Magazine*, vol. 19, pp. 61-72.

A Signature Detection Scheme for Distributed Storage

R. Hegarty, M. Merabti, Q. Shi and R. Askwith

School of Computing and Mathematical Sciences, Liverpool John Moores University, James Parsons Building, Byrom Street, Liverpool, L3 3AF, U.K.
R.C.Hegarty@2006.ljmu.ac.uk, {M.Merabti, Q.Shi, R.J.Askwith}@ljmu.ac.uk

Abstract

Cloud computing is an emerging model of computing that offers elastic scalable computing resources to many concurrent users worldwide. It provides resources that are paid for as they are consumed, dynamically scaled to suit the demands of the user, which makes it attractive to organisations that wish to consolidate resources by creating their own elastic resource platforms or outsource to obtain more flexible cost effective computing resources. The scale and dynamic nature of cloud computing creates significant challenges for their management, including investigating malicious activity and/or policy failure. Digital forensics is the practice of analysing computers for evidence of crime or breach of policy. Among the various techniques employed to forensically analyse computer systems, file signatures are commonly used. This paper identifies the barriers to applying existing signature detection techniques to the large scale distributed storage platforms provided by cloud computing. The focus of this paper is the development of a model to determine a suitable signature length for use in the forensic analysis of a large distributed set of files. By reducing the signature length we show that we can reduce the amount of data required to carry out signature detection as this is one of the constraints preventing exiting techniques from being applied to cloud platforms. Through experimentation we validate our model and show that it is possible to use shorter length signatures to accurately carry out forensic analysis if factors such as the scale of the data undergoing analysis and the scale of the signature set used for the analysis are taken into account.

Keywords

Digital forensics, cloud computing, signature detection

1. Introduction

The amount of data stored in distributed systems is growing as they move from being the domain of scientists (Huang et al. 2006) to the domain of everyday users via cloud computing and utility computing platforms (Foster et al. 2008). Signature detection is the process of comparing a set of known signatures against signatures generated from a set of files to determine if any matches are present, it entails analysis of vast repositories of data to detect the presence of known illicit files (Richard III & Roussev 2006). Current digital forensic signature detection techniques were not developed to target distributed environments and therefore do not possess the capability to process data and signatures at cloud scale. Cloud scale systems contain Exabyte's of distributed data negating the ability of a single computer to analyse the files stored within them. Therefore a distributed approach is required. The signature sets which play a key role in forensic analysis must therefore be distributed across multiple analysis nodes within the distributed forensic analysis system. As these signature sets are themselves large in scale often containing many millions of signatures their deployment introduces storage, computation and network overheads. As the scale of the data undergoing analysis increases so too does the number of analysis nodes required to carry out signature detection. This in turn increases the signature set deployment overheads' as it increases the duplication of the signature set. To make feasible the scalable distribution of signature sets a more efficient signature creation scheme is required to reduce the burden of signature distribution placed on cloud infrastructure to make signature detection across a distributed forensic analysis system feasible.

This paper proposes a model to determine what length signature is most appropriate for use in a signature detection scheme applied to distributed storage. With the goal of minimising the burden of signature dissemination, to enable a distributed signature detection process to be developed. Section 2 provides background on cloud computing and the existing computer forensic techniques that are applied both to analyse distributed environments and utilise distributed environments to analyse single computers. Section 3 provides details of our models for signature creation and signature detection accuracy when various length signatures are used in the signature detection process. Section 4 provides details of the experiments we carried out to and result we obtained to verify our models. Section 5 contains a conclusion about the effectiveness of our approach and introduces the future work we have identified as necessary in order to enable forensic analysis of cloud computing environments.

2. Related Work

Cloud computing is a computing paradigm where users request and consume computer resources as and when they require them (Armbrust et al. 2009) in much the same way as utility companies provide access to water, electricity and gas on demand (Foster et al. 2008) (Armbrust et al. 2009). Through a combination of distributed computing and virtualisation (Barham et al. 2003) techniques resources are allocated in an elastic manner scaling up and down to suit demand (Rappa 2010). The three broad categories of cloud computing are (Rimal et al. 2009) Infrastructure as a Service (IaaS), Platforms as a Service (PaaS) and Software as a Service (SaaS). IaaS provides users with hardware and software as a service, and its resources (processing power, memory, and storage) are dynamically scalable, enabling adaptation to suit the users changing requirements and providing cost savings (Delic & Walker 2008). PaaS provides an environment in which developers can create distributed scalable applications using the API's provided by the service provider. SaaS provides users with applications hosted on a distributed architecture to be accessed using a Web browser. This enables developers to create cross platform applications and for end users to access applications from any computer with a Web browser. All of these models provide storage as a service in some form or other, storage is also offered as a service individually by providers such as Amazon via their S3 service (Amazon n.d.) and Dropbox (Dropbox n.d.) a storage service for end users. The detection of illicit data stored in these large scale storage platforms is the target of the forensic analysis techniques proposed in this paper.

While cloud computing is efficient (Delic & Walker 2008) and flexible it introduces barriers to current digital forensic analysis techniques, which typically rely on having physical access to a data storage device in order to image (create a bit by bit copy of the device) (Allen 2005) and search the device for known illicit files. Storage device access is restricted in cloud computing as the distributed storage often spans multiple data centres worldwide and is used to store multiple concurrent users' data (Reilly et al. 2010).

Various authors have identified the potential to utilise distributed computing platforms to perform forensic analysis or store images (Garfinkel 2007). In (Golden G. Richard, Vassil 2006) (Roussev & Richard III 2004) the authors identify the need to apply distributed analysis techniques to the task of analysing computer hard drives. They cite the complexity of investigations and ever increasing storage capacities as barriers to existing standalone techniques. They also identify the features of forensic analysis techniques, which can benefit from informed design choices such as avoiding unnecessary memory-to-memory copies and disk I/O particularly writes (Golden G. Richard, Vassil 2006). However ultimately they posit that the performance gains alone from well designed software will not be sufficient and a distributed approach is required.

In (Golden G. Richard, Vassil 2006) the acquisition phase of forensic analysis is identified as an area which needs improvement as capturing all possible data is costly (Golden G. Richard, Vassil 2006). A system to load entire disk images into main memory, distributed across multiple worker nodes and coordinated by a central control node is proposed in (Golden G. Richard, Vassil 2006). This allows the disk image to be read into memory once for subsequent analysis by multiple worker nodes reducing the I/O overheads imposed through multiple reads. The author also criticises the current sequential query/response/query model used by current tools for their lack of concurrency. While the paper successfully identifies the requirements for a distributed processing technique it does not implement and test any techniques nor does it address the emerging trend of large-scale distributed storage on the Internet often referred to as cloud computing.

A distributed forensic analysis architecture proposed by (Liebrock et al. 2007) utilises a database wrapper to enable workstations to request the results of a distributed analysis technique from a parallel machine. The distributed analysis technique is not described and the overall architecture appears to be simplistic. They do not consider the requirements identified by previous work in this field.

The Forweb technique proposed and tested in (Haggerty et al. 2008) utilises a more efficient block signature search technique Forsigs (Haggerty & Mark Taylor 2006) to analyse blocks from images retrieved from the Internet by a web spider. The approach was developed to analyse image files uploaded and stored in distributed storage platforms accessible via the World Wide Web using a single analysis host to target specific websites. While the technique results in accurate signature detection when searching compressed file types it is not accurate when searching for non-compressed file types and does not scale due to its reliance on a single host for analysis.

3. Distributed Forensic Analysis

The existing work cited in the previous section identifies either the requirement to distribute the forensic analysis of single host machines or the requirement to analyse data stored in distributed platforms. However, to our knowledge to date no attempt has been made to bring together these requirements to enable distributed forensic analysis of the large scale distributed data repositories found in cloud computing. To achieve these goals we need to develop a distributed signature detection technique. This paper focuses on the first stage of this task, which is the creation of signatures with a low storage overhead for use in a distributed signature detection process. We make the following assumption about the overall system to enable this work to be carried out. We assume that multiple analysis nodes will be created within the cloud environment, each of which will receive a copy of the signature set being used to carry out the first round signature detection. These analysis nodes will receive the reduced length signature sets which are the subject of this paper and carry out comparison with signatures they create from their local subset of files. Any matches in the first round stage will result in a second round search being carried out using the corresponding full length MD5 hash values retrieved following the first round search to confirm or deny that a file signature matches. The overall aim being to reduce the quantity of data required to store and distribute the signature sets needed for forensic analysis by reducing the storage requirement per signature for the first round and reducing the number of MD5 hash values required for the second round.

Our work aims to provide a set of metrics for use in signature detection to determine the most suitable length signatures to use for signature detection based on any given set of criteria. The criteria include the availability of time, required accuracy and computational resources available. By creating and disseminating reduced length signatures from known target files forensic analysis of large distributed storage platforms can be carried out. MD5 signatures for a set of target files may be hundreds of megabytes so significantly reducing the size of these enables a distributed approach to signature detection where many analysis nodes carry out signature detection simultaneously resulting in an approximately linear reduction in the amount of time required to carry out analysis.

3.1. Signature Creation and Detection Models

Our model can determine how many signatures a signature set will contain. By taking into account the number of hashes the signatures are created from and the length of the signatures in the set. The purpose of a signature is to provide pseudo unique identification of the file or hash value they were generated from. We calculate the theoretical number of signatures that a theoretical evenly distributed signature set would hold if we input x hash values and compressed them to length m using equation 1.

Equation 1 sums the probability of each of the hash values being input resulting in a unique signature. This is determined by calculating the probability that each signature will be unique. The probability of a signature being unique is reduced as signatures are added to the set. To calculate the probability of a signature already being in the set we divide the number of signatures in the set by the capacity of the set. To determine the probability of the signature not being in the set we divide 1 over the probability that the signature is already in the set. The capacity of the set is determined by the length of the signatures. As each bit in the signature can represent 2 values the capacity of the set is 2^m. If s calculated in equation 1 is greater than the sets capacity we substitute s with the set's capacity. Thus we can determine how many unique signatures are theoretically held in the set of signatures of a given length.

$$s = \left(\frac{x}{\sum_{i=1}^{z}\frac{1}{i}}\right)2^m$$

Equation 1. Probable number of signatures created

$$r = \frac{s}{2^m}$$

Equation 2. Probable false positive rate

$$t = (128 f r) + ms$$

Equation 3. Total amount of search data for both search rounds

Symbol	Meaning
s	Number of signatures in the set
x	Number of hash values input
m	Length of the signatures being created
z	The smaller of x and 2^m
r	False positive rate as a %
f	Number of files undergoing analysis
t	Total amount of search data for both search rounds.

We analyse the impact of reduced length signatures on the accuracy of a search using reduced length signatures. The probability of a file signature matching a signature in the signature set is directly related to the percentage of the signature set that is occupied by signatures. Equation 2 of our model illustrates this relationship.

We combine both the signature creation and signature detection equations to create equation 3 which calculates the total amount of data required to represent the signatures in the first round signature set. This is added to the total amount of data required to represent the 128bit MD5 hash values used in the second round search which are required to rule out the false positives induced through the use of the shorter length signatures in the first round search.

4. Results

To verify our signature creation and detection models we employed two signature creation techniques. The first technique SPLIT takes the first n bits of a MD5 hash value and uses them as a signature. The second XOR technique splits an MD5 hash value into a even number of pieces and combines them using bitwise exclusive or to create a signature n bits in length. Both techniques where applied to sets of randomly generated unique MD5 hash values to create signature sets for the various signature lengths.

4.1. Signature Creation

We created a Python script to create and calculate the total number of signatures in each set using the SPLIT and XOR techniques to create various length signatures. The script generated 10,000 MD5 hash values and processed them to create the signature sets. The script was executed 100 times and the average number of signatures in each signature set recorded for signatures of length 4 – 40 bits. Both of the SPLIT and XOR techniques resulted in very similar results to our theoretical model as illustrated in table 1 and figure 1.

	4	8	12	16	20	24	28	32	36	40
Model	16	256	2744	9216	9952	9997	9999	9999	9999	9999
XOR	16	256	3732	9266	9951	9996	9999	10000	10000	10000
SPLIT	16	256	3720	9273	9958	9994	10000	10000	10000	10000

Table 1: Actual and theoretical signature set size

The actual results largely follow the trend of the theoretical model. Figure 1 compares the average of the actual results obtained from the XOR and SPLIT techniques with the theoretical results from our model. Initially the results are identical as the number of signatures in the signature sets is equal to their capacity. For signature sets containing signatures of lengths from 10 bits to 16 bits, there is some divergence between the theoretical and actual results. This divergence is expected as our mathematical model assumes perfectly even byte value distribution for the signatures at each length.

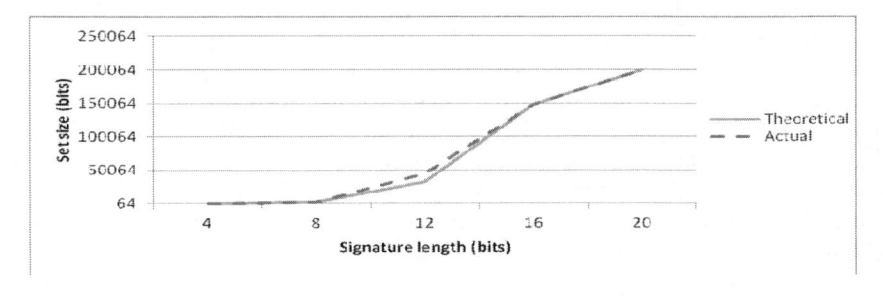

Figure 1: A comparison of the actual and theoretical signature set sizes

This is of course not the case in reality. The MD5 hash values input into the signature creation techniques have near even byte value distribution across their length. However the signature creation techniques create a shorter signature which may contain byte values which are less evenly distributed across the length of the signature. The effect of any skew in byte value distribution is not observed when the signature set is full to capacity. Likewise when the capacity of the signature set is much larger than the number of signatures in the signature set the effect is not observed as the probability of the byte value distribution skew resulting in a collision where two or more difference MD5 hash values are processed resulting in the same reduced length signature is much smaller. For signatures of length 20 bits – 40 bits the results from our experiments converge with those of our model and follow a linear trend.

4.2. Signature Detection

We created a Python script which generated two distinct sets of hash values. The first set represented the signature set and contains 10,000 hash values. The second set represents the files undergoing analysis and contains 100,000 hash values. Using the XOR and SPLIT techniques the hash values were used to create signature sets containing signatures of lengths 4,8,12...40. For each length and type of signature, comparison was carried out between the sets to determine the number of matches. As the initial hash values generated by the script formed two distinct sets containing 10,000 and 100,000 unique hash values we expect zero matches to be found therefore any matches between the sets where viewed as false positives. We executed the script 100 times and calculated the average number of false positives for each signature type at various lengths.

Signature Length	4 bits	8 bits	12 bits	16 bits	20 bits	24 bits	28 bits	32 bits	36 bits	40 bits
Theoretical	100%	100%	67.0%	14.1%	0.95%	0.06%	0.004%	0.0002%	<0.0002%	<0.0002%
XOR	100%	100.%	91.6%	14.1%	0.94%	0.06%	0.003%	0.0002%	<0.0002%	<0.0002%
SPLIT	100.%	100%	91.8%	14.2%	0.95%	0.06%	0.004%	0.0002%	<0.0000%	<0.0000%

Table 2: False positive rates when searching for 10,000 signatures in 100,000 signatures.

Table 2 illustrates the percentage false positive rate for signatures of length 4 to 40 bits determined by our model and those generated by our experiment. The results more or less follow the trend determined by our model. The false positive rate was initially 100% as the signature sets containing 4 and 8 bit signatures are filled to 100% capacity by signatures. This results in 100% of the file signatures matching signatures in the set. As the percentage of signatures in the signature sets is reduced due to the increased signature length the percentage of false positives also falls. In Figure 2 we compare the results of our experiment with our model, for signature lengths 4 – 24 bits. The false positive rates between 24 and 40 bits are either identical to the graph generated by our model in figure 2 or show negligible difference. As the results produced by the XOR and SPLIT techniques are almost identical they are represented on the graph by a single line which is the average of the two.

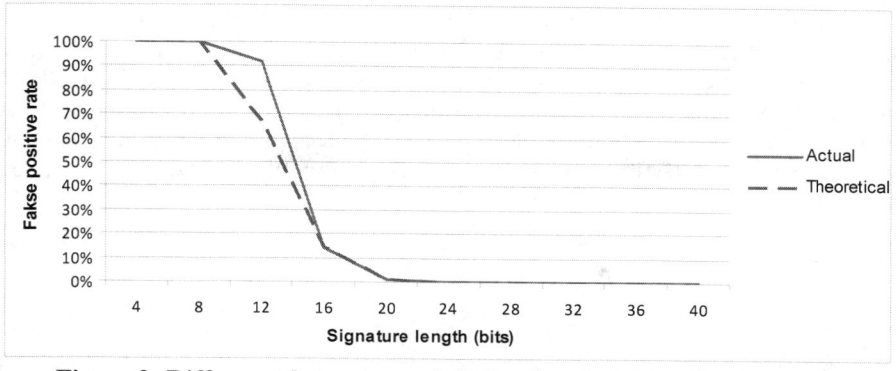

Figure 2: Difference between modelled and actual false positive rates.

The marked difference between the modelled and actual results for signature lengths 10 – 16bits is not unexpected. As explained in the previous section the possible skew in the byte value distribution induced by the SPLIT and XOR signature creation techniques is reflected in the false positive rates for signatures at these lengths. When the signature length is 16 bits or greater the signatures are more evenly distributed across the set and occupy a much smaller percentage of the signature sets capacity making collisions and therefore false positives much less probable. The results of our experiment for signatures with lengths 24 – 40 bits closely match our model with the false positive rate rapidly decaying to a small fraction of a percent.

Our model can fairly accurately determine the size of a signature set when a given length signature is used. It can also determine the accuracy of a signature detection process which utilises the signatures. This is useful as it allows decisions to be made about what length signature to use when analysing a set of files.

Using equations 1 and 2 from our model we can compare determine the false positive rate of reduced length signatures and the amount of round one search data required to carry out signature detection. Figure 3 shows the relationship between signature length and accuracy.

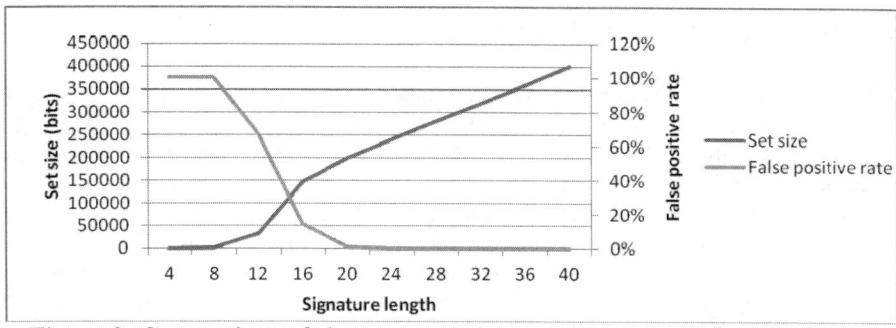

Figure 3: Comparison of signature set size and accuracy for various length round one signatures

This satisfies the requirement to reduce the size of the signature set used for forensic analysis of a distributed storage platform and enables us to determine the accuracy levels likely to be achieved if we use signatures of a given length. This allows tradeoffs to be made when determining which length signature to use for the first round of a signature detection technique, taking into account the size of the resulting signature set and the potential burden it will impose of the signature detection process.

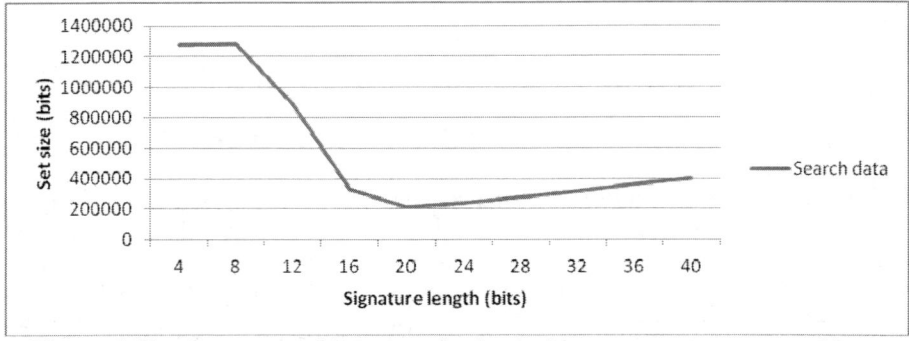

Figure 4. Total amount of data required to achieve accuracy comparable to existing techniques.

Using equation 3 from our model we calculate the total amount of data required to represent the signatures for both the first and second round searches. Taking into account the number of round two MD5 hash values that are required to rule out any false positives induced through the use of shorter signatures in the first round. The results are graphed in figure 4 which illustrate how we can achieve accuracy comparable with that of a single round search using MD5 hash values while reducing the combined size of the signature sets using our model for a two round search. In the case of our experiment using 24 bit signatures in the first round search provides a reduction in the overall signature set size from 1280000 to 240689 an 81% reduction. Obviously if files with matching signatures in the first round also match signatures in the second round there will be an increase in the size of the required search data.

5. Conclusion and Further Work

Reduced length signatures can be used to reduce the scale of signature sets and make feasible forensic analysis of large scale distributed storage platforms. We have considered the scale of the signature set and the scale of the data undergoing analysis as factors that influence the selection of signature lengths when analysing data. We can now determine an appropriate signature length for a given sized signature set and number of files. This enables us to avoid two negative situations which could occur if incorrect signature lengths where selected for use in the analysis process. The first of situation may occur if the signature length selected was too short, and the result would be many false positives in the first round of the search. Resulting in the requirement for the vast majority of the hash values generated for the round two of the search to be disseminated. This would increase the burden on both the network and analysis nodes, reducing the ability of the analysis technique to scale. The second situation arises where the signatures selected were too long. This would again result in an increased burden on the network and analysis nodes and limit the ability of the analysis technique to scale.

While there are existing techniques such as Bloom filters (Bloom 1970) available which provide time and space efficient searches, the nature of digital forensics is such that we need to determine which signature matches rather than just that a match has occurred. Our technique provides this and enables us to look up the metadata associated with the signature to continue the investigation. For example we may want to categorise our signatures based on a set of criteria or know when a signature was first detected to enable link analysis to be carried out.

We will run further experiments using a distributed network of analysis nodes to enable us to determine the effect of distributing our signatures and take into account factors such as the availability of bandwidth and other constraints when determining an appropriate signature length to enable large scale distributed analysis.

To distribute our signature detection scheme we are working on a publish subscribe model where analysis nodes can register with a server to receive signature sets as well as command and control information to initialise, execute and report the results of our distributed signature analysis technique. When a node registers it receives a copy of the reduced size round one signature set. The files on or local to the node are processed to produce reduced size signatures which are compared with those in the set to determine if a match can be found. If a match is found, the details of the file are logged and its second round signature requested. The second round search will be executed using the MD5 hash values which correspond to the round one signatures which resulted in a match.

6. References

Allen, W.H., 2005. Computer forensics. *Security & Privacy Magazine, IEEE*, 3(4), pp.59-62.

Amazon, Amazon Simple Storage Service (Amazon S3). *http://aws.amazon.com*. Available at: http://aws.amazon.com.

Armbrust, M. et al., 2009. *Above the clouds: A berkeley view of cloud computing. EECS Department, University of California, Berkeley, Tech. Rep. UCB/EECS-2009-28.*

Barham, P. et al., 2003. Xen and the art of virtualization. In *OSP '03 Proceedings of the nineteenth ACM symposium on Operating systems principles*. Bolton Landing, NY, USA, p. 164.

Bloom, B., 1970. Space/time trade-offs in hash coding with allowable errors. *Communications of the ACM*, 13(7), p.422–426.

Delic, K. a & Walker, M.A., 2008. Emergence of the Academic Computing Clouds. *ACM Ubiquity*, 9(21).

Dropbox. *http://www.dropbox.com/*. Available at: http://www.dropbox.com/.

Foster, I. et al., 2008. Cloud Computing and Grid Computing 360-Degree Compared. *Grid Computing Environments Workshop, 2008. GCE '08*, pp.1-10.

Garfinkel, S., 2007. Commodity grid computing with amazon s3 and ec2. *Usenix*, pp.7-13..

Golden G. Richard, Vassil, R., 2006. Next-generation digital forensics. *Communications of the ACM*, 49(2), pp.76 - 80.

Haggerty, J., Llewellyn-Jones, D. & Taylor, M., 2008. Forweb: file fingerprinting for automated network forensics investigations. In *Proceedings of the 1st international conference on Forensic applications and techniques in telecommunications, information, and multimedia and workshop*. Adelaide, Australia: ICST (Institute for Computer Sciences, Social-Informatics and Telecommunications Engineering), p. 29..

Haggerty, J. & Taylor, Mark, 2006. "FORSIGS: Forensic Signature Analysis of Hard Drive Multimedia File Fingerprints." *FIP TC11 International Information Security Conference* (Vol. 232). Sandton, South Africa.

Huang, W. et al., 2006. A case for high performance computing with virtual machines. In *Proceedings of the 20th annual international conference on Supercomputing - ICS '06*. Cairns, Queensland, Australia: ACM Press, p. 125.

Liebrock, L.M. et al., 2007. A preliminary design for digital forensics analysis of terabyte size data sets. *Proceedings of the 2007 ACM symposium on Applied computing - SAC '07*, p.190.

Rappa, M., 2010. The utility business model and the future of computing services. *IBM Systems Journal*, 43(1), pp.32-42.

Reilly, D., Wren, C. & Berry, T., 2010. Cloud computing: Forensic challenges for law enforcement. In *Internet Technology and Secured Transactions (ICITST), 2010 International Conference for*. London, UK, pp. 1-7.

Richard III, G.G. & Roussev, V., 2006. Digital forensics tools: the next generation. *Communications of the ACM*, p.75.

Rimal, B.P., Choi, E. & Lumb, I., 2009. A Taxonomy and Survey of Cloud Computing Systems. In *Proceedings of the 2009 Fifth International Joint Conference on INC, IMS and IDC*. Washington, DC, USA: IEEE Computer Society, pp. 44-51.

Roussev, V. & Richard III, G.G., 2004. Breaking the performance wall: The case for distributed digital forensics. In *Proceedings of the 2004 digital forensics research workshop (DFRWS 2004)*. DFRWS, pp. 1-16.

LUARM – An Audit Engine for Insider Misuse Detection

G. Magklaras, S.M. Furnell and M. Papadaki

Centre for Security, Communications and Network Research, University of Plymouth, Plymouth, UK
e-mail: cscan@plymouth.ac.uk

Abstract

'Logging User Actions in Relational Mode' (LUARM) is an open source audit engine for Linux. It provides a near real-time snapshot of a number of user action data such as file access, program execution and network endpoint user activities, all organized in easily searchable relational tables. LUARM attempts to solve two fundamental problems of the insider IT misuse domain. The first concerns the lack of insider misuse case data repositories that could be used by post-case forensic examiners to aid an incident investigation. The second problem relates to how information security researchers can enhance their ability to specify accurately insider threats at system level. This paper presents LUARM's design perspectives and a 'post mortem' case study of an insider IT misuse incident. The results show that the prototype audit engine has a good potential to provide a valuable insight into the way insider IT misuse incidents manifest on IT systems and can be a valuable complement to forensic investigators of IT misuse incidents.

Keywords

Insiders, misuse, detection, auditing, logging, forensics

1. Introduction

The problem of insider IT misuse is a very real threat for the health of IT infrastructures encompassing both intentional activities (e.g. targeted information theft and accidental misuse (e.g. unintentional information leak). Numerous studies have tried to define an "insider" in the context of Information Security. A generic definition from Probst et al. (2009) is "a person that has been legitimately empowered with the right to access, represent, or decide about one or more assets of the organization's structure".

The most widely known insider misuse cases are usually about intellectual property theft. The arrest of Lan Lee and Yuefei Ge by FBI agents (Cha, 2008) is a classic case. The arrested men were engineers of NetLogic Microsystems (NLM) until July 2003. During the time of their employment, they were downloading trade sensitive documents from the NLM headquarters into their home computers. These documents contained detailed descriptions of the NLM microprocessor product line. Eventually, their ties to the Chinese government and military were discovered by investigators. However, both mass media case descriptions and relevant security surveys do not provide the tools or the methodology to systemically study and mitigate the problem. Insider IT misuse is a multi-faceted problem and one of the things insider misuse researchers really need is a repository of more detailed case descriptions with a focus on the impact insider misuse actions have at computer system level (NSTISSAM). This is the area of Insider Threat Specification, the core concept behind the proposed logging engine which is examined in the next section.

2. Insider Threat Specification and modelling

Threat specifications follow the principles of intrusion specification, a concept which is not new in the information security world. Techniques to describe threats exist for an entire range of information security products, from anti-virus software to several intrusion detection/prevention systems (IDS/IPS) (Bace, 2000), where threats are specified by anomaly detection, pattern matching (also known as misuse detection) mechanisms or a heuristic-based combination of the two. Insider Threat Specification is the process of using a standardized vocabulary to describe in an abstract way how the aspects and behaviour of an insider relate to a security policy defined misuse scenario. Figure 1 shows the information flow of a typical IT misuse detection system. The security specialist translates the Security (and resulting monitoring policy) into a set of misuse scenario signatures, standard descriptions of IT misuse acts that describe the behaviour of a user at process execution, filesystem and network endpoint level (Magklaras et al, 2006). The misuse scenario signatures and collected audit data (Bace, 2000) from the IT infrastructure are fed into a misuse detection engine.

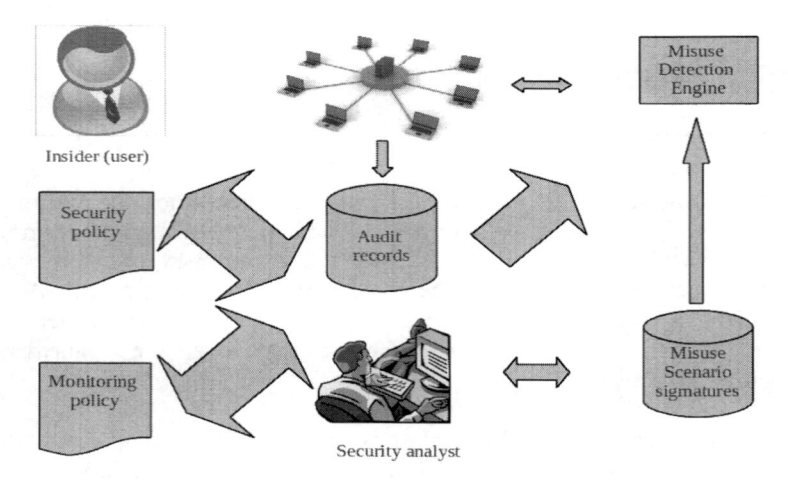

Figure 1: Information flow in an insider misuse detection system

Vital to insider threat specification is the structure and content of the audit record, at the center of Figure 1. If the audit record is incomplete, in terms of the type of information we need to log or unavailable, because the data are vanished due to bad system design or intentional data corruption, the specification of insider threats is useless. This is one of the primary objectives that LUARM tries to address by providing an evidence rich and reliable audit record format.

3. Insider misuse detection auditing requirements

Bace (Bace, 2000) discusses intrusion detection (and hence misuse detection) as an audit reduction problem. Audit reduction is the process of filtering the relevant information out of the audit records, in order to infer a partially or fully realized threat and excluding information that is irrelevant or redundant. The structure of an audit record is important for a misuse detection system. A good structure has well defined fields that can be easily parsed. Moreover, the structure of the audit record should easily facilitate relational type queries. It is necessary for the information to be applied on the disjunction (OR), conjunction (AND), and negation (NOT) operators, in order to increase the query versatility and speed of response.

A desired aspect of a suitable crafted audit record format for insider misuse detection is clear user accountability. This means that the audit record should be able to reliably and easily associate user entities to recorded actions. The wealth and replication of vital information in various types of audit records is a requirement for proper event correlation and step instance selection (Meier, 2004).

Another important issue of audit record engines is that of referencing time. In large IT infrastructures that span several networks and time zones, audited systems might report in different time formats. They can also experience 'clock skew', a difference in time recorded amongst computer systems due to computer clock hardware inaccuracies, especially when an NTP (Mills et al, 2010) server is not available to provide a reliable time source.

One of the most recent and commonly referenced works that concern the format of audit records is the Common Criteria for Information Technology Security Evaluation (Common Criteria Portal, 2009) standards. The Common Criteria (CC) effort does not fully address the previously mentioned audit record requirement omissions of its predecessor, the Orange Book (DOD 5200.28-std, 1985). However, some of its high level functional audit requirements are interesting. In particular, CC requirement 88 of section 8.2 states that: "At FAU_GEN.2 User identity association, the TSF shall associate auditable events to individual user identities." In CC terminology TSF stands for Target of evaluation Security Functionality, meaning essentially the software and hardware under evaluation. In addition, CC mentions a set of requirements that concern various aspects of the audit record storage. Once again, the requirements are given in high-level terms, specifying that:

- unauthorized deletion and/or modification of audit records
- any other condition that could cause storage failure.

should be mitigated.

The next section discusses whether today's audit engines satisfy these requirements.

4. Existing audit record engines

Audit record engines have existed since the very early days of operating systems. However, not all of them fit the requirements of misuse detection engines, as discussed in the previous section.

The most common variety of audit record engines uses information that comes directly from the Operating System. Characteristic examples of this category of engines are Oracle's Basic Security Module (BSM) auditing system (Oracle Corporation, 2010) and its open source implementation OpenBSM (Trusted BSD Project portal, 2009), the psacct audit package (psacct utilities, 2003), as well as the syslogd (Gerhards, 2009) and WinSyslogd (Monitorware, 2010) applications.

After examining these engines, serious deficiencies can be located in terms of use for insider threat prediction. Firstly, many engines consolidate information from various different devices and operating system vendors, but they are far from describing sufficiently issues in an operating system agnostic way. In addition, process accounting tools might not cover sufficiently the variety of different system level information (file, process execution and network level). In fact, some of them might miss data as described in (HP Portal, 2003). A logging engine that cannot facilitate the description of both static and live forensic insider misuse system data at the network, process and filesystem layer could hinder a forensic examination of an IT misuse incident. Static digital forensic analysis is employed by most forensic tools and cannot portray accurately the non-quiescent (dynamic) state of the system under investigation. Information such as active network endpoints, running processes, user interaction data (number of open applications per user, exact commands), as well as the content of memory resident processes may not be recorded accurately on non-volatile media. (Hay et al, 2009) discuss the shortcomings of static digital forensics analysis in detail. In order to overcome the barriers of static analysis, Adelstein et al. (2006) discuss the virtues of non-quiescent or live analysis, which essentially gathers data while the system under-investigation is operational.

Several audit record systems do not report consistently the timing of audit record generation. For instance, many implementations of the syslog audit standard and psacct tools generate the audit record by entering the time stamp of the client system. If the client system does not have a reliable time source, this generates inaccurate information and could seriously hinder event correlation.

Finally, one of the most serious drawbacks of existing audit approaches is the inability to store the audit information in a form that can utilize relational queries. Section 3 discussed the reasoning behind this requirement. In one sense, some people might argue that this is an audit management feature rather than an audit log design issue. However, as section 3 discussed the advantages of using a relational schema to form audit queries in a structured log record, the author's view is that everything that increases the expressive power of an audit log query should be incorporated in the structure of the audit log, rather than being left as an 'add-on' feature.

5. The LUARM audit engine

LUARM is a prototype Open Source audit record engine (LUARM portal, 2010) that uses a Relational Database Management System (RDBMS) for the storage and organization of audit record data. The employment of an RDBMS is a core design choice for the LUARM engine. Beyond the relational type query support discussed in Section 3, an RDBMS offers the necessary data availability, integrity and scalability features, because most RDBMS tools are explicitly designed to organize and store large amounts of data, as dictated by many CC requirements. The Structured Query Language (SQL) facilitates instance selection and completion, as well as data correlation can be performed by using clauses such as 'FROM' and 'WHERE'.

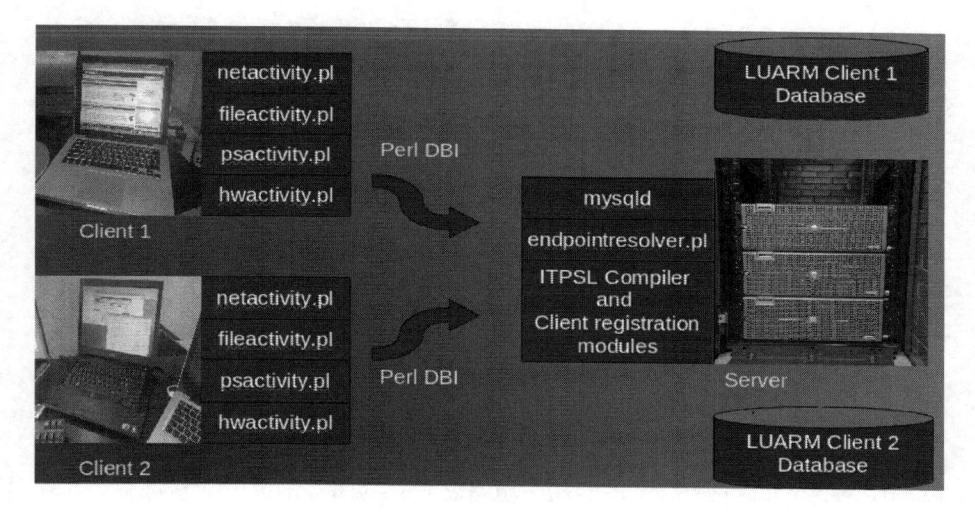

Figure 2: The LUARM architecture

Fileinfo table			Netinfo table			Procinfo table			Hwinfo table	
fileaccessid	bigint		endpointinfo	bigint		psinfo	bigint		hwdevc	bigint
md5sum	text		md5sum	text		md5sum	text		md5sum	text
filename	varchar		transport	tinytext		username	tinytext		devbus	tinytext
location	varchar		sourceip	tinytext		pid	smallint		devstring	text
username	tinytext		sourcefqdn	tinytext		ppid	smallint		devvendor	text
application	text		destip	tinytext		pcpu	decimal		application	text
fd	tinytext		destfqdn	tinytext		pmem	decimal		userslogged	text
pid	int		sourceport	smallint		command	text		cyear	int
size	bigint		destport	smallint		arguments	mediumtext		cmonth	tinyint
cyear	int		ipversion	smallint		cyear	int		cday	tinyint
cmonth	tinyint		cyear	int		cmonth	tinyint		chour	tinyint
cday	tinyint		cmonth	tinyint		cday	tinyint		cmin	tinyint
chour	tinyint		cday	tinyint		chour	tinyint		csec	tinytint
cmin	tinyint		chour	tinyint		cmin	tinyint		dyear	int
csec	tinytint		cmin	tinyint		csec	tinytint		dmonth	tinyint
dyear	int		csec	tinytint		dyear	int		dday	tinyint
dmonth	tinyint		dyear	int		dmonth	tinyint		dhour	tinyint
dday	tinyint		dmonth	tinyint		dday	tinyint		dmin	tinyint
dhour	tinyint		dday	tinyint		dhour	tinyint		dsec	tinyint
dmin	tinyint		dhour	tinyint		dmin	tinyint			
dsec	tinyint		dmin	tinyint		dsec	Tinyint			
			dsec	Tinyint		username	tinytext			
			username	tinytext		pid	int			
			application	text						

Figure 3: LUARM relational table structure

Figure 2 depicts the module client-server architecture of the LUARM audit engine. On the left of the figure, we can see a set of audited computer clients. Every client is running a unique instance of a set of monitoring scripts. Each of the client scripts audits a particular system level aspect of the operating system: 'netactivity.pl' audits the addition and creation of endpoints, 'fileactivity.pl' records various file operations, 'psactivity' provides process execution audit records and 'hwactivity.pl' keeps a log of hardware devices that are connected or disconnected from the system. The right hand side contains the centralized server part of the architecture where audit data are stored, maintained and queried in a MySQL (Oracle MySQL portal, 2010) based RDBMS (other RDBMS systems could be used as well). The Perl programming language is used to implement the modules and the communication between client and server is performed via a Perl DBI (CPAN-DBI, 2010) interface.

The client-server architecture avoids leaving the data in vulnerable clients. The central host MySQL server has its own authentication system responsible for controlling who has access to the audit data. By authenticating audit reviewers against the RDBMS authentication system, we de-couple the users being audited from the auditors, a desirable property that ensures that audited insiders cannot easily manipulate audit data. Furthermore, by assigning a separate database instance per audited client, we reduce the likelihood of compromising the data for all clients. If the database access credentials of one client are compromised, the damage is limited to the audit data for that client only.

Figure 3 displays the relational table format for the four main types of recorded audit data in LUARM: fileaccess, process execution, network endpoint and hardware device information. Temporal information is provided by event creation time stamps (cyear, cmonth, cday,chour,cmin,csec) and respective event destruction time stamps (dyear,dmonth,dday,dhour,dmin,dsec). The combination of the two types of timestamps can pinpoint exact time intervals for events in a consistent format for all recorded event types. In contrast, most audit systems may provide only event creation time references without hinting for the duration of an event.

The sampling of events is done at 100ms intervals and is adjustable by means of modifying certain variables on each monitoring module. At first, this might seem problematic as many attack steps can occur much faster than that amount of time. However, in an event sampling loop, one has to account for the time delay to update the database, which can vary from 10ms to 60-70 ms intervals on heavily loaded clients and servers. In addition, time resolution varies amongst operating systems. For these reasons, LUARM relies on the Perl Time::HiRes module (CPAN-HiRes, 2010) to bridge the gap between the different operating system timer implementations. A time granularity of 100 ms is also a good compromise between accuracy and scalability. The more granular the time resolution, the greater the computational load for both the client and the server LUARM parts.

Another important design decision that concerns the format of the audit table was to include common attributes amongst different event tables for the purposes of increasing the ability to correlate events and provide user entity accountability. For instance, fields such as 'username' (user entity), pid (numeric process ID of the program responsible for the event creation) and application (string that represents the name of the application that matches the pid) can be found in most of the event tables. This enables the audit reviewer to use SQL and relate events, so he can form queries of the type "Find the network endpoint created by program x of user y" in an easy manner.

The 'fileinfo' table stores file access related events. The filename specification consists of two parts. The 'filename' field which holds the filename with the file extension (i.e. data.txt) and the 'location' field which contains the absolute path of the file. The fact that the two are divided in separate fields makes it easier to search by location or by field name only, increasing the versatility of mining file data. In order to populate the data on this table, LUARM relies on the 'lsof' utility (Pogue et al, 2008). The utility is versatile and can record a variety of events including file and network endpoints in real time. It exists for an entire range of UNIX/Linux and MACOSX operating systems, covering a large spectrum of computing devices.

The 'netinfo' table logs the creation and destruction of network endpoints. In the context of LUARM, the term 'network endpoint' refers to the operating system data structures employed to facilitate network connectivity via the TCP/IP protocol suite. Network endpoint activity is considered as live forensic data. A series of table fields are used to record endpoint details ('sourceip', 'destip', 'sourceport' , 'destport' and 'transport' record source and destination IP addresses, source and destination port and transport protocol respectively). The fields 'sourcefqdn' and 'destfqdn' hold the DNS (Mockapetris, 1987) resolved Fully Qualified Domain Name (FQDN) for the source and destination hosts.

The 'sourcefqdn' and 'destfqdn' fields are not populated by the client LUARM routines. In contrast, they are populated on the LUARM server side. Due to the criticality of correct DNS data for the audit records, the frequent DNS configuration errors (Barr, 1996), aspects of DNS operational security (Bauer, 2003) and client performance, the endpoint name resolution is left on the server side. This provides a greater control on DNS derived data and does not rely on vulnerable clients (malicious insiders or software vulnerabilities) for auditing network connections.

Process execution activity is recorded in the 'psinfo' table (Figure 3). This table records 'live' forensic data. The table includes both the proces ID ('pid') and parent process id ('ppid'), so that process execution flow can be traced back to the original process. In order to speed up process execution searches, the LUARM engine also separates the executed command ('command') from its arguments ('arguments'). One might like to search them separately in the process of mining process execution data. The 'ps' UNIX/Linux utility (Pogue et al, 2008) is used to collect process information. For all active processes (whose d* temporal fields are NULL), LUARM updates in near real time these two fields.

The 'hwinfo' table logs 'live' device connection and disconnection events. All events generated by devices that connect to the Peripheral Component Interconnect (PCI and PCI-Express) and Universal Serial (USB) buses. These two buses are commonly found on a large array of computing devices. For instance, an audit reviewer or forensics analyst might correlate file activity to a portable storage medium connection, as part of an intellectual property theft scenario. In that case, the 'hwinfo' table logs information in various fields that help identify the attached device ('devstring', 'devvendor'), the bus the device was connected to ('bus') and correlate the device attachment event against a number of users that are logged into the system at the time of the device attachment ('userslogged').

6. LUARM in action

Having a proposed structure and content for the various categories of audit events as described in the previous section, we can now issue sample SQL statements to illustrate how audit data mining is performed. Figure 4 displays sample queries that demonstrate the expressiveness of LUARM's audit record content and structure.

There are a few important observations to make about the example LUARM SQL queries. The first one concerns the embedding of system specific knowledge inside the statement. In essence, the third example of Figure 4 defines a step of an insider trying to transfer a sensitive file to a portable medium. One has to know the name of the sensitive file 'prototype.ppt' and also the fact that '/media' is used as a mount point for portable media for that host. Additional possible destination locations could be specified by means of OR operators. The use of the 'RLIKE' operator (RLIKE

RegExp, 2008), always in relation to the second and third examples of Figure 4. The operator implements a regular expression type of match. Apart from the conjunction operator (OR), regular expressions give the specification polymorphic properties (one specification string, many matching results), a desirable property for compact misuse detection language statements.

> Find all accesses of the file 'prototype.ppt' by users 'toms' OR 'georgem' between 9:00 and 14:00 hours on 23/10/2009.
> SELECT * FROM fileinfo WHERE filename='prototype.ppt' AND ((username='toms') OR (username='georgem')) AND cyear='2009' AND cmonth='10' AND cday='23' AND chour >= '9' AND chour <= '13' AND cmin >= '0' AND cmin >= '59';

> Find all USB devices that were physically connected to the system when users 'toms' OR 'georgem' were logged on 23/10/2009.
> SELECT * from hwinfo WHERE devbus='usb' AND ((userslogged RLIKE 'toms') OR (userslogged RLIKE 'georgem')) AND cyear='2009' AND cmonth='10' AND cday='23' AND chour >= '9' AND chour <= '13' AND cmin >= '0' AND cmin >= '59';

> Find whether users 'georgem' or 'toma' have tried to move or copy a file called 'prototype.ppt' (irrespective of location) under the directory '/media' between 9:00 and 13:00 hours on the 23rd of October 2009.
> select * FROM psinfo WHERE ((command='cp') OR (command='mv')) AND (arguments RLIKE 'prototype.ppt' AND arguments RLIKE '/media') AND ((username='georgem') OR (username='toms')) AND cyear='2009' AND cmonth='10' AND cday='23' AND chour >= '9' AND chour <= '13' AND cmin >= '0' AND cmin >= '59';

Figure 4: Using SQL to mine data in LUARM

LUARM was tested on a variety of simulated insider misuse scenarios. The scenarios were derived by real world LUARM captured data. However, permission to publish the original audit data was not obtained by the organizations in question. Thus, we had to reconstruct the misuse incidents by means of writing down a text based description of each incident and ask a team of users to re-enact it under a controlled IT infrastructure. The following paragraphs will present one of these incidents and demonstrate how the correlation versatility of the LUARM relational audit log structure can shed forensic light into the actions of a malicious insider. The scenario is provided below:

> 'Autobrake' Corp is a company designing car braking systems. Their engineering department is the most information sensitive work area. The braking system design process takes place in high performance Linux workstations, one for each design engineer. The engineers have normal user rights to the workstations. Superuser rights (root) is given only to the IT admin. The designs reside on the local hard drives of the workstations and the company's IT policy forbids any transfer of sensitive data to portable media. Autobrake's system administrator has requested a salary raise various times. This has been denied by management. The system administrator is lured by a competing company that asked him to deliver schematics of the new and revolutionary Autobrake's RGX9 SUV braking system in return for a large amount of money. Enjoying the trust of everyone and having full control of the engineering CAD workstations, the system administrator decides to take the offer of the competing company. He performs the intellectual property theft by following a well designed approach which is summarized below:

- He carefully chooses the user account of a mechanical engineer (username 'engineer3') that had some disputes over work issues with management. He aims to avoid detection by means of masquerading as the engineer in question.

- After successfully masquerading as the engineer in the IT system he uses a portable USB key to obtain the commercially sensitive RGX9 schematic, leaving only the traces of the engineer "actions".

Assuming that a third party auditor manages the audit process and monitors the logging (ensuring that the logging infrastructure works) and that all Engineering workstations are monitored by LUARM, we are now tasked to find the offender and clear the name of 'engineer3'. The reader should consult the LUARM relational table structure (Figure 3), in order to follow the SQL queries presented below.

The investigation begins from the most important file, that of RGX9, and the people that work on it. From the audit record of the workstations with name 'proteas', we utilize LUARM to find out who has been using the file:

mysql> select username,pid,cday,chour,cmin,location,filename from fileinfo where filename RLIKE 'RGX9' OR location RLIKE 'RGX9' \G

From the many hits we get from the data base, we focus our attention on the following ones:

*************************** 111. row ***************************
username: engineer3
pid : 8301
cday: 4
chour: 15
cmin: 30
location: /storage/users/engineer3/work/designs
filename:RGX9.jpg
...
*************************** 118. row ***************************
username: engineer3
pid: 28538
cday: 4
chour: 15
cmin: 32
location: /media/U3SAN03-12
filename: RGX9.jpg

The reason these file access patterns looked suspicious is that they were different than the normal pattern of accessing the file by the staff engineer. Normally, user 'engineer3' would access the file by means of certain design and image editing applications, under its usual directory (/storage/users/engineer3/work/designs). This time, however, things look a bit different, if one follows the association of file access to process execution, in order to confirm which programs performed the file transaction. The following SQL queries achieve the desired association:

mysql>select username,pid,command,arguments,cyear,cday,chour,cmin from psinfo where username='engineer3' AND pid='8031' AND cyear='2011' AND cday='4' AND chour='15' AND cmin='30';

*************************** 1. row ***************************
username: engineer3
pid: 8031
command: /bin/cp
arguments: work/designs/RGX9.jpg /tmp/
cyear: 2011
cday: 4
chour: 15
cmin: 30

mysql>select username,pid,command,arguments,cyear,cday,chour,cmin from psinfo where username='engineer3' AND pid='8031' AND cyear='2011' AND cday='4' AND chour='15' AND cmin='30';

*************************** 1. row ***************************
username: root
pid: 28538
command: mv
arguments: RGX9.jpg /media/U3SAN03-12
cyear: 2011
cday: 4
chour: 15
cmin: 32

Essentially, the previous results verify that the file was first copied from the normal directory to /tmp and then was moved to the /mnt/usb. At this point, a little bit of system specific knowledge comes into light, as /mnt/usb is the usual mount point where Linux links portable storage media to the filesystem. Hence, the question to raise is whether a portal storage medium was connected to the workstation, prior to the 'mv' file transaction. The query result yields a positive answer:

mysql> select * from hwinfo where cyear='2011' AND cmonth='01' AND cday='04' AND chour='15'\G
*************************** 1. row ***************************
hwdevid: 71
md5sum: a16e7386f14de769a7a9491da2071f5b
cyear: 2010
cmonth: 12
cday: 4
chour: 15

cmin: 30
csec: 28
devbus: USB
devstring: Cruzer Micro U3
devvendor: SanDisk Corp.
userslogged: engineer3,root
dyear: 2010
dmonth: 1
dday: 4
dhour: 15
dmin: 33
dsec: 38

This database hit seems to be in line with the actions of engineer3, as it indicates a device connection before the execution of the 'mv' command and a disconnection well after the mv command. Thus, everything seems to point out that 'engineer3' violated the company policy and transferred a sensitive file to a USB medium, against the company IT regulations. However, this had been categorically denied by the actual person. A good but non IT based alibi for the staff engineer was that he exited the building with his security card token around 14:50, returning back to his desk at 15:50, a wide gap for him. Clearly, something else was going on and the clue was the 'userslogged' field of the last LUARM result. This 'hwinfo' LUARM table field contains the usernames for accounts that are logged into the workstation at the time of the device connection. Apart from 'engineer3' we note the root account being active, which is clearly the only other choice that, under the circumstances, could have performed the mount procedure.

Based on the time stamp of the mv operation, a careful investigation of the root account actions reveals a key command execution, derived from the 'psinfo' table:

mysql> select * from psinfo where pid='27865' AND cyear='2011' AND cday='4' AND cmonth='1' AND chour='15' AND cmin >= '20' AND cmin <='33' \G
*************************** 1. row ***************************
psentity: 97654
md5sum: 7067284f2e1aefc430339ef091b4e41b
username: root
pid: 27865
ppid: 26407
pcpu: 0.0
pmem: 0.0
command: su
arguments: - engineer3
cyear: 2011
cmonth: 1
cday: 4
cmin: 28
chour: 15

csec: 36
dyear: 2011
dmonth: 1
dday: 4
dhour: 15
dmin: 28
dsec: 39

The 'su' command is used routinely by administrators to switch user credentials, in order to test environment settings and perform system tasks (Garfinkel et al, 1996). However, it can be easily used as a masquerading tool to covertly perform actions using the credentials of somebody else. A further investigation also found the USB key on the desk of the IT administrator with the RGX9.jpg file. The hwinfo table device identifier data ('devstring', 'devvendor') as well as the mount point identifier (/media/U3SAN03-12) from the psinfo commands contributed towards strengthening the final piece of the puzzle.

This case shows the versatility of the relational structure of the LUARM record that showed the way from simple file operation to related program execution and other events that can provide strong evidence and lead to the misuser. In addition, LUARM has also been used successfully to provide evidence about security incidents of external origin (Magklaras, 2011). Thus, it offers a valuable complement of existing logging mechanisms.

7. Conclusions

A very important tool to mitigate Insider IT misuse is an audit record which is specifically designed to address its various needs, as well as complement existing forensic tools when security specialists perform a post-mortem incident examination. LUARM is an audit engine that provides a detailed log of user actions at file, process execution and network endpoint level stored in a Relational Database Management System. Its file, process and network endpoint data provide a dynamic forensic view of the system, a useful complement to existing forensic tools that offer only static data in their majority. The relational storage layer increases the correlation versatility amongst the different types of audit data, as it is vital to be able to perform various associations during the investigation of an incident (process to file, process to network activity) and reliably relate actions to user entities.

The results are promising, showing a much better way to examine a system than looking at static text files which are difficult to parse and even more difficult to correlate. However, LUARM is a work in progress. It has its deficiencies and needs many improvements, in order to become a production real-world audit engine for insider misuse.

The first issue that was identified relates to the sampling frequency of user processes execution. After examining carefully the consistency of audit logs, it became evident that LUARM was losing process execution data. A fault was located at the process execution monitoring module. Due to the way the sampling loop was written in that module, the effective sampling frequency could exceed by far the desired 100 millisecond sampling frequency. As a result, LUARM would miss processes that executed by various users in the system. The module was re-written using an entirely different process execution sampling philosophy. A Linux kernel technique called 'execve wrapping' was employed by adopting the Snoopy logger open source software (Snoopylogger portal, 2000). A modified 'execve wrapper' logger like 'Snoopy' logger provides a way to log the process execution and its arguments without relying on a sampling loop and is thus a more efficient interface to capture live process execution data. This solved the problem of losing process execution data due to a slow sampling rate and thus corrected an important deficiency of LUARM.

Addressing the issue of user privacy is not so straightforward. There is always a tension between insider IT misuse monitoring and privacy. LUARM needs to retain and collect data about a user's behavior, in order to help the analyst infer IT misuse. In direct contrast, privacy dictates the right of individuals to define whether somebody will collect data about their online actions and the extent or way the data can be used. The best compromise between these two opposing needs is to control the amount and type of logged data. This can be achieved by pseudo-anonymizing certain parts of the audit record, in order to protect certain aspects of the user privacy but still be able to infer IT misuse reliably. The term 'Privacy-Respecting Intrusion Detection' (Flegel, 2007), encompasses all the efforts of achieving a good compromise between the need to monitor and the need to respect user privacy.

The achievement of the LUARM prototype has been to demonstrate that structured evidence based logging for IT misuse is feasible. The authors welcome feedback and participation to the development of its code base. The prototype is not yet ready for production deployment, but it should be suitable for experimentation and has already proved its value on a number of insider IT misuse incidents.

8. Acknowledgements

The authors wish to thanks the University of Oslo IT engineers Harald Dahle, Jean Lorentzen and Melaku Tadesse for helping with the simulation of various misuse scenarios.

9. References

Adelstein F. (2006), "Live Forensics: Diagnosing Your System without Killing it First", Comm. ACM, vol.49, no.2, 2006, pp. 63-66.

Bace R. (2000), "Intrusion Detection", Macmillan Technical Publishing, Indianapolis, USA, ISBN: 1-578701856, pp. 38-39 discuss the terms 'misuse detection' and 'anomaly detection' in an intrusion specification context, pp. 47-66 discuss various audit record issues.

Barr D. (1996), "Common DNS Operational and Configuration Errors", Internet Engineering Task Force (IETF) Request For Comment (RFC) 1537, February 1996.

Bauer M. (2003), "Building secure servers with Linux", O'Reilly & Associates, ISBN: 0-596-00217-3: Chapter 6, pp. 154-196.

Cha A.E. (2008), "Even spies embrace China's free market.", WashingtonPost,February15,2008,www.washingtonpost.com/wpdyn/content/article/2008/02/14/AR2008021403550.html (Accessed 03 March 2011)

Common Criterial Portal (2009), "The Common Criteria for Information Technology Security Evaluation", Version 3.1, Revision 3, July 2009. Part 2: Functional security components,www.commoncriteriaportal.org/files/ccfiles/CCPART1V3.1R3.pdf (Accessed 03 March 2011)

CPAN-DBI (2010), "The Perl Database Interface (DBI) module" at the Comprehensive Perl Archive Network (CPAN),search.cpan.org/~timb/DBI-1.615/DBI.pm (Accessed 03 March 2011)

CPAN-HiRes (2010), "The Perl High Resolution Timer module" at the Comprehensive Perl Archive Network (CPAN),search.cpan.org/~jhi/Time-HiRes-1.9721/HiRes.pm (Accessed 03 March 2011)

DOD 5200.28-std (1985), "Department of Defense Trusted Computer System Evaluation Criteria", National Computer Security Center: Orange Book, DOD 5200.28-std, December 1985.

Flegel U. (2007), "Privacy-Respecting Intrusion Detection", Advances in Information Security, Springer, ISBN: 978-0-0387-34346-4 .

Furnell S. (2004), "Enemies within: the problem of insider attacks", Computer Fraud and Security, Volume 2004 Issue 7, pp. 6-11.

Garfinkel S, Spafford G. (1996), "Practical UNIX and Internet Security", Second Edition, O'Reilly and Associates, Sebastopol, CA, ISBN: 1-56592-148-1

Gerhards R. (2009), "The Syslog Protocol", Internet Engineering Task Force (IETF), Request for Comment (RFC) 5424, March 2009.

Hay B., Nance K., Bishop M. (2009), "Live Analysis Progress and Challenges", IEEE Security & Privacy, Volume 7, Number 2, pp. 30-37.

HP Portal (2003), "psacct process accounting misses some commands", HP IT ,forums11.itrc.hp.com/service/forums/questionanswer.doadmit=109447626+1286381845785+28353475&threadId=1413576 (Accessed 02 February 2011)

LUARM portal (2010),luarm.sourceforge.net/ (Accessed 03 March 2011)

Snoopylogger (2000), http://sourceforge.net/projects/snoopylogger/ (Accessed 04 May 2011)

Magklaras G., Furnell S., Brooke P. (2006), "Towards an Insider Threat Prediction Specification Language", Information Management & Computer Security, (2006) vol. 14, no. 4, pp. 361-381.

Magklaras G. (2011), "Catching an undesired guest in the penguin /tmp room", Epistolatory Blogspot, epistolatory.blogspot.com/2011/02/catching-undesired-guest-in-penguin-tmp.html (Accessed 03 March 2011)

Meier M. (2004), "A Model for the Semantics of Attack Signatures in Misuse Detection Systems", K. Zhang and Y. Zheng (Eds.): ISC 2004, Springer-Verlag Berlin, Heidelberg, LNCS 3225, pp. 158–169.

Mills D., Delaware U., Martin J., Burbank J., Kasch W. (2010), "Network Time Protocol Version 4: Protocol and Algorithms Specification", Internet Engineering Task Force (IETF) Request For Comment (RFC) 5905, June 2010.

Mockapetris P. (1987), "Domain Names – Implementation and Specification", Internet Engineering Task Force (IETF) RFC 1035, November 1987.

Monitorware (2009), www.winsyslog.com/en/product/ (Accessed 03 March 2011)

NSTISSAM (1999), "The Insider Threat To US Government Information Systems", U.S. National Security Telecommunications And Information Systems Security Committee, NSTISSAM INFOSEC /1-99.

Oracle Corporation (2010), "System Administration Guide:Security Services", Solaris 10 Operating System, Part No: 816–4557–19 , September 2010, pp. 559-672,dlc.sun.com/pdf/816-4557/816-4557.pdf, (Accessed 03 March 2011)

Oracle MySQL portal (2010), www.mysql.com (Accessed 03 March 2011)

Pogue C., Altheide C., Haverkos T. (2008), "Unix and Linux Forensic Analysis DVD Toolkit", Syngress, 2008, ISBN: 978-1-59749-269-0.

Probst C., Hunker J., Bishop M., Gollman D. (2009), "Countering Insider Threats", ENISA Quarterly Review Vol. 5, No. 2, June 2009, pp. 13-14.

Psacct utilities (2003), Utilities for process activity monitoring, linux.maruhn.com/sec/psacct.html (Accessed 03 March 2011)

Rivest R. (1992), "The MD5 Message-Digest algorithm", Internet Engineering Task Force (IETF) Request For Comment (RFC) 1321, April 1992.

RLIKE RegExp (2008), "String Regular Expression Operator", MySQL 5.1 Manual, Oracle Corporation,dev.mysql.com/doc/refman/5.1/en/regexp.html (Accessed 03 March /2011)

Trusted BSD Project portal (2009), "OpenBSM: Open Source Basic Security Module (BSM) Audit Implementation",www.trustedbsd.org/openbsm.html (Accessed 03 Match 2011)

Issues on Selecting Image Features for Robust Source Camera Identification

Y. Hu[1,2], C-T. Li[1], C. Zhou[3] and X. Lin[2]

[1]Department of Computer Science, University of Warwick,
Coventry CV4 7AL, UK
[2]School of Electronic and Information Engineering,
[3]College of Automation Science and Engineering,
South China University of Technology, Guangzhou 510641, China
e-mail: Yongjian.Hu@dcs.warwick.ac.uk; eeyjhu@scut.edu.cn;
c-t.li@warwick.ac.uk

Abstract

Image feature selection is an important issue for source camera identification. Well-selected features should make camera classifiers accurate, efficient as well as robust. Current source camera identification schemes select image features mainly based on classification accuracy and computational efficiency. In this work, we demonstrate that robustness should also be considered for classifiers which aim at real-world tasks. Besides, we reveal what impact the reduced feature subset will have on the robustness of camera classifiers. The dimensionality reduction is often necessary for computational efficiency.

Keywords

Image Forensics, Camera Identification, Image Feature Selection, Robustness, Dimensionality Reduction

1. Introduction

Statistical image features are important clues for uncovering image origin and tracing back source imaging devices. Most statistical image features employed for these purposes were investigated in steganalysis, for example, the statistics of wavelet-like decomposition of natural images and the statistics of prediction errors of wavelet coefficient magnitude (Farid and Lyu, 2002), and the image quality metrics (IQMs) (Avcibas et al., 2003). These statistics and their variants are easily found in previous image forensic studies such as (Kharrazi et al., 2004), (Tsai et al., 2006), (Gou et al., 2009), (Khanna et al., 2009), (Filler et al., 2008), (Tsai et al., 2007), and (Tsai et al., 2008). Usually, specific statistical features related to camera and/or scanner pipelines, e.g., CFA (colour filter array) configuration (Kharrazi et al., 2004), (Tsai et al., 2006), demosaicing algorithms (Gallagher and Chen, 2008), (Cao and Kot, 2009), colour processing/transformation, and the photo response non-uniformity noise (PRNU) (Filler et al., 2008) are used along with steganalysis features. Although there are many similarities in technique between steganalysis and source camera/scanner identification, their difference is fundamental. For the former, we can assume that a stego image has not been changed since the hidden message is embedded. Such an assumption is reasonable; otherwise the hidden message may not be losslessly extracted). For the latter, however, this assumption is often not feasible. In practice, we often have little knowledge about the image in question. A test image may have undergone some image processing and thus becomes a processed one, or it may remain unchanged since it is generated by cameras or scanners so that it keeps an unprocessed one. Consequently, the statistical image features associated with the purpose of forensic investigation should ideally remain unchanged or practically change very little for a test image which has undergone some innocuous image processing.

Since in general, existing camera/scanner identification methods are deemed quite reliable in laboratory tests, one might be tempted to apply them in practice as well. However, little is known about the robustness of forensic algorithms (Gloe et al., 2007). In this work, we use a variant algorithm of (Kharrazi et al., 2004) and (Tsai et al., 2006) as an example to investigate the robustness of camera classifiers as well as the impact the reduced subset of features has on the robustness.

The rest of the paper is organized as follows. In Section 2, we construct our sample camera classifier and evaluate its performance on ten different cameras. In Section 3, we evaluate the performance of our classifier on images under three common image manipulations. In Section 4, we first adopt a classical feature selection algorithm in pattern recognition to search for a suboptimal subset of features, and then evaluate the performance of the camera classifier on unprocessed and processed images, respectively. We will conclude our work in Section 5.

2. A Sample Camera Classifier and its Performance

2.1. Construction of Feature Vector

In (Kharrazi et al., 2004), Kharrazi et al. proposed a prototype of camera classifier based on the statistical image features derived from steganalysis as well as the statistical features related to camera pipelines. That method was re-implemented by Tsai and Wu on different camera models (Tsai et al., 2006). Their feature vector consists of three types of image features: 9 wavelet features, 12 colour features and 12 image quality metrics (IQMs). The wavelet features consist of the mean of high-frequency subband coefficients in each orientation and at one scale. The colour features consist of the average value of each colour band, the correlation pair between two different colour bands, the neighbour distribution centre of mass for each colour band, and three energy ratios. The IQMs features are directly borrowed from (Avcibas, 2001) and consist of three pixel difference-based features, i.e., Minkowski difference, the mean absolute error, and the mean square error; three correlation-based features, i.e., the structural content, the normalized cross correlation, and Czekonowski correlation; six spectral features, i.e., the spectral magnitude error, the spectral phase error, the spectral phase-magnitude error, the block spectral magnitude error, the block spectral phase error, and the block spectral phase-magnitude error. The reader is referred to (Kharrazi et al., 2004), (Tsai et al., 2006) and (Avcibas, 2001) for more detailed information about the IQMs.

In this work, we propose a variant algorithm of (Kharrazi et al., 2004) and (Tsai et al., 2006) as our sample camera classifier. We adopt all the 33 features in (Tsai et al., 2006). Besides, we add the standard deviation (STD), skewness and kurtosis of high-frequency subband coefficients in each orientation and at one scale in order to more comprehensively reflect the characteristics of wavelet coefficients. As a result, we have $3\times3\times4=36$ wavelet features, which form our Feature Set I. The colour features and IQMs listed in (Tsai et al., 2006) form our Feature Sets II and III, respectively. By combining Feature Sets I, II and III, we generate a new feature vector of 60 dimensions, which is used as the input of our camera classifier. Like (Kharrazi et al., 2004) and (Tsai et al., 2006), we adopt the LIBSVM toolbox (Chang and Lin, 2001) with a nonlinear RBF (Radial Basis Function) kernel to build our camera classifier.

2.2. Performance of Our Sample Classifier on Unprocessed Images

Ten cameras employed in our test are five Canon cameras: A40, A620-1, A620-2, A720, 450D; two Nikon cameras: L3-1, L3-2; two Sony cameras: DSC-T10, DSC-W90; one Olympus camera: U820. For simplicity, we represent the above ten cameras as $X1$, $X2$, $X3$, $X4$, $X5$, $X6$, $X7$, $X8$, $X9$, and $X10$ in sequence. To evaluate the capability of these image features in identifying individual cameras, we purposely use two Canon A620 cameras and two Nikon L3 cameras. Exactly, the photos taken by $X3$ and $X7$ are not what we captured ourselves but downloaded from the well-known free photo website: http://www.flickr.com/. Each camera takes 300 photos of natural scenes including buildings, trees, blue sky and clouds, streets and people. All the photos are saved in JPEG format at the highest resolution each camera can support. To facilitate fair comparison, we take a 1024×1024 test image block from each photo. Based on the previous analysis (Li, 2010), each test image is cut from the centre of a photo to avoid saturated image regions. This selection strategy makes the test image better reflect the original image content. For each camera, we randomly choose 150 images to form the training set while the rest 150 images form the test set. Experimental results are shown in the form of confusion matrix, where the first column and the first row are the test camera index and the predicted camera index, respectively. To prevent obscuring significant statistics, a classification rate below 3% is simply denoted as∗ in the tables.

	X1	X2	X3	X4	X5	X6	X7	X8	X9	X10
X1	96	*	*	*	*	*	*	*	*	*
X2	3	96	*	*	*	*	*	*	*	*
X3	*	*	87	7	*	*	*	*	*	*
X4	*	*	*	96	*	3	*	*	*	*
X5	*	*	*	*	96	*	3	*	*	*
X6	*	*	*	*	*	95	*	*	*	*
X7	5	3	*	*	15	7	63	*	*	*
X8	*	*	*	*	*	*	*	99	*	*
X9	*	*	*	*	*	*	*	*	95	*
X10	*	*	*	*	*	*	3	*	*	91

Table 1: Confusion matrix for our sample classifier using all the three feature sets. Accuracy = 91% (1370/1500)

From Table 1, our classifier achieves the average classification accuracy of 91%. It demonstrates that our sample camera classifier is very effective in classifying unprocessed images. As for X3 and X7, the correct rates are 87% and 63%, respectively. We owe the decline in accuracy to different image content. As mentioned before, the photos from X3 and X7 are downloaded from a free photo website. So we are unable to know whether the photos have been altered or not. The only thing we can observe is that the image content from X3 consists of artificial products with various textile patterns and those images looks bright, while the image content from X7 mainly consists of indoors scenes and those images looks dark. In contrast, the content of our photos mainly consists of natural scenes with middle intensity. Our detection results coincide with the observation that identification rate is affected by image content (Tsai et al., 2007), (Li, 2010).

	X1	X2	X3	X4	X5	X6	X7	X8	X9	X10
X1	95	*	*	*	*	*	*	*	*	*
X2	*	97	*	*	*	*	*	*	*	*
X3	*	*	83	7	*	*	7	*	*	*
X4	*	*	*	91	*	6	*	*	*	*
X5	*	*	*	*	94	*	*	*	*	*
X6	*	*	*	*	*	95	*	*	*	*
X7	*	*	*	*	5	3	87	*	*	*
X8	*	3	*	*	*	*	*	97	*	*
X9	5	*	*	*	*	*	*	*	91	*
X10	*	*	*	*	*	*	6	*	*	93

Table 2: Confusion matrix for our sample classifier using Feature Set I. Accuracy = 92% (1382/1500)

	X1	X2	X3	X4	X5	X6	X7	X8	X9	X10
X1	64	*	*	*	6	8	*	*	9	7
X2	20	40	*	*	13	9	*	3	8	5
X3	*	*	81	3	*	7	*	*	*	3
X4	7	17	*	45	4	9	*	5	*	9
X5	4	7	*	5	38	17	*	3	12	9
X6	15	6	*	12	11	43	*	3	6	*
X7	6	9	13	7	7	*	43	*	9	4
X8	3	11	*	7	24	15	*	29	*	5
X9	9	10	7	9	13	13	*	3	35	*
X10	*	5	*	9	4	12	*	10	5	51

Table 3: Confusion matrix for our sample classifier using Feature Set II.
Accuracy = 47% (702/1500)

We further investigate the performance of each individual feature set. Table 2 indicates that the average accuracy is 92% when only Feature Set I is used. So wavelet features have better identification power than the combined effect of all the three feature sets. In other words, even without Feature Sets II and III, this camera classifier can still achieve satisfactory accuracy for these ten cameras. On the other hand, Table 3 shows that the colour features lead to the average accuracy of 47% while Table 4 shows that the IQMs have the average accuracy of 66%. Apparently, both Feature Sets II and III are not as effective as Feature Set I. In terms of computational complexity, these two feature sets are redundant in this case.

	X1	X2	X3	X4	X5	X6	X7	X8	X9	X10
X1	77	7	*	11	*	*	*	*	*	*
X2	20	61	*	9	*	*	*	*	*	*
X3	*	*	81	11	*	*	*	*	*	*
X4	11	13	6	58	*	5	*	*	*	*
X5	5	*	*	*	88	*	5	*	*	*
X6	4	5	*	*	4	70	*	4	10	*
X7	*	7	*	7	12	*	52	5	4	7
X8	*	4	4	5	5	*	17	56	3	*
X9	*	4	*	*	6	11	17	13	45	*
X10	*	*	*	4	3	*	11	9	*	69

Table 4: Confusion matrix for our sample classifier using Feature Set III.
Accuracy = 66% (987/1500)

3. Robustness of Our Sample Classifier

Incidental image processing is usually not a malicious attack but a feasible way for saving storage space or emphasizing image regions of interest. Camera identifiers should have the capability in tackling images that have undergone invisible image manipulations. We evaluate the robustness of our classifier under three common image manipulations: JPEG compression, image contrast stretching and image sharpening. Each test image has undergone only one manipulation under each test. We do not consider the combined effect of different manipulations to avoid making our analysis biased. As will be seen, colour features, which have mediocre performance for unprocessed/untouched images, outperform both wavelet features and IQMs for processed images.

3.1. Experimental Results under Compression

We take JPEG compression using MATLAB with quality factor 70. The image quality under that level is often acceptable for saving storage space. Table 5 indicates that the average accuracy is 36%. Compared with Table 1, the performance of the classifier greatly decreases. We further investigate the performance of each individual feature set. From Feature Sets I to III, the corresponding correct identification rates are 21%, 46% and 31%, respectively. Apparently, the performance of every feature set degrades. Feature Set I has the sharpest decline in performance. However, the behaviour of Feature Set II is a little surprising. It leads to the average accuracy of 46%. Compared with the accuracy before compression (47%), there is only a slight decline. This result implies that compression has a small impact on Feature Set II. This is because the colour features do not have much relation to the image details which the JPEG compression often discards. So we can say that colour features are more robust than the wavelet features and the IQMs for compressed images.

	X1	X2	X3	X4	X5	X6	X7	X8	X9	X10
X1	89	*	*	*	*	*	7	*	*	*
X2	68	11	*	*	*	*	17	*	*	*
X3	41	5	25	*	*	4	19	*	*	*
X4	30	*	*	*	4	*	47	*	*	14
X5	*	*	*	*	81	*	17	*	*	*
X6	48	*	*	*	3	13	29	*	*	6
X7	15	*	*	*	10	*	72	*	*	*
X8	22	*	*	*	39	*	36	*	*	*
X9	29	*	*	*	26	7	34	*	*	*
X10	26	*	*	*	3	*	7	*	*	63

Table 5. Confusion matrix for our sample classifier using all the three feature sets under compression. Accuracy = 36% (534/1500)

	X1	X2	X3	X4	X5	X6	X7	X8	X9	X10
X1	94	*	3	*	*	*	*	*	*	*
X2	10	86	3	*	*	*	*	*	*	*
X3	*	*	88	7	*	*	*	*	*	*
X4	*	*	*	97	*	*	*	*	*	*
X5	*	*	*	*	89	*	5	*	*	*
X6	*	*	4	7	*	89	*	*	*	*
X7	5	3	7	*	17	4	54	*	*	5
X8	*	*	*	*	*	*	*	97	*	*
X9	*	*	*	*	*	*	*	*	89	*
X10	*	*	*	5	*	*	4	*	*	87

Table 6. Confusion matrix for our sample classifier using all the three feature sets under contrast stretching. Accuracy = 87% (1305/1500)

3.2. Experimental Results under Contrast Stretching

Contrast stretching is a common image processing operation when people want to emphasise image content within an interval of image grey levels. To simulate the process of suppressing some grey-level pixels while emphasising others, we stretch pixel values on each test image with the following contrast stretching function

$$f(x) = \begin{cases} 0, & 0 \leq x \leq 20 \\ \frac{255}{210}(x-20), & 20 < x < 230 \\ 255, & 230 \leq x \leq 255 \end{cases} \quad (1)$$

According to Table 6, the average accuracy of the sample classifier is 87%. So the average accuracy of our sample classifier only decreases by 4 percentage points compared with Table 1. From Feature Sets I to III, the corresponding correct identification rates are 90%, 42% and 46%, respectively. Feature Set I only has a slight decline in performance compared with Table 2, but Feature III loses almost 20 percentage points in accuracy. Therefore, the wavelet features are quite robust against contrast stretching while the IQMs do not behave well in this circumstance. In essence, contrast stretching directly changes the shape of the histogram of pixel values and it has little influence on the high frequency wavelet coefficients, so the good performance of Feature Set I is understandable.

	X1	X2	X3	X4	X5	X6	X7	X8	X9	X10
X1	*	*	97	*	*	*	*	*	*	*
X2	5	*	95	*	*	*	*	*	*	*
X3	*	*	100	*	*	*	*	*	*	*
X4	*	*	99	*	*	*	*	*	*	*
X5	*	*	84	16	*	*	*	*	*	*
X6	*	*	100	*	*	*	*	*	*	*
X7	3	*	65	20	*	6	4	*	*	*
X8	75	*	15	*	*	*	*	9	*	*
X9	*	*	91	*	*	*	*	*	7	*
X10	*	*	99	*	*	*	*	*	*	*

Table 7: Confusion matrix for our sample classifier using all the three feature sets under sharpening. Accuracy = 12% (186/1500)

3.3. Experimental Results under Image Sharpening

Image sharpening is often used for enhancing object edges. In our simulation, a weighted median filtering-based sharpening algorithm is used with the recommended parameter (Bovik, 2006). Table 7 shows the average accuracy is 12%. Apparently, image sharpening has the greatest impact on our sample classifier. From Feature Sets I to III, the corresponding correct identification rates are 11%, 43% and 12%, respectively. It means that using the wavelet features or the IQMs can hardly identify cameras correctly. By contrast, the use of the colour features only loses 4 percentage points in accuracy compared with Table 3. Therefore, the colour features are robust against image sharpening. In fact, image sharpening often equally alters pixels on red, blue and green bands, so the selected colour features are not very sensitive.

4. Dimensionality Reduction and its Impact on Robustness

Feature selection is one of the important problems in pattern recognition. There are many reasons for reducing the number of features, for instance, computational complexity. The problem in Feature Selection (FS) can be stated as the search for a sufficiently reduced subset of, say, d features out of the total number of available ones, D, without significantly degrading (or even improving in some cases) the performance of the resulting classifier when using either set of features (Ferri et al., 1994). Some FS algorithms have been introduced to optimize camera classifiers. Tsai and Wang once used the SFFS (Sequential Floating Forward Selection) algorithm (Pudil et al., 1994) as an adaptive feature selection tool to find a suboptimal subset of features which was supposed to improve the classification precision of their SVM-based camera classifier (Tsai et al., 2008). The top 20 important features were selected from 34 features employed in (Kharrazi et al., 2004). In this work, we use the SFFS algorithm to select a subset from our 60 features, but our focus is to investigate the effect of this reduced subset on the robustness of the camera classifier. As will be seen, the SFFS algorithm is able to find a suboptimal subset which enables our sample classifier to achieve almost the same average identification accuracy as the original 60 features. However, the selected feature subset has no way to guarantee the robustness. In fact, feature selection algorithms such as SFFS aim at efficient pattern classification and the criterion functions in SFFS are defined on the basis of classification accuracy.

4.1. SFFS and the Criterion Function

The Sequential Forward Selection (SFS) and its backward counterpart (SBS) are suboptimal methods. Both of them suffer from the so-called "nesting effect". Attempts to prevent the nesting of feature subsets led to the development of the plus l - take away r method. The plus l - take away r method or called (l, r) method, consists of applying SFS during l steps followed by r steps of SBS with the cycle of forward and backward selection until the required number of features is reached. However, it is not easy to find the best parameters l and r. The improved version of (l, r) method is the SFFS algorithm, which consists of applying after each forward step a number of backward steps as long as the corresponding subsets are better than the previously evaluated ones at that level (Ferri et al., 1994).

The criterion function determines which feature should be included in and which should be excluded from the subset in the SFFS. Two popular class separability criteria are divergence and scatter matrices. Computation of divergence is not easy for non-Gaussian distribution. Hence, this work uses the criterion function defined on the basis of scatter matrices. Suppose S_w, S_b and S_m are Within-class scatter matrix, Between-class scatter matrix and Total mixture matrix, respectively. Our criterion function is defined as $J = |S_m|/|S_w|$, where $|.|$ represents determinant. The reader is referred to (Theodoridis, 2006) for more information about its calculation.

4.2. Performance of the Reduced Feature Subset

After performing the SFFS, 26 features are selected from the original 60 ones to form our new feature vector. They are 15 wavelet features (i.e., 7 coefficient averages, 5 STD, 2 skewness values and 1 kurtosis value), 6 colour features (i.e., 2 average values, 2 correlation pairs and 2 energy ratios) and 5 IQMs (i.e., 3 pixel difference-based features and 2 spectral features).

We use these 26 features to repeat our experiments in Subsection 2.2 and Section 3. For unprocessed images, the camera classifier has the average classification accuracy of 90%. Compared with Table 1, the reduced subset achieves very close identification accuracy as the original 60 features. Next we evaluate its performance under three image manipulations. For compressed images, the reduced subset leads to the average accuracy of 29%. Compared with Table 5, it loses 7 percentage points in accuracy. For contrast stretched images, the average accuracy is 86%. Compared with Table 6, it loses only 1 percentage point in accuracy. As for image sharpening, these 26 features have the same identification power (i.e., 12%) as the original 60 features. From the above experiments, we can observe that the performance of these

26 features is very close to that of the original 60 features when test images are not subject to image processing; for processed images; however, the reduced subset may cause the classifier to lose robustness to some extent.

5. Conclusions

Image feature selection is an important issue for feature-based camera classifiers. Although different statistical image features have been proposed for camera identification, their robustness has not been thoroughly discussed; moreover, the robustness of the reduced subset of features has seldom been discussed. In this work, we have used a variant of a classical camera classifier as an example to investigate these two aspects. Our experiments have revealed that different statistical image features have different robustness against image manipulations and the reduced subset of features usually does not have the same robustness as the original feature vector. Our work also indicates that the selection of an accurate, efficient and robust reduced subset of image features is a difficult issue since we can not predict which features will be selected by common SF algorithms. This topic is significant for the design of practical camera classifiers and needs further study.

6. Acknowledgement

This work is partially supported by the EU FP7 Digital Image and Video Forensics project (Grant Agreement No. 251677, Acronym: DIVeFor) and NSF of China 60772115.

7. References

Avcibas, I. (2001), Image Quality Statistics and their Use in Steganalysis and Compression. Ph.D. Thesis, Bogazici University, Turkey, 2001.

Avcibas, I., Memon, N. and Sankur, B. (2003), "Steganalysis Using Image Quality Metrics", *IEEE Transaction on Image Processing*, Volume 12, Number 2, January 2003, pp. 221-229.

Bovik, A.C. (2006), Handbook of Image and Video Processing (Communications, Networking and Multimedia). Academic Press, Orlando, FL. 2006.

Chang C.-C. and Lin, C.-J. (2001), LIBSVM: A Library for Support Vector Machines 2001. http://www.csie.ntu.edu.tw/cjlin/libsvm

Cao H. and Kot, A.C. (2009), "Accurate Detection of Demosaicing Regularity for Digital Image Forensics", *IEEE Transactions on Information Forensics and Security*, Volume 4, Number 4, December 2009, pp. 899-910.

Farid, H. and Lyu, S. (2002), "Detecting Hidden Messages Using Higher-Order Statistics and Support Vector Machines", *Proceedings of 5th International Workshop on Information Hiding*, Springer-Verlag, Berlin, Heidelberg, Volume 2578, 2002, pp. 340-354.

Ferri, F.J., Pudil, P., Hatef, M. and Kittler, J. (1994), "Comparative Study of Techniques for Large-Scale Feature Selection", *Pattern Recognition* in Practice IV. Elsevier, Amsterdam, 1994, pp. 403-413.

Filler, T., Fridrich, J. and Goljan, M. (2008), "Using Sensor Pattern Noise for Camera Model Identification", *Proceedings of IEEE International Conference on Image Processing*, 2008, pp. 1296-1299.

Gallagher A. and Chen, T. (2008), "Image Authentication by Detecting Traces of Demosaicing", *Proceedings of IEEE International Conference on Computer Vision and Pattern Recognition*, Alaska, US, 2008, pp. 1-8.

Gloe, T., Kirchner, M., Winkler, P. and Bohme, R. (2007), "Can We Trust Digital Image Forensics", *Proceedings of the 15th ACM International Conference on Multimedia*, September 23-28, 2007, pp.78-86.

Gou, H., Swaminathan, A. and Wu, M. (2009), "Intrinsic Sensor Noise Features for Forensic Analysis on Scanners and Scanned Images", *IEEE Transactions on Information Forensics and Security*, Volume 4, Number 3, September 2009, pp. 476-491.

Kharrazi, M., Sencar, H.T. and Memon, N. (2004), "Blind Source Camera Identification", *Proceedings of IEEE International Conference on Image Processing*, Singapore, October 24-27, 2004, pp. 709-712.

Khanna, N., Mikkilineni, A.K. and Delp, E.J. (2009), "Scanner Identification Using Feature-based Processing and Analysis", *IEEE Transactions on Information Forensics and Security*, Volume 4, Number 1, March 2009, pp. 123-139.

Li, C.-T. (2010), "Source Camera Identification Using Enhanced Sensor Pattern Noise", *IEEE Transactions on Information Forensics and Security*, Volume 5, Number 2, June 2010, pp. 280-287.

Pudil, P., Novovicova, J. and Kittler, J. (1994), "Floating Search Methods in Feature Selection", Pattern Recognition Letters, Volume 15, Number 11, 1994, pp. 1119-1125.

Tsai, M.-J. and Wu, G.-H. (2006), "Using Image Features to Identify Camera Sources", *Proceedings of IEEE International Conference on Acoustics, Speech and Signal Processing*, Volume 2, 2006.

Tsai, M.-J., Lai, C.-L. and Liu, J. (2007), "Camera/Mobile Phone Source Identification for Digital Forensics", *Proceedings of IEEE International Conference on Acoustics, Speech and Signal Processing*, 2007, pp. 221-224.

Tsai M.-J. and Wang, C.-S (2008), "Adaptive Feature Selection for Digital Camera Source Identification", *Proceedings of IEEE International Symposium on Circuits and Systems*, May 2008.

Theodoridis S. and Koutroumbas, K. (2006), Pattern Recognition (Third Edition). Academic Press, London, 2006.

A Social Network Discovery Model for Digital Forensics Investigations

A. Karran[1], J. Haggerty[2], D. Lamb[1], M. Taylor[1] and D. Llewellyn-Jones[2]

[1]School of Computing and Mathematical Sciences, Liverpool John Moores University, James Parsons Building, Liverpool L3 3AF
[2]School of Computing, Science and Engineering, University of Salford, Newton Building, Manchester, M5 4WT
e-mail: A.J.Karran@ljmu.ac.uk; J.Haggerty@salford.ac.uk; D.J.Lamb@ljmu.ac.uk; M.J.Taylor@ljmu.ac.uk; D.Llewellyn-Jones@ljmu.ac.uk

Abstract

Our continued reliance on email communications ensures that this type of data remains a major source of evidence during a digital investigation. Due to the many applications and data types, there is no standard email format. Therefore, much current work in the forensic investigation of emails has focused on data extraction. This paper focuses on the investigatory process and posits a model for social network discovery for use in digital investigations. This model is applied to the widely used Enron email corpus to demonstrate its applicability.

Keywords

Digital forensics; social network analysis; visualisation

1. Introduction

With our reliance on email as a communications medium, particularly within the workplace, it is likely to continue to feature as a major resource of evidence during a digital investigation. The identification of both tangible and intangible evidence from large volumes of data is a major challenge for digital investigations involving emails. Social network analysis and visualisation techniques can significantly contribute to evidence discovery and collection by identifying and understanding relationships and data flow between actors and events within the email network.

Digital forensics investigatory models do not currently differentiate between email and any other data. However, intangible evidence such as relationship data is a defining feature of social networks (Wasserman & Faust, 1994) and may provide information pertinent to an investigation. Much work on digital investigations involving email data focus on techniques for the extraction of evidence, for example by focusing on data mining (Wei *et al*, 2008) or clustering algorithms (Bird *et al*, 2006). Recently there has been some focus on process models for investigations that involve email data. These approaches generally provide a theoretical framework or software application (Debbabi *et al*, 2009), which details a process or methodology for the visualisation and extraction of specific email artefacts or features. However, these approaches focus on particular aspects of email data rather than the process itself.

This paper therefore presents a model for social network discovery through email data and is organised as follows. Section 2 presents related work. Section 3 posits the model for social network discovery for investigations involving emails. Section 4 presents a case study and results of applying the approach to the Enron email data set. Finally, we make our conclusions and suggest future work.

2. Related Work

Social network analysis was first formalised as a scientific field by Moreno in the 1930s (Moreno, 1951). It has since become a widely used method of mapping and understanding social structures, adopted in many fields to investigate the underlying structure of interactions and relationships between actors. It can therefore be used to highlight the significance of members within communities. Social network analysis tools and techniques have been used in a wide range of inter-disciplinary studies. For example, this approach has been used to map local communities (Hawe, 2008), highlight voting patterns and regional political affiliations (Faust, 1997), uncloak terrorist networks (Krebs, 2002) and map parts of the Internet in terms of social communities (Cocciolo *et al*, 2007).

Recently, social network analysis has been proposed as an aid for digital investigations. For example, Haggerty *et al* (2009) proposed the Email Extraction Tool (EET) for the extraction and visualisation of email data resident in files on the hard drive. Dellutri *et al* (2009) focus on the identification of social networks through data on smartphones and Web information. This approach aims to reconstruct a user's profile by combining the smartphone's data with social relationships found on the Internet. Wiil *et al* (2010) provide an analysis of the 9/11 hijackers' network and focus on the relationships between actors. This study uses a number of measures associated with social network analysis to identify key nodes. However, these approaches have in common that they focus on the details of extracting and identifying data within specific environments to identify the social network rather than developing the procedures surrounding this activity.

The Enron email data set contains data from about 150 users, predominantly senior management at the company (Cohen, 2010). The data set provides real data that can be used as a test bed in a number of ways. For example, Lin (2010) uses this data set to demonstrate the applicability of their approach in predicting sensitive relationships identified in email communications. Alternatively, Zhou *et al* (2010) use this data set for text analysis which employs a wide variety of statistical techniques to identify value profiles of Enron employees. Alternatively, Collingsworth *et al* (2009) use network analysis of this data set to assess organisational stability. Therefore, this data set provides a means by which the social network discovery model may be tested.

3. A Model for Email Investigation

This section presents a new process model for use in digital forensics investigations of email data. In particular, this model focuses on incorporating social network analysis techniques into digital forensics investigations to elucidate intangible data, i.e. relational information.

Figure 1 illustrates the processes involved in a digital forensics investigation of email data. These processes do not differ much to any other investigation. However, the Analysis stage reflects the need to identify and assess relational information using centrality measures and visualisation techniques. The Investigation column breaks down these processes into further detail of the stages related specifically to email data. The Case Study column illustrates the specific processes used in section 4

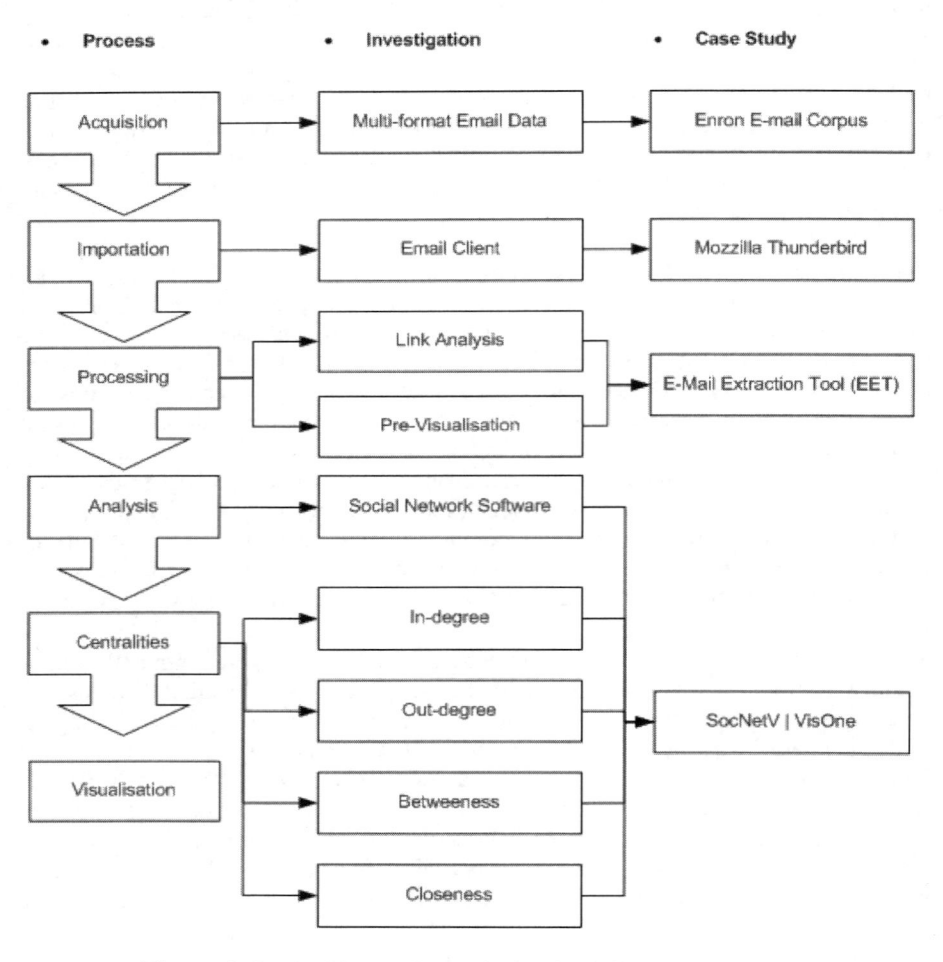

Figure 1: Social Network Analysis of emails methodology.

Process. This column in figure 1 reflects the overall procedures involved in digital forensics investigations. As with any investigation, the data must be acquired in a robust manner, ensuring that the data maintains its integrity. Therefore, when data is imported for analysis, this is done in 'read only' to ensure that data is not modified. As with other investigations, the data has to be processed and analysed. However, with email, the application of analysis techniques such as centrality analysis and visualisation will be applied. These centralities provide alternative views of the social network dynamics (Wiil et al, 2010).

Investigation. This column reflects the investigation process as it relates to email evidence. The acquisition of email data during an investigation is problematic due to the many email formats available depending on the application used by the suspect. Therefore, importation of the data will depend on the client used, for example, Mozilla Thunderbird stores email data in plain text whilst Microsoft Outlook uses a bespoke format. The data is processed to provide an initial visualisation of links to give the examiner an initial view of the social network. Analysis of the evidence is then conducted using other social network tools. These tools, such as Pajek, SocNetV and VisOne, provide different viewpoints of the network by using statistical measures. These are as follows: *in-degree centrality* indicates a node's receptivity or "popularity" in the network and can be used to identify key network facilitators; *out-degree centrality* indicates the expansiveness of ties within the network that an actor possesses; *betweeness centrality* identifies potential points of information control within the network; *closeness centrality* highlights an actor's ability to interact with other members of the network. Wasserman and Faust (1994) provide a comprehensive description and analysis of these measures.

Case study. This column illustrates how the investigation in this paper has been achieved. The Enron email data set is downloaded and the data converted to Mozilla Thunderbird format due to its plain text format. The initial processing and triage is achieved using the EET tool (Haggerty et al, 2009) and provides an initial visualisation of the network. It also provides the platform for easy exportation to other common social network analysis formats, such as Pajek. SocNetV and VisOne tools are used to measure and further analyse the network within this paper.

4. Case Study and Results

This section presents the results of applying the social network discovery model, as detailed in figure 1, to the Enron email data set. This section first places the case study in context by discussing the background to the case. As the data has already been collected, this stage of the model is bypassed, although procedures discussed in (Haggerty et al, 2009) would be used. This section presents the link analysis of the data visualised and triaged through EET. It then identifies the social network groups discovered within the data. The data is analysed using social network centrality measures. Finally, the results are discussed.

A. Case Study Background

Enron was a large energy company that had expanded from its beginnings in 1985 to employ thousands of workers across 40 countries. The Enron fraud caused shockwaves within the business community when it was revealed in 2001 due to the extent and scale of the case. The fraud resulted in the bankruptcy of the company and dissolution of a large accountancy and audit company. The fraud occurred due to the lack of transparency in the firm's accountancy procedures. The main executives in the company used a series of techniques to perpetrate the fraud, such as accountancy loopholes, employing special purpose entities and poor accountancy practices, in order to hide billions of dollars of debt that the company had accrued.

The main actors are as follows: Jeffrey Skilling, former President of Enron Corporation and responsible for Enron's introduction of accounting methods that treated anticipated profits as if they were real gains; Kenneth Lay, Enron Chairman and Chief Executive Officer from 1985; Andrew Fastow, Chief Financial Officer who set up a network of off-balance-sheet companies controlled by Enron to hide Enron losses; Jeffrey McMahon and Ben Glisan, former Enron Treasurers Executive; Ken Rice, former Enron executive and President of Enron's broadband service.

The email data used in this paper is from the Enron corporate business network. This data has been released by the Federal Energy Regulatory Committee (FERC) and is sanitised for use (Cohen, 2010). The data consists of a snapshot of the email folders of a large proportion of Enron employees taken in the final year of business and at the time of criminal proceedings for fraud against members of the Enron organisation. This data set comprises approximately 500,000 emails. This case study uses a selection of user email folders to cover the five most important users based on their position within the Enron hierarchy.

B. Link Analysis

Figure 2 illustrates the data set comprising 118 emails and 215 actors visualised in EET. Aggregating the data in this way helps to counter the issue of source-centricity often found in the analysis of email data. Node sizing is used to gain an overall impression of the importance of the main actors in this network, i.e. the larger the node size, the more emails they have sent and/or received. Ten main actors can be identified from this view. These actors have been manually teased out of the main body to give a better impression of how the emails are linked and how information flows around this network group.

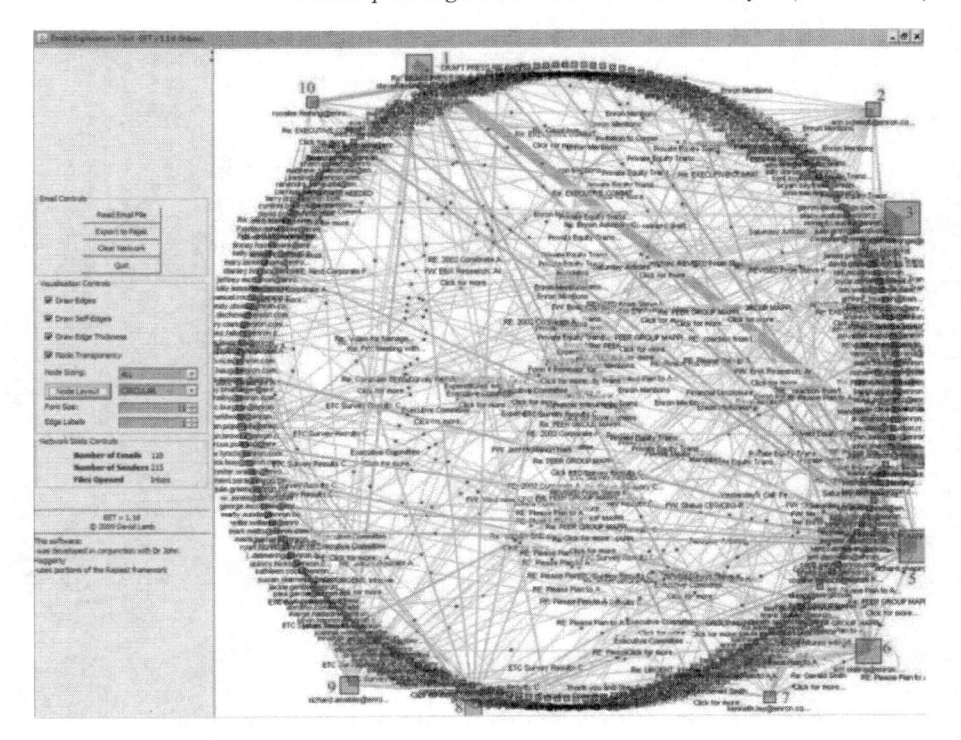

Figure 2: Aggregated data set link analysis.

In the link analysis, email headers reveal that Actors 1 and 4 discuss draft press releases about financial disclosure, with Actor 5 receiving overviews and sending them to Actor 6. This communication could be a part of standard corporate operating procedure. The significance becomes apparent only when the nature and content of these emails are considered. Several of the emails used in this aggregated dataset later appeared as exhibits used in evidence. This supports the potential value of triaging through link analysis.

C. Social Network Group Discovery

Figure 3 illustrates the node mapping graph for the discovered social networks, which identifies six distinct social structures. The first network shows a social network with Actor X at its centre. The directed information shows a typical star layout, indicative of a reporting structure. The second structure of significance has Actor Y at its centre. In this network Actor Z can be seen reporting to Actor Y. This is the first appearance of Actor Z in the analysis of the data sets.

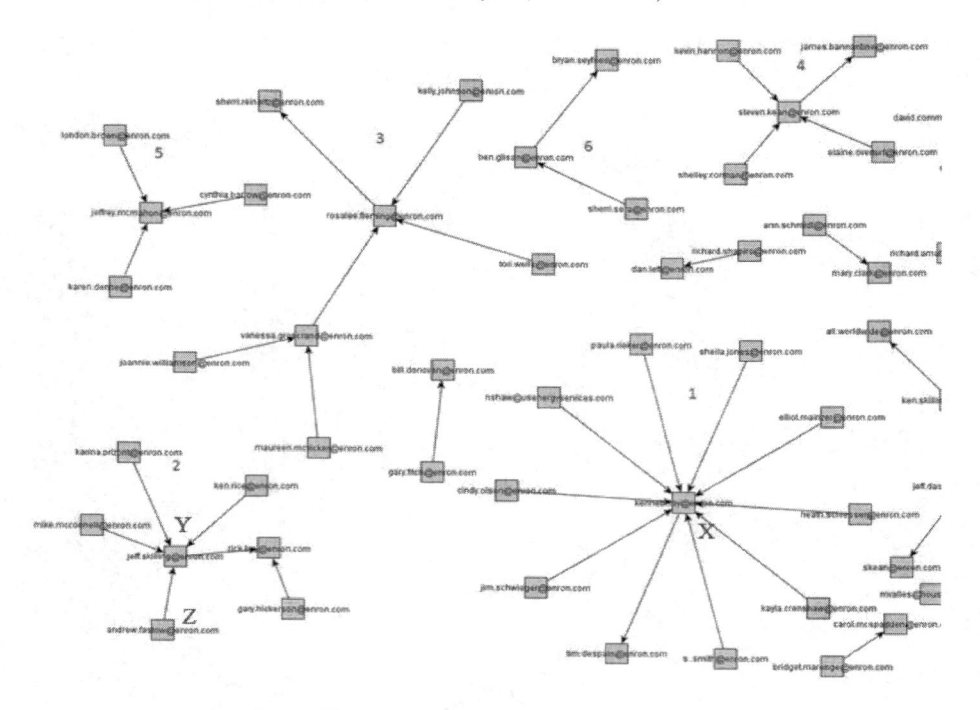

Figure 3: Aggregated data set social network group discovery.

The third social structure features a member of the Enron executive oversight committee and the personal assistants of Actor Y and Actor X. The fourth network features another member of the oversight committee and a public relations executive. The fifth and sixth networks feature two actors of significance in the financial dealings with Enron's strategic partnership companies. The link analysis and node mapping combine to give a financial context to the analysis, highlighting the major actors within the dataset. If the hypothesis for the process model holds true, the centrality analyses that are considered next should demonstrate this context. That is, it is expected that the actors who are heads of financial matters and those whose position in Enron grants access to this information should prove significant.

D. *Centrality Measures*

This section details the analysis of the centrality measures used within the case study and presents the quantitative analysis of the email data as a centrality graph, which allows for qualitative interpretation. These circular radial graphs are interpreted by observing the position of nodes (actors); the closer a node is to the centre of the graph, the higher the measure of that node by the centrality measure and therefore of greater interest within a digital investigation. Line thickness indicates the strength of the ties (relationships) with other nodes within the graph. Three centrality measures are used in this study to demonstrate the applicability of the approach to provide the digital examiner with different views of the email network; betweeness centrality, in-degree centrality and out-degree centrality.

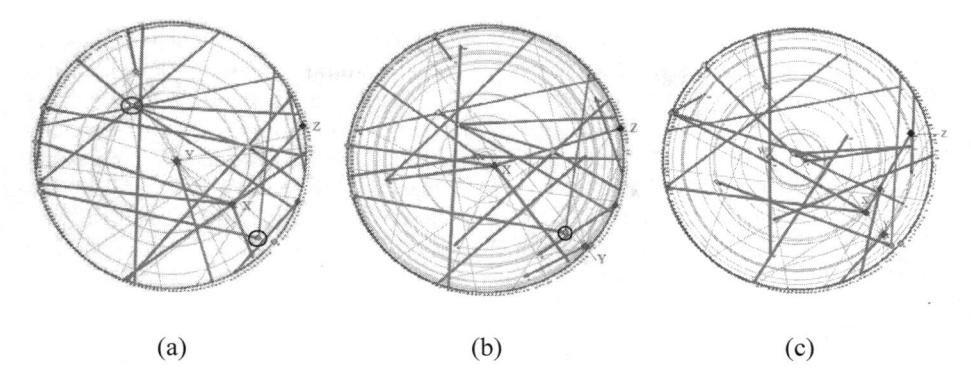

(a)　　　　　　　　　　(b)　　　　　　　　　　(c)

Figure 4: Significant actors identified by (a) betweeness centrality (b) in-degree centrality (c) out-degree centrality.

Figure 4(a) displays the betweeness centrality of the aggregated data. Actors closer to the centre of the graph have a higher betweeness centrality, indicating a greater control over information being sent by email. We can see therefore that the graph indicates that Actor X is most central for communications involving Actor Z. Documents pertaining to the downfall of Enron (Findlaw, 2009) show that collaboration between Actor X, Actor Z and Actor Y sustained the proliferation of the Enron fraud. Within figure 4(a), these actors are highlighted by this quantitative analysis and qualitative information shows that Actor X is central in the network at the time when Enron's financial situation was being called to account. Actor X was able to receive the bulk of network information from both strong and weak ties to other actors within the network. Overall this graph suggests a close-knit social structure able to shape and disseminate financial information to suit the needs of those in prominent roles.

Figure 4(b) illustrates actor in-degree centrality with those having more incoming emails (i.e. information) placed closer to the centre of the disc. In this graph the former treasurer shares the highest in-degree measure with actor X. An interesting observation in this graph is the position of the replacement treasurer marked with a circle. The FERC Enron investigation timeline supports such an inference indicating that the position of treasurer within Enron was in flux and changing hands. They therefore had not had time to have made as many connections within the email network as the previous treasurer. From a digital investigation viewpoint, this may suggest that they will not be able to provide as much evidence.

Figure 4(c) illustrates the out-degree centrality for actors within the data set, with those having more outgoing connections being closer to the centre. In this graph the personal assistants for Actor X and Actor Y are the most prominent, indicating the volume of information they send into the network on behalf of their superiors. These would be actors not necessarily under investigation but would be able to provide a wealth of information to the investigatory team.

The next actor of significance is Actor W, the head of the Enron broadband division. This is the first time his presence is evident in the centrality measures. This signifies that this actor was in a position, both within Enron and the network, to disseminate information widely across the network. This information took the form of financial "overviews" of the market position of Enron broadband. It was later reported that this was code for fraudulent disclosure of financial information (Murphy, 2006). Actor W was seen as a *protégé* of Actor Y. Actor W's position in the graph of Figure 4(c) indicates a relationship in which he reports directly to Actor Y, who then disseminated the fraudulent reports to the rest of the network.

E. Discussion

The social network discovery model illustrated in figure 1 provides a framework by which digital forensics investigators may analyse email data and explore intangible evidence contained therein. Link analysis visualisation provides a rudimentary visualisation of the email data and can be used to effectively triage the potentially large data sets to identify just key actors within the network. This can then be used to inform the social network group discovery, whereby relevant subnets within the data may be assessed. Finally, the application of social network analysis tools and techniques to measure the network not only provides different viewpoints of the network, but also quantifies an actor's role, and therefore potentially their culpability, in an event or set of events. The results obtained from applying the model to the Enron data concur with those established during the FERC investigation, indicating that the techniques used provide a valid indication of real world activity. Moreover, the case suggests that the most significant results can be gained by aggregating key actor data into a single data set, given the source-centric nature of email data. This aggregation provides the additional benefit of enabling the investigator to recreate the role of actors whose data may have been excised or obfuscated.

When combined with supporting evidence, the qualitative and quantitative analysis of this social network provides some indicative and interesting conclusions. The executive oversight committee of Enron took a stronger stance on the financial dealings of the company and its strategic partnership companies. The previous financial controller was an unwilling participant in fraudulent activities. His replacement was promoted and co-opted on the basis of tractability and willingness to commit fraudulent acts. The holder of this role (Actor W) became a prominent actor within the management reporting structure of the network. This position allowed the doctoring of information that flowed around the network so as to benefit the prominent actors. Actor Z, the architect of the strategic partnership fraud methodology, is seen in these graphs but with a low profile. The information they received from the network appears to come from two more prominent sources – Actors X and Y – indicating strong ties to these actors. These actors and relational information are identified by applying the model posited in this paper.

5. Conclusions and Future Work

Our reliance on email communications, particularly within the workplace, ensures that this type of data will continue to feature during digital forensics investigations. Email data provides not only evidence of the flow of information through a network, but also an indication of actor relationships. This relational information may not only identify potential sources of evidence in cases involving many actors, but also when measured, it may provide a quantified assessment of a suspect's culpability in an event or set of events.

Recent work in digital forensics email analysis has focused on the identification and extraction of specific artefacts due to a lack of standardisation across these applications. Little work beyond those proposing specific tools has been conducted into proposing general frameworks for the wider digital investigation of email data. Therefore, this paper has posited a social network discovery model for email investigations. This model reflects the processes required to triage, visualise, analyse and quantify both tangible and intangible information contained within the network. The model has been applied to the Enron email data set to demonstrate its applicability.

Future work aims to develop the model further by highlighting relevant actors in email social networks in an automated way and testing the methodology by using data for case studies from other domains.

6. References

Bird, C., Gourley, A., Devanbu, P., Gertz, M., and Swaminathan, A. (2006), "Mining e-mail social networks", Proceedings of the 2006 international Workshop on Mining Software Repositories, Shanghai, China, 2006, pp. 137-143.

Cocciolo, A. Chae, H. S., Natriello, G. (2007), "Using social network analysis to highlight an emerging online community of practice", Technical Report available at http://edlab.tc.columbia.edu/files/cscl_final_1.pdf (accessed 28 February, 2011).

Cohen, W.W., 2010. "Enron Email Dataset", http://www.cs.cmu.edu/~enron/, 21 August, 2010 (accessed 26 February, 2011).

Collingsworth, B., Menezes, R., Martins, P. (2009), "Assessing Organizational Stability via Network Analysis", Proceedings of IEEE Symposium on Computational Intelligence for Financial Engineering, Nashville, USA, 2009, pp. 43-50.

Debbabi, M. Hadjidj, R. Lounis, H. Iqbal, F. Szporer, A. Benredjem, D. (2009), "Towards an integrated e-mail forensic analysis framework", Digital Investigation, Volume 5, Issues 3-4, March 2009, pp.124-137.

Dellutri, F., Laura, L., Ottaviani, V., Italiano, G.F. (2009), "Extracting Social Networks from Seized Smartphones and Web Data", Proceedings of the 1st International Workshop on Information Forensics and Security, London, UK, 2009, pp. 101-105.

Faust, K. (1997), "Centrality in Affiliation Networks", Social Networks, Volume 19, pp. 157-191.

Findlaw, http://fl1.findlaw.com/news.findlaw.com/wsj/docs/enron/sicreport/chapter2.pdf (accessed 28 February, 2011).

Haggerty, J., Lamb, D. & Taylor, M. (2009), "Social Network Visualization for Forensic Investigation of E-Mail", Proceedings of the 4th Annual Workshop on Digital Forensics and Incident Analysis, Athens, Greece, 2009, pp. 81-92.

Hawe, P., Ghali, L. (2008), "Use of social network analysis to map the social relationships of staff and teachers at school", Health Education Research, Volume 23, 2008, pp. 62-9.

Krebs, VE. (2002), "Uncloaking Terrorist Networks", First Monday, Volume 7, Number 4, April 2002.

Lin, H. (2010), "Predicting Sensitive Relationships from Email Corpus", Proceedings of the 4th International Conference on Genetic and Evolutionary Computing, Shenzhen, China, 2010, pp. 264-267.

Moreno, J. L. (1951), Sociometry, Experimental Method and the Science of Society: An Approach to a New Political Orientation, Beacon House, Beacon, New York.

Murphy, K. (2006), "No Love Lost at the Enron Trial", Business Week, February 15, 2006, http://www.businessweek.com/bwdaily/dnflash/feb2006/nf20060215_9015_db017.htm (accessed 28 February, 2011).

Wasserman, S., Faust, K. (1994), Social Network Analysis: Methods and Applications, Cambridge University Press, Cambridge.

Wei, C., Sprague, A., Warner, G., Skjellum, A. (2008), "Mining spam e-mail to identify common origins for forensic application", Proceedings of the 2008 ACM Symposium on Applied Computing, Fortaleza, Brazil, 2008, pp.1433-1437.

Wiil, U.K., Gniadek, J., Memon, N. (2010), "Measuring Link Importance in Terrorist Networks", Proceedings of the 2010 International Conference on Social Networks Analysis and Mining, Odense, Denmark, 2010, pp. 225-232.

Zhou, Y., Fleischmann, K.R., Wallace, W.A. (2010), "Automatic Text Analysis of Values in the Enron Email Dataset: Clustering a Social Network Using the Value Patterns of Actors", Proceedings of the 43rd Hawaii International Conference of System Sciences, Hawaii, USA, 2010, pp. 1-10.

Author Index

Askwith, R.	122	Oliver, M.S.	17
Balan, C.	69	Magklaras, G.	133
Bihina Bella, M.A.	17	Martini, A.	55
		Merabti, M.	122
Dija, S.	69	Mitchell, I.	44
		Mouton, F.	108
Eloff, J.H.P	17		
		Pangalos, G.	55
Furnell, S.M.	133	Papadaki, M.	133
		Patel, A.	81
Glisson, W.B.	1		
		Sant, P.	33
Haggerty, J.	160	Shi, O.	122
Hegarty, R.	122	Spyridopoulos, T.	93
Hewling, M.	33		
Hu, Y.	149	Taylor, M.	160
		Thomas, K.L.	69
Illioudis, C.	55	Tobona, A.Z.	1
		Tryfonas, T.	55
Jones, D.	76		
		Venter, H.S.	108
Kalajdzic, K.	81	Vidyadharan, D.S.	69
Karran, A.	160		
Katos, V.	93	Zaharis, A.	55
		Zhou, C.	149
Lamb, M.	160		
Li, C-T.	149		
Lin, X.	149		
Llewellyn-Jones, D.	160		